The Discursive Construction
of National Identity

Critical Discourse Analysis Series

Series Editor: Norman Fairclough

Discourse in Late Modernity: Rethinking Critical Discourse Analysis
Lilie Chouliaraki and Norman Fairclough

The Discursive Construction of National Identity

Ruth Wodak, Rudolf de Cillia,
Martin Reisigl and Karin Liebhart

Translated by Angelika Hirsch
and Richard Mitten

Edinburgh University Press

© Ruth Wodak, Rudolf de Cillia, Martin Reisigl,
Karin Liebhart, 1999

Translation © Angelika Hirsch and
Richard Mitten

This book is a considerably abbreviated version
of the German edition, published by Suhrkamp,
Frankfurt am Main, 1998

Edinburgh University Press Ltd
22 George Square, Edinburgh

Typeset in Garamond
by Norman Tilley Graphics, Northampton,
and printed and bound in Great Britain
by The University Press, Cambridge

A CIP record for this book is available from
the British Library

ISBN 0 7486 1080 4 (paperback)

The right of Ruth Wodak, Rudolf de Cillia,
Martin Reisigl and Karin Liebhart
to be identified as authors of this work
has been asserted in accordance with
the Copyright, Designs and Patents Act 1988.

Contents

Series Preface

Critical Discourse Analysis (henceforth CDA) starts from the perception of discourse (language but also other forms of semiosis, such as visual images) as an element of social practices, which constitutes other elements as well as being shaped by them. Social questions are therefore in part questions about discourse – for instance, the question of power in social class, gender and race relations is partly a question of discourse. And careful linguistic and semiotic analysis of texts (for example, newspaper articles or advertisements) and interactions (for example, conversations or interviews) therefore has a part to play in social analysis.

CDA has attracted a great deal of interest since the 1970s, not only amongst specialists in linguistics and language studies, but also within other social science disciplines. Just to give one example: the Department of Urban Studies at Glasgow University held well-attended and successful conferences on discourse in relation to aspects of urban policy in 1998 and 1999, where many of the presentations drew upon CDA. The current interest in CDA reflects, I believe, an upsurge in critique of language within contemporary society. There is widespread cynicism about the rhetoric of advertising and the simulated personalness ('have a nice day') of people working in impersonal commercial organisations, and a developing consciousness of linguistic forms of racism and sexism.

Why this enhanced critical consciousness about language? Language (and more generally, semiosis) has become an increasingly salient element of contemporary social practices. For instance, language has become more important economically. With the shift to 'knowledge-based' economies, many of the 'goods' that are produced have a linguistic or partly linguistic character – the language used by service workers is part of the service they provide, and the products of the advertising industry are semiotic products. Moreover, key areas of social life (such as politics) have become increasingly centred upon the mass media, and those involved in these areas have consequently become increasingly self-conscious about the language they use. These changes have led to an increase in conscious interventions to shape linguistic and semiotic elements of social practices in accordance with economic, organisational and political objectives. Language has become subject to the wider contemporary preoccupation with design; it has become 'technologised' in the sense that it is increasingly seen as another material to which social technologies can be applied in the search for greater profit or better performance. Enhanced critical consciousness of language is at least in part a response to these colonisations of language.

It is clear that these tendencies are growing. A critical perspective on discourse is therefore a socially and politically important element in contemporary social and language study. The Critical Discourse Analysis series launched by Edinburgh University Press is on one level a recognition of this need. It also aims to contribute to the development and consolidation of CDA as a field of study. In the latter regard, the series is intended to address a number of themes and needs. First, the development of CDA has raised a number of theoretical problems, some of which need more sustained attention than they have so far received – for instance, the theorisation of discourse as an element of social practice, or the relationship between discourse and ideology. More generally, a debate is needed about the relationship between CDA and critical and post-structuralist social theory. Second, the series is intended to reflect the considerable range of social issues and problems where CDA has a contribution to make – in the media, politics, law, the workplace and so forth. Third, we hope the series will encourage authors to explore the exciting possibilities for working across disciplines, as well as the problems of interdisciplinarity. The series encourages books written by two or more authors based in different disciplines, as well as books co-authored by discourse analysts and practitioners in the domain in focus, for example journalists, lawyers or doctors. Fourth, a number of relatively distinct positions and approaches have been developed within CDA, and the series aims to reflect that range and explore relationships between them. Fifth, the series is international in scope, bringing together work by scholars who are developing and using CDA in various parts of the world.

Norman Fairclough
Series Editor

Acknowledgements

We are grateful to many people in many different capacities for making this book possible.

First of all, we would like to express our gratitude to two institutions which have supported our work: the Internationales Forschungszentrum Kulturwissenschaften (IFK) generously financed the research project from which the present book emerged, as well as two workshops where we were able to discuss the preliminary results of our studies with scholars from around the world; the Zentrum für Internationale und Interdisziplinäre Studien of the University of Vienna (ZIIS) was also involved in the organisation of the initial international workshop which provided invaluable feedback at an early stage.

Two colleagues, Dilek Cinar and Bernd Matouschek, were associated with the research project in its initial phase. The many ideas and suggestions they contributed during the study's first year proved stimulating throughout the entire period of research. In addition, it was Bernd Matouschek who, along with Ruth Wodak, developed the original research proposal. At this early stage Richard Mitten and Peter A. Ulram offered valuable comments on earlier drafts of this proposal, from which it benefited enormously.[1] To all these we would like to express our deepest appreciation.

The present volume is a considerably abbreviated version of the German edition, published by Suhrkamp, Frankfurt am Main, in 1998. Maria Kargl and Klaus Hofstätter, two members of the research team and co-authors of the German book, deserve special mention here for their earlier work and their assistance in preparing the German edition.

The original unabridged final report, and the Suhrkamp volume, have both benefited greatly from the criticism and suggestions we received from Michael Agar, Gertraud Benke, Peter A. Bruck, András Kovacs, Lutz Musner, Anton Pelinka and Christoph Reinprecht. We would like gratefully to acknowledge their contributions, while underlining that they bear no responsibility for any remaining deficiences the book might possess.

The translation of the German manuscript book would not have been possible without grants from the Austrian Ministry of Science and Transport (Bundes-

---

1. Rudi de Cillia directed the project during Ruth Wodak's sabbatical in the autumn of 1995.

ministerium für Wissenschaft und Verkehr) and from the Vienna Municipal Council (Gemeinde Wien). We would like to express our sincere appreciation for this support.

We are particularly grateful to Angelika Hirsch and Richard Mitten for the precision and commitment they brought to the English translation. We owe a special debt to Richard Mitten for supplying his expertise as historian and for editing the English version.

Thanks should also go to Lieselotte Martin, who efficiently managed the research budget; to Thomas Gamperl, Patricia Herzberger, Sabine Mayr and Maria Sedlak, who transcribed the audio-tapes with great care; and to the co-ordinators of the focus group discussions. We owe a special thank you to all the people who took part in the discussions and interviews and shared their ideas about Austrian identity with us.

To our publisher, Edinburgh University Press, and in particular to Jackie Jones, who provided much expert advice and support, as well as to Anna Claybourne, who copy-edited the typescript so carefully, we would like to express our sincere appreciation.

Finally, our warmest thanks go to Norman Fairclough for his interest in and encouragement of our work, and for his invaluable support in making it known to an English readership.

Vienna, May 1999

Chapter 1

Introduction

In *The Xenophobe's Guide to the Austrians* (James 1994) author Louis James writes: 'When a Stone Age Austrian popped out of a glacier in Tyrol in 1991, he was claimed by the Italians as one of them. A learned commission established that maybe he was lying just over the border by a metre or two, and a television reporter inquired satirically why they didn't just look at his passport" (1994, p. 11).

The moral of this story is that even after all those years in cold storage, the iceman (Ötzi) suffers from a certain confusion as to his identity, a trait he ostensibly shares with all other Austrians. Of course, this nationalist tug-of-war between Austria and Italy, to which James ironically refers, really tells us nothing about Ötzi's identity, for national(ist) ideas and sentiment did not emerge before the age of modernity, centuries after Ötzi's demise. Still, the attempts by both Austria and Italy to adorn their respective 'national pasts' with a historically highly significant archaeological find reveal a typical strategy, metaphorically described by Rudolf Burger (1996, p. 40) as the 'nationalist dilation of time'. In this view, similar problems of identity seem to beset the English too. Past contingencies (in this case, a casual discovery) are appropriated by the contemporary nation by mythically expanding the nation into a transhistorical, and thus eternal, entity.

In a companion volume, *The Xenophobe's Guide to the English*, Antony Miall writes: [As far as] 'the English are concerned, all of life's greatest problems can be summed up in one word – foreigners'. And he continues: 'English views on foreigners are very simple. The further one travels from the capital in any direction, the more outlandish the people become' (1993, pp. 5–6). It is obvious that the ego-, ethno- and nation-centric view described by Miall with respect to English people is not so much an English peculiarity as a general cross-cultural feature of ethnicist and nationalist patterns of perception of others.

We could go on almost *ad infinitum* with such more or less serious anecdotal remarks about nationality or the alleged mentality of nations. While this can be amusing to a certain extent, we are also aware of how often nationalist attitudes and ethnic stereotypes articulated in discourse accompany or even determine political decision-making, and we note with concern the increase in discriminatory acts and exclusionary practices conducted in the name of nationalism in many parts of Europe.

This book is about the manifold attempts to imagine and construct national identity. Although our study focuses on Austria, it is by no means restricted to it. Many of its insights, especially its theoretical and methodological approach, which was specially developed for this investigation, are equally applicable to other western European states.[1]

Austrian national identity has been exposed to particularly strong challenges in the wake of the opening up of eastern Europe in 1989 and the subsequent geo-political transformations in Central Europe. Similarly, in the run-up to Austria's referendum on whether or not to join the European Union, the Austrian population was frequently reassured that nothing was going to change and that there was no cause for concern about a possible loss of identity. It is the aim of this book to investigate the tension in Austria's attempts both to maintain and to transform its national identity, a phenomenon that can be observed across Europe.

Two important Austrian anniversaries, both of which were characterised by intensive identity management and increased public self-reflection, prompted this study: the year 1995 marked the fiftieth anniversary of the founding of the Second Republic, and 1996 was dedicated to the 'Austrian millennium', celebrating the thousand-year anniversary of the first documented occurrence of the country's name. The mention of the word *Ostarrichi* in a 996 Roman document was eagerly taken up as the basis of an Austrian 'myth of origin'.

Our investigation was carried out within the tradition of Critical Linguistics (Wodak 1995, Fairclough and Wodak 1997, Van Dijk (in print)), and in particular Critical Discourse Analysis, as it has been developed in a number of previous studies on topics such as postwar Austrian antisemitism (Wodak et al. 1990), Austria's 'coming to terms' with its Nazi past in the context of the commemorative year 1988 (Wodak et al. 1994) and the political and discursive exclusion of Romanian refugees after the fall of the Iron Curtain (Matouschek, Wodak and Januschek 1995). In contrast to many studies carried out within the framework of Critical Linguistics, we do not limit ourselves to theory-building, but place great emphasis on the analysis of our empirical data (cf. Wodak 1996). Our analytical working model integrates both the synchronic and diachronic dimensions (cf. Wodak 1996, Harvey 1996) and combines social science methodologies of data collection and fieldwork with the 'discourse-historical' approach developed by the Vienna School of Discourse Analysis, which in many ways transcends the concerns of traditional sociolinguistics. In turn, our theoretical concepts derive from detailed analysis of our empirical data. We do not, however, regard our findings as conclusive and definitive, as the emergence of new information may always entail the reconsideration and re-evaluation of data (Fairclough and Wodak 1997). However, it is important to state at the outset that our research is grounded in the political and ethical grid of values of Critical Theory.

'Since every search for identity includes differentiating oneself from what one is not,' writes Seyla Benhabib (1996, pp. 3f.):

identity politics is always and necessarily a politics of the creation of difference.

One is a Bosnian Serb to the degree to which one is not a Bosnian Moslem or a Croat. ... What is shocking about these developments, is not the inevitable dialectic of identity/difference that they display but rather the atavistic belief that identities can be maintained and secured only by eliminating difference and otherness. The negotiation of identity/difference ... is the political problem facing democracies on a global scale.

The prime objective of our study, therefore, is to conceptualise and identify the various macrostrategies employed in the construction of national identities and to describe them using a hermeneutic-abductive approach. We understand the concept of identity on which we base our study to be context-dependent and dynamic (cf. Chapter 2). We assume further that the various discursive constructs of national identity are given different shapes according to the context and to the public in which they emerge, all of which can be identified with reference to content, strategies and argumentation patterns, as well as according to how they are expressed in language (linguistic realisation). The publics we investigate are not separate entities, but interrelate in highly complex ways, a fact we have tried to account for, at least at certain points of our study, by including reception analysis (cf. Chapter 7). In order to trace some of these interrelations, what are called 'intertextualities', we look at how different types of discursive practices on one and the same topic interconnect and how individual argumentation patterns are reformulated and recontextualised in different contexts (Bernstein 1996, Fairclough 1995, Iedema 1997, Wodak and Van Leeuwen 1999). Readers might ask why we have included group conversations and qualitative interviews to illustrate such an eminently political topic as the construction of national identities, why we have not instead just analysed political speeches or samples of media discourse. The answer is simple: our concept of 'political' is far broader than that in common usage and not only concentrates on the language of the powerful élites, but also includes discursive acts which, according to Paul Chilton and Christina Schaeffner, 'involve power, or its inverse, resistance' (1997, p. 212) in many different contexts, including non-official and informal ones. To be able to understand the impact of the discourse of the élites, we believe that it is necessary to investigate its reception and recontextualisation in other domains of society, in other words, in the lifeworld (in Habermas's sense). We hope that our study will demonstrate that methods such as focus groups and topic-oriented interviews are excellent tools in Critical Discourse Analysis, which allow us, for example, to observe the processes through which important concepts like 'nation' are being 'co-constructed' during an ongoing discussion.

At this point, we would like to introduce several hypotheses which underlie our analytical framework and to which we will frequently have occasion to recur in the course of our study.

Firstly, following Benedict Anderson (1983, pp. 15f.), we assume that nations are mental constructs, 'imagined communities', which nationalised political subjects perceive as discrete political entities.

Secondly, we assume that national identities, as special forms of social identities, are produced and reproduced, as well as transformed and dismantled, *discursively*.

Thirdly, we assume 'national identity' to imply a complex of similar conceptions and perceptual schemata, of similar emotional dispositions and attitudes, and of similar behavioural conventions, which bearers of this 'national identity' share collectively and which they have internalised through socialisation (education, politics, the media, sports or everyday practices). This conception of national identity relates to Bourdieu's concept of habitus. In our case, the common *conceptions* shared by Austrians include ideas of a *homo Austriacus*; of a common culture, in the past, present and future; of a distinctive national territory; and of notions of and attitudes towards other national communities and their culture, history, and so on. The shared *emotional dispositions* relate to the attitudes members of a given ingroup have towards other members of that ingroup, as well as those towards members of an outgroup. In our case, disposition would be towards solidarity with one's own group as well as towards excluding the 'others' from this constructed collective.

Fourthly, we assume that the institutional and material social conditions and practices interrelate dialectically with discursive practices. Different social fields of action can, however, conflict with each other; for example, if official political ceremonial discourse attempts to justify, gloss over or obscure discriminatory practices and thus helps to maintain the status quo.

Fifthly, we assume that discursive constructs of nations and national identities – and here we also draw upon research conducted within the field of Cultural Studies (cf. Hall 1996a, 1996b, Martin 1995) – primarily emphasise national uniqueness and intra-national uniformity but largely ignore intra-national differences. In imagining national singularity and homogeneity, members of a national community simultaneously construct the distinctions between themselves and other nations, most notably when the other nationality is believed to exhibit traits similar to those of one's own national community, similar to what Freud called the 'narcissism of small differences' (1982 [1930], p. 243).

Sixthly, we assume that there is – in an essentialist sense – no such thing as *one* national identity. We believe rather that different identities are discursively constructed according to audience, setting, topic and substantive content. National identities are therefore malleable, fragile and, frequently, ambivalent and diffuse. In order to trace the reciprocal relations between the models of identity formulated by the political élites or the media and those forged in 'everyday discourse' (the recontextualisation of élite discourse), we investigate five different sets of data from public, semi-public and private spheres, of which three are represented in detail in this book; for reasons of space the other two are only briefly addressed (cf. Wodak et al. 1998).

We distinguish certain core areas in the discursive construction of national identities at the content-level, i.e. a collective past, a collective present and future, a common culture, a common territory, and a *homo nationalis*. Again, for reasons of space, we have confined ourselves to the discussion of four main content-related areas we feel to be of particular relevance, as they can easily be applied to other countries: the concept of nation, the *homo nationalis* (in our case, the *homo Austriacus*), the construction of a collective past, and 'Europe and Austrian neutrality'.

Finally, we assume that the clear dichotomy between the concepts of *Staatsnation* and *Kulturnation*[2] is an idealised abstraction. If *Staatsnation* and *Kulturnation* are viewed as mutually exclusive concepts, they cannot adequately account for the national processes of identification in a particular nation-state. Discourses of national identity constructed by residents of any given state will always contain or imply both cultural and political elements. The principal reason to maintain the distinction is to highlight differences in national self-perception within a country – be it between different political or ideological camps or even within one and the same political group.

The above-mentioned assumptions were developed on the basis of a critical survey of the relevant social science and historical literature, and tested on our data. Thematically, this study highlights the general tension between nation-state and globalisation more generally and its effects on the conceptualisation of Austrian identity. Moreover, although Austria has always had close ties with Germany, since 1945 it has attempted more self-consciously to differentiate itself. Finally, Austria has been trying to find its place in the European Union, which it joined in 1995. Its membership in this organisation has led to a reformulation of one of the pillars of Austrian identity – neutrality – within the larger context of European integration.

If, as argued above, many of the theoretical insights gained are applicable to any number of national cultures, it is important to emphasise that for these concepts and tools to be useful, they must take careful note of the historical and cultural features specific to the nation being investigated. Accordingly, we would like to sketch here some of the features that are unique to the Austrian case we have studied.

At the intersection between identity and history, both the 'Austro-fascist' period (1934–8) and the National Socialist era (1938–45) have shaped the 'collective memory' of the Austrian nation, each in its own specific way (cf. Botz and Sprengnagel 1994). In Austria, the 'victim thesis', which defines Austria as having been the first victim of Nazi Germany, occupied a central place in the construction of Austrian identity up to 1986, the year of the Waldheim affair (cf. Wodak et al. 1990, 1994, Mitten 1992). Since the celebrations commemorating the fiftieth anniversary of the Nazi occupation and the 'November Pogrom' (*Reichskristallnacht*) in 1938, the pendent 'perpetrator thesis' has increased in significance. One consequence of this has been a rewriting of recent Austrian history and the emergence of new patterns of argumentation in public discourse. The denial of Austria's participation in Nazi crimes was the principal reason for its particularly strong differentiation from Germany, which has taken an altogether different course in dealing with its Nazi past (Stern 1991). However, a closer inspection reveals that the relationship between Austria and Germany has remained rather ambivalent, and that the autonomy of Austrian identity with respect to the 'German question' has proved to be fragile. This is particularly evident in the evaluation of German as a national language in Austria. Although the German language is crucial in the construction of Austrian identity – even for members of linguistic minorities whose native languages do not have equal status – the primary linguistic level of identification of German-speaking Austrians is the dialect, which results in a low awareness of an independent

(Austrian) standard variety of German (de Cillia 1996, 1998a). For reasons of space, these dimensions of the Austrian identity could not be considered in this book; they are, however, dealt with extensively in the German edition.

Similarly, two case studies dealing with Austria's decision to join the European Union – an analysis of the advertising campaigns preceding the 1994 referendum on membership of the EU, and an analysis of the media coverage of 'security policy and neutrality' in Austrian daily newspapers immediately after the referendum – could not be included here. The most salient findings of these two case studies are, however, briefly summarised in the concluding chapter.

Taking the current scholarly literature as a point of departure, Chapter 3 explores the dimensions of Austrian national identity and introduces the thematic blocks of Austrian identity which are central to our study. The subsequent three chapters test the analytical tools we have developed and the assumptions outlined above by examining three case studies of the construction of Austrian national identity in different publics. Chapter 4 analyses political speeches commemorating the foundation of the Second Republic during the celebrations in April and May 1995; Chapter 5 investigates semi-public discourse on the basis of seven focus groups in different Austrian provinces; and Chapter 6 is based on twenty-four extensive topic-oriented 'deep' interviews.

The concluding chapter presents what in our view are the most important theoretical and methodological findings of our study, which, leaving aside certain Austrian particularities, can also be fruitfully applied in the investigation of other western European nation-states. What has emerged in the course of this study is that strictly disjunctive and static concepts such as *Staatsnation* or *Kulturnation* have proven analytically insufficient. Moreover, a nuanced discourse-analytical apparatus which systematically combines contents, strategies and linguistic realisations is much more valuable than the usual exclusively quantitative procedures of social science. Finally, we would like to point out that the purpose of this study is not to provide definitive answers, but to open up and enrich discussion in a field which holds great potential for future work.

NOTES

1. The present book is an abbreviated English version of Ruth Wodak, Rudolf de Cillia, Martin Reisigl, Karin Liebhart, Klaus Hofstätter and Maria Kargl, *Zur diskursiven Konstruktion nationaler Identität*. Frankfurt am Main: Suhrkamp, 1998.
2. See Chapter 2.2.6.1. for a discussion of these concepts. The use of the terms 'discourse', 'discourses', 'discursive practices' and 'texts' is extensively discussed in Chapter 2.1 and in Wodak 1996 as well as in Wodak and Reisigl 1999.

Chapter 2

The Discursive Construction of National Identity

2.1 CRITICAL DISCOURSE ANALYSIS: DISCOURSE AS SOCIAL PRACTICE[1]

Since the 1970s, the term 'discourse' has become common currency in an everyday research sense in a variety of humanities and social science disciplines, including the applied branches of linguistics. Because of the wide-ranging use of this term, a variety of meanings have been attributed to it (see Ehlich 1993, p. 145, and Ehlich 1994), which has led to considerable semantic fuzziness and terminological flexibility. In the following we will briefly describe the concept of discourse as it is currently employed in the context of the research activities carried out at the University of Vienna, which have also informed the present investigation, and place this usage within the international research context (for an overview of research on discourse analysis in Austria, see Menz 1994).

The paradigm of Critical Discourse Analysis is not homogeneous. The British variety, represented by such figures as Gunther Kress, Robert Hodge, Roger Fowler, Norman Fairclough and Theo Van Leeuwen, has drawn upon Foucault's theory of discourse and, in its linguistic dimension, is closely associated with the systemic linguistic theory formulated by William Firth and M. A. K. Halliday, as well as with Halliday's social semiotics. The cognitive-oriented approach of Dutch Critical Discourse Analysis, exemplified by the work of Teun van Dijk, uses a triadic model to show how personal and social cognition mediates between social structures and discourse structures. German Critical Discourse Analysis, as practised by Utz Maas, Siegfried Jäger and Jürgen Link, has been influenced even more strongly by Foucault's concept of discourse than has the British.

The Vienna School of Discourse Analysis, which also has roots in Bernstein's sociolinguistic approach, situates itself within Critical Discourse Analysis (cf. among others Fairclough and Wodak 1997, Fairclough 1995, Wodak 1995, Wodak 1996, *Discourse & Society* 4/2/1993) as well as within the philosophical and sociological tradition of Critical Theory. In the analysis of historical and political topics and texts, the historical dimension of discursive acts is considered in two ways. Firstly, the discourse-historical approach always attempts to integrate as much available information as possible on the historical background and the original historical sources in which discursive 'events' are embedded. Secondly, a number of investigations (Wodak et al. 1990, Wodak et al. 1994, Matouschek, Wodak and Januschek 1995) have traced the diachronic change, which particular types of discourse undergo during a specified period of time.

Critical Discourse Analysis centres on authentic everyday communication in institutional, media, political or other locations rather than on sample sentences or sample texts constructed in linguists' minds. Critical Discourse Analysis regards both written and spoken 'discourse' as a form of social practice (Fairclough and Wodak 1997). It assumes a dialectical relationship between particular discursive acts and the situations, institutions and social structures in which they are embedded: the situational, institutional and social contexts shape and affect discourse, and, in turn, discourses influence social and political reality. In other words, discourse constitutes social practice and is at the same time constituted by it.

Through discourses, social actors constitute objects of knowledge, situations and social roles as well as identities and interpersonal relations between different social groups and those who interact with them. Furthermore, discursive acts are socially constitutive in a variety of ways. Firstly, they are largely responsible for the genesis, production and construction of particular social conditions. Secondly, they can contribute to the restoration, legitimation or relativisation of a social status quo (ante). Thirdly, discursive acts are employed to maintain and reproduce the status quo. Fourthly, discursive practice may be effective in transforming, dismantling or even destroying the status quo. In view of these social macrofunctions, we distinguish in this book between constructive, perpetuating and/or justifying discursive strategies as well as strategies of transformation and dismantlement or disparagement (cf. section 2.3.3.2 and table 2.5).

On a social level, through linguistic representation in various dialogic contexts, discursive practices may influence the formation of groups and serve to establish or conceal relations of power and dominance between interactants, between social groups and classes, between men and women and between national, ethnic, religious, sexual, political, cultural and subcultural majorities and minorities. The aim of Critical Discourse Analysis is to unmask ideologically permeated and often obscured structures of power, political control, and dominance, as well as strategies of discriminatory inclusion and exclusion in language use. In contrast to other types of discourse and conversation analysis, Critical Discourse Analysis does not pretend to be able to assume an objective, socially neutral analytical stance. Indeed, practitioners of Critical Discourse Analysis believe that such ostensible political indifference ultimately assists in maintaining an unjust status quo. Critical Discourse Analysis, which is committed to an emancipatory, socially critical approach, allies itself with those who suffer political and social injustice. Its aim is therefore to intervene discursively in given social and political practices. In this book, this 'intervention' is primarily analytical, in contrast to previous, more practically oriented studies on communication in various institutional contexts carried out by researchers in Vienna. The earlier work aimed, among other things, to break down language barriers in hospitals, schools, courts, public authorities and the media. In the analysis of the discursive construction of national identity, the kind of 'intervention' we envision will, among other things, serve to uncover manipulative manœuvres in politics and the media, which aim at linguistic homogenisation or discriminatory exclusion of human beings, and to heighten the awareness of the rhetorical strategies which are used to impose certain political beliefs, values, and goals. In other words, the aim of the present study is to throw light on the largely contingent and imaginary character of nation and to sharpen awareness of dogmatic, essentialist and naturalising conceptions of nation and national identity which, according to Habermas (1996, pp. 172ff.), threaten or make impossible what he has described as 'difference-sensitive inclusion', that is, equal pluralistic coexistence of various ethnic groups, language communities, religious communities and forms of life.

Critical Discourse Analysis is faced with the twofold task of revealing the relationship between linguistic means, forms and structures and concrete linguistic practice, and making transparent the reciprocal relationship between discursive action and political and institutional structures. In contrast to other discourse-analytical approaches such as functional pragmatics (see, for example Ehlich 1986 and Brünner and Graefen, 1994), Viennese Critical Discourse Analysis places more emphasis on this second aspect. The main concern of the Vienna School is not to study the linguistic system and its functional and semantic potential in all its dimensions *per se*, but rather to establish the linguistic relations between specific linguistic subsystems and social structures (Wodak 1997), in order to explore the specific social significance and function of a concrete linguistic or grammatical option.

In accordance with this second aim, exploring the interconnectedness of discursive practices and extra-linguistic social structures, the Vienna School of Critical Discourse Analysis employs the principle of triangulation (cf. Cicourel 1969). Triangulation means that discursive phenomena are approached from a variety of methodological and theoretical perspectives taken from various disciplines. For example, in exploring the phenomenon of national identity, our interdisciplinary approach combines historical, socio-political and linguistic perspectives in a methodologically pluralistic approach. In our study, the principle of triangulation implies using various methods of data collection and the analysis of different sets of data – political speeches, newspaper articles, posters and brochures, interviews and focus groups – which enable us to provide a detailed picture of the Austrian identity in public and semi-private settings exhibiting various degrees of formality, and to identify and contrast competing configurations of national identity as well as divergent narratives of identity.

Our choice of the principle of triangulation is based on our understanding of 'context' (cf. Wodak 1996, pp. 20ff.). The first aspect of context, which we take into consideration is the immediate linguistic co-text, that is the semantic environment of an individual utterance about Austrian identity, and the local interactive processes of negotiation and conflict avoidance – if the discussions under investigation are dialogue-based. The second aspect we focus on concerns extra-linguistic social variables and institutional settings of the specific situation of an utterance. Thirdly, our notion of context comprises the intertextual or interdiscursive references in the text.

We will explore the local co-textual environment on the basis of selected linguistic analyses of group discussions and individual interviews. These analyses will examine the influence of a preceding text or spoken discourse on an utterance made in the discussion or interview itself (for example, the resumption of a certain theme). From the co-textual environment, we also try to infer psychological factors or motives of speakers. For example, we examine the extent to which positive emotional and cognitive connotations associated with certain concepts can serve as indicators of a certain national feeling or national consciousness, or how certain features of oral communication such as fragmented sentences, hesitation and modifications indicate self-censorship or uneasiness when discussing topics with negative associations. Individual factors such as a participant's health, how he or she feels on the particular day of discussion or interview, or whether he or she is an introvert, cannot be considered. Instead we have tried to consider possible factors which can influence a given utterance: the degree of formality of the speech situation; the place, the occasion and the speaker's addressees; and sociological factors such as the participants' ages, occupations, education and training as well as their social, regional, ethnic, national, sexual and religious memberships (as defined by themselves and by others), and other factors such as the political affiliation and position of individual speakers. Finally, we pursue a number of interdiscursive leads (these occur principally as allusions or evocations in politicians' statements, but also as quotations or hidden borrowings in public commemorative addresses from publications by historians, political scientists, and others) and explore how stereotypical formulations or arguments from political and media discourse are taken up in semi-public and quasi-private discourse.

An unavoidable contextual factor is the setting of the interviews and focus groups themselves. The very method of data acquisition and the use of tape recorders and video cameras may distort the interaction. Thus, we tried to minimise such disturbing effects by creating a more informal atmosphere (for example, by offering coffee and other refreshments). The interviews were conducted almost exclusively at people's homes so that the interviewees could talk about their views on national identity in a relaxed atmosphere.

2.2 FROM IDENTITY TO NATIONAL IDENTITY

2.2.1 Static and Dynamic Conceptualisations of Identity

Identity has been a topic of a wide variety of logical, philosophical, psychological (in both social and developmental senses), sociological, political and other discussions for quite some time. In view of the mass of literature on this topic, which is quite controversially debated, it would be impossible to present here a detailed discussion of even all the most important identity theories. Consequently, we have chosen to discuss only those theoretical interpretations of identity that seem necessary for the heuristic understanding of our own conceptual interpretation of the phenomena complex of identity in general and of national identity in particular.

At first sight, the concept of identity may seem to possess considerable explanatory force. Formally and logically, 'identity' is a relational term. It defines the relationship between two or more related entities in a manner that asserts a sameness or equality. If one were to use this semantic definition of identity in reference to 'real' objects, individual people or groups of people, one would immediately encounter a number of objections. In the first place, such an absolute sameness criterion is highly questionable when referring to members of a group. However, the idea of an individual or even a lifeless object staying the same would also be untenable. Individual people change constantly in the course of their lives, be it physically, psychologically or socially. Even an object changes constantly in its material constitution, as is revealed by a microscopic examination if not otherwise obvious. In this way, the concept of identity (apart from the formal sense of the term used in logic and mathematics) never signifies anything static, unchanging, or substantial, but rather always an element situated in the flow of time, ever changing, something involved in a process. This applies, of course, to all forms of personal and social identity as well as to 'ego identities', all of which will be addressed in more detail below.

Banal as this observation may seem, and despite the fact that it was integrated into early social theories of identity such as that of the social philosopher George Herbert Mead (1967), it does not seem to have become self-evident in everyday scholarship. Consequently, Denis Martin was able to observe critically as late as 1995 that the concept of identity loses all analytical power when it is used to explain the political and military conflicts in ex-Yugoslavia, Africa, Latin America or Canada (Martin 1995, p. 5). Used as a completely static idea, the concept wrongly suggests that people belong to a solid, unchanging, intrinsic collective unit because of a specific history which they supposedly have in common, and that as a consequence they feel obliged to act and react as a group when they are threatened. Understood in this way, this concept is incapable of explaining why the social actors involved act in a certain way and how such political and military conflicts could arise. Given the assumption of homogeneity and constancy, the term in this sense cannot do sufficient justice to the complexity of the relationships a more comprehensive definition of identity must consider. According to Martin (1995), Paul Ricœur's philosophical theory of identity (1992) is capable of paying due attention to the dynamic, relational complexity of identificational processes. Although it necessarily involves oversimplifying the theory in parts, we would like to give a general description of some of the cornerstones of Ricœur's theory, as they are important for our own conceptualisation of identity.

2.2.2 Sameness and Selfhood

In his hermeneutics of the self, Ricœur (1992) distinguishes two sub-components of the equivocal term 'identity': identity as sameness (in Latin *idem*, in German *Selbigkeit*, in French *mêmeté*) and identity as selfhood (in Latin *ipse*, in German *Selbstheit*, in French *ipséité*).

Ricœur characterises 'sameness' as a concept of relation and as a relation of relations (1992, p. 116). He divides the conceptual structure of sameness, or *idem* identity, into three semantic components:

> First comes *numerical* identity: thus, we say of two occurrences of a thing, desig-
> nated by an invariable noun in ordinary language, that they do not form two
> different things, but 'one and the same' thing. Here, identity denotes oneness: the
> contrary is plurality (not one but two or several). To this first component of
> the notion of identity corresponds the process of identification, understood in
> the sense of the reidentification of the same, which makes cognition recognition:
> the same thing twice, *n* times.
>
> (Ricœur 1992, p. 116)

This numerical identity is associated with the category of quantity, whereas the (second) *idem* identity operates with the criterion of quality:

> In second place we find *qualitative* identity, in other words, extreme resemblance:
> we say that *x* and *y* are wearing the same suit – that is, clothes that are so similar
> that they are interchangeable with no noticeable difference. To this second
> component corresponds the operation of substitution without semantic loss, *salva
> veritate*.
>
> (Ricœur 1992, p. 116)

In the case of great temporal distance between a recollection from the remote past and a present perception, the qualitative criterion of similarity often proves to be very weak, so that the third element of *idem* identity gains significance for the recognition or re-identification of someone or something. Ricœur describes this component as '*uninterrupted continuity* between the first and last stage in the development of that which we consider to be the same individual. This criterion is predominant whenever growth and aging operate as factors of dissemblance and, by implication, of numeri-cal diversity' (Ricœur 1992, p. 117). Therefore the assumption or demonstration of uninterrupted continuity is capable of replacing or supplementing the criterion of similarity. Exposing this continuity consists in the ordered stringing together of slight changes 'which, taken one by one, threaten resemblance without destroying it. ... As we see, time is here a factor of dissemblance, of divergence, of difference' (Ricœur 1992, p. 117). The threat to identity posed by the lasting continuity of change is no longer present when a principle of temporal constancy, which underlies both similarity and uninterrupted continuity of transformation, is assumed, for example in that the concept of structure is applied as a criterion of identity. Ricœur illustrates his relational concept of structure as a criterion of identity using the example, among others, of the permanence of genetic code of a biological individual and the example of the invariable structure of a tool, all of whose parts have gradually been replaced (Ricœur 1992, p. 117). Applied to communities and groups, the con-cept of structure can be demonstrated by the example of social institutions.

The concept of identity as sameness operates in a dialectical relationship to identity as selfhood, or *ipséité*. *Ipse* identity, as Ricœur understands it, is far more difficult to grasp conceptually than sameness. In his 1995 article cited above, Martin proposed 'uniqueness', meaning 'singularity' or 'unmistakability', as one translation of Ricœur's *ipséité* (1995, p. 6).

Although the terms 'uniqueness', 'singularity' and 'unmistakability' are not semantically equivalent to 'selfhood' (the German *Selbstheit*, the French *ipséité*), we have nonetheless chosen to employ them in elaborating our own notion of identity. We will not, however, include Ricœur's own term 'selfhood' among the conceptual instruments we use. We would like to explain the basis for this decision.

Ricœur (1992) developed his concept of identity on the basis of the single individual, to whom he applies the concept of 'selfhood'. In our opinion, applying the expression 'selfhood' to refer to a collective group such as an entire nation would not only make little sense, it would also bring about an extremely misleading and questionable conceptual and ideological hypostatisation. Ricœur himself was not yet wholly immune to the temptation of such a hypostasing, personifying analogy between individuals and communities:

> The notion of narrative identity also indicates its fruitfulness in that it can be applied to a community as well as to an individual. We can speak of the self-constancy of a community, just as we spoke of it as applied to an individual subject. Individual and community are constituted in their identity by taking up narratives that become for them their actual history.
>
> (Ricœur 1988, p. 247)

Moreover, that which Ricœur wishes to denote with his term 'selfhood' cannot be transferred to a nation. Selfhood is conceptually very closely associated with what is frequently referred to as the 'ego identity' in other identity theories, for example, in those of Erikson (1959), Erving Goffman (1990) and Jürgen Habermas (1976), and an imagined community such as a nation cannot have such an 'identity of the self'. However, in Ricœur's work (1992) there are no references to the identity concepts of Mead, Goffman, Erikson and Habermas. Thus, the analogy between the concepts of 'selfhood' and 'ego identity' should be viewed with caution, as it is only intended to suggest possible reference points in the semantic jungle of identity discussions. A comprehensive clarification of the implications of this terminological debate would indeed deserve a study of its own.

Whereas 'personal' and 'social' identity are ascribed to the individual from the outside, the 'ego identity' according to Goffman, is 'one's own subjective feeling about one's own situation and one's own continuity and uniqueness' (Goffman 1990, p. 129). Mead's theory contains an approximate conceptual match for 'ego identity' in the term 'I', which Mead distinguishes from 'me'. The ego identity synthesises and mediates between the various 'me' forms. In this context, 'me' means either my idea of the picture that others have of me, or the internalisation of the attitudes and expectations of others. Among other things, the ego identity is the authority which enables people to direct their own behaviour. It includes the ability to shape social roles, the ability to interpret (others') expectations of these roles and the ability to distance oneself from one's own internalisations (cf. Dreitzel 1980, p. 55).

For reasons of space we cannot discuss in detail the identity of selfhood and its relationship to the identity of sameness. However, let us make one observation: the identity of selfhood is rooted in a model of constancy which corresponds to the temporality of human existence, while the identity of sameness is based on the constancy of a farthest-reaching invariant. *Ipse* identity covers a spectrum of meaning which reaches from one extreme pole to another; at one pole, *ipse* identity reaches a point at which it is congruous with the identity of sameness, and at the other it is completely distinct from sameness.

2.2.3 Narrative Identity

Sameness and selfhood stand in a dialectical relationship to each other. In Ricœur's theory the notion of 'narrative identity' functions as an intermediary between these two identity elements in the ordering of temporality. It oscillates between both poles of identity and integrates the changeable and dynamic elements in a temporal permanence. Narrative identity is an identity seen as identity of a character (*personage*) (Ricœur 1992, p. 141); a figure is that part of a fable composition which executes the plot. The fable composition aims to synthesise heterogeneous elements by combining heterogeneous factors in linked plots and events to form a narrative. It functions 'to integrate with permanence in time what seems to be its contrary in the domain of sameness-identity, namely diversity, variability, discontinuity, and instability' (1992, p. 140). The narrative configuration has to mediate between concordance and discordance in such a way that the story told can be understood as a whole by its recipients.

By means of this narrative operation, a dynamic concept of identity is formed which also includes the concept of transformation. In correlation to the narrated story, the identity of a person unfolds dialectically: it is moulded by the narrative plot in such a way that on the one hand the singular temporal unity of his or her life is conveyed (along the lines of the ordering principle of concordance), and on the other hand this unity is threatened by unexpected 'twists of fate' along the lines of discordance. Narrative identity allows various, different, partly contradictory circumstances and experiences to be integrated into a coherent temporal structure, thus making it possible to sketch a person's identity against the background of a dynamic constancy model which does justice to the coherence of a human life. Thus the concept of narrative identity can go beyond the one-sided model of an invariant, self-identical thing. It can take into account the idea that the self can never be grasped without the other, without change.

The quintessence of Ricœur's concept of narrative identity is that the person as a narrative figure draws his or her identity from the identity of the story's plot (Martin 1995, p. 7). One's own identity is conveyed to others in the form of a narrative, and in this process it is possible to arrange and interpret, to rearrange and to reinterpret past events in one's own life. The narration (in this context, narration is not understood in the narrow linguistic-narratological sense) offers the possibility of bringing the often conflicting elements of constancy and transformation into harmony with each other:

> Narrative identity, being at the same time fictitious and real, leaves room for variations on the past – a 'plot' can always be revisited – and also for initiatives in the future. It is an open-ended identity which gives meaning to one's practice, which makes any one act meaningful'.

> (Martin 1995, p. 8)

An 'other' is also always found in a person's narrative identity to the extent that the person changes over the course of time. In other words, the person who was different yesterday from the way she or he is today in turn will be different tomorrow from the way she or he is today. This process of change, which is often characterised by fractures, is told as a more or less coherent life story. The narrated self, however, is also an 'other' to the extent that at least a part of an individual narrative arises from the internalised attitudes, values, behavioural dispositions and patterns of action taken from important role models.

Internalisation is one of the interfaces at which social identities impinge upon the lives of individuals. The authority of the 'conscience', or in psychoanalysis the superego, is constituted by means of the internalisation processes. It is not co-incidental that Ricœur points out the significance of the narrative component of psychoanalytical 'case histories'. In the psychoanalytical process of 'working through', something aims at:

> Replacing the equally incomprehensible and unbearable fragments of a story with a coherent and acceptable story in which the subject of analysis can recognise her or his *ipséité*. Psychoanalysis thus presents an especially instructive laboratory for the specific philosophic investigation of the concept of narrative identity. Here one can actually see how a life story is constituted by a series of rectifications which are performed on earlier narrations.

> (Ricœur 1991, p. 247)

According to Ricœur, the same applies to the history of a people, a collective group or an institution. It proceeds 'from the series of corrections that new historians bring to their predecessors' descriptions and explanations, and step by step, to the legends that preceded this genuinely historiographical work. As has been said, history always proceeds from history' (Ricœur 1991, p. 247).

2.2.4 Individual and System-related Identities

If we now turn to the topic of social or collective identities, which has largely been excluded from our discussion up to now, we must make an important distinction in advance which may at least help to avoid the danger of the confusion of terms which looms constantly on the slippery ice of identity discussions. As Holzinger (1993b, pp. 10ff.), borrowing from Frey and Hausser (1987) makes clear, in its interplay between individual and society identity is discussed mainly from two perspectives in modern social science and the humanities.

On the one hand, the individual person or his or her 'individual identity' is the focus of the investigations. In such cases, 'social identity' refers to an individual person. This person is ascribed certain social characteristics (age, sex, class, and so on) and assigned role expectations and memberships from outside, which people then actually do take on in their images of themselves or which at least are seen by others to be their external attributes. From precisely this perspective, Goffmann distinguishes between 'actual' and 'virtual' social identity. The object of identification in this case is a person, and the subject is the other people (Frey and Hausser 1987, p. 3).

On the other hand, there is another analytical perspective that considers identity in relation to systems. From this standpoint, the concept of identity is used for the characterisation of social systems, and so-called 'collective identities' are the focus of interest: 'The object of identification is not individual people, but rather groups, organisations, classes, cultures. The subject is people who reveal the social system through descriptions' (Frey and Hausser 1987, p. 4). The latter group would include members of this system who talk about themselves as, say, Austrians, Viennese people, Tyroleans, farmers, and so on, and also those who find themselves outside of the system and who cast judgements on 'the Germans', the 'Swiss', 'civil servants', and other groupings.

The element that links these two perspectives is the fact that they both conceive of the identity characteristics of both individual and collective objects as being defined from the outside. The fact that the distinction made here is not made clearly or consistently enough in some theoretical debates on identity and that this often leads to a confusion of terms – which Holzinger also points out (Holzinger 1993b, p. 12) – is definitely linked to the fact that individual-related and system-related identities overlap a great deal in the identity of an individual. To a certain extent, individuals bear the characteristics of one or more collective groups or systems to which they belong.[2]

2.2.5 Multiple Identities

The previously mentioned idea of one person belonging to more than one collective group or system brings us to the term 'multiple identity'. This term is intended to describe the fact that individuals as well as collective groups such as nations are in many respects hybrids of identity, and thus the idea of a homogeneous 'pure' identity on the individual or collective level is a deceptive fiction and illusion. The members of any *Staatsnation* are enculturated in many heterogeneous and often conflicting regional, supraregional, cultural, linguistic, ethnic, religious, sexual, political and otherwise defined 'we'-identities (cf. also Smith 1991, pp. 3–8, who uses the term 'identity' as generally synonymous with the term 'role'). Even in the identity of any given individual several of these social identities or their components – identity fragments, so to speak – are intertwined. A member of a wide variety of social groups and networks has at her or his disposal a wide spectrum of sources of identification, from which he or she selects more or less voluntarily, depending on the context and situation, and thus 'composes' her or his multiple identity (the quotation marks here are intended as an orthographic means of distancing ourselves from the autonomous, voluntary meaning of the verb, which we do not wish to praise too highly).

If one assumes that every identity inevitably involves inclusion and exclusion (Pelinka 1995, p. 29), then hybrid, multiple identities represent a potential corrective element which can counteract the practices of exclusion and differentiation. Wherever different social identities overlap, certain lines of conflict will fade into the background. For example, religious and linguistic differences in Switzerland are reciprocally toned down because approximately 50 per cent each of the French-speaking and German-speaking Swiss are Catholic and the other 50 per cent of each group are Protestant (Pelinka 1995, p. 30; see also Pelinka 1993, p. 44 on the mitigation of ethnic tensions as a result of religious fragmentation in Switzerland). In contrast, in cases where an identity directed against others is one-sidedly overemphasized or overestimated and all 'identity-distance' (Saner 1986, pp. 42 f. borrows from Hegel in his interpretation of this term: 'the identity which includes the non-identity' or the 'identity of identity and non-identity') is lost – which is the case in every form of fundamentalism – conflicts can escalate to dangerous proportions. As Saner suggests:

> However, the most dangerous indeed is cultural overidentification. It manifests itself at its crassest level in the undistanced oversocialisation of entire peoples under charismatic leaders in ideological systems. It is the source of the most and the worst crimes against humanity. The fact that figures such as *Höss* and *Eichmann* themselves were not bloodhounds but professional mass murderers nonetheless was astonishing to some, and they suspected a breach in identity as the reason. Maybe the opposite is true. Socialized by obedience and a submissive mentality to the point that all cultural distance of identity disappeared, they obeyed banally to the very end, completely in line with their idols.
>
> (1986, p. 50)

The conclusion Saner draws from such 'catastrophes of identification' is 'short and to the point: it is necessary to gain distance from identity in order not to make it into a ridiculous and damaging phantom and to remain a real person' (Saner 1986, p. 50) The more people become aware that they are the bearers of multiple identities, the easier it is to fulfil Saner's demand.

Stuart Hall, the main representative of Cultural Studies, is one of several who has pointed out that the process of globalisation, which is controlled by market economics, creates favourable circumstances for cultural hybridisation (1996a, 1996b). In comparison to traditional societies in which identities were still relatively stable – they were also hybrid in the sense that socially internalised 'others' have always been integrated into the selves of these 'pre-modern' people (and in all people at all times) – late modern societies, according to Hall (1996a, p. 600) and Laclau (1990), are increasingly characterised by 'differences' and split by various societal rifts and antagonisms which produce a large number of various 'subject positions', or identities for individuals. Indeed, political groupings, in a simplified response to complex diversity, have tried and still try to 'combine' these cultural differences in ways that have frequently included violent conquest and suppression of cultural diversity (Hall 1996a, p. 616). It was not until after the violent beginnings of nations, and thus after many of the differences had been 'forgotten' as a consequence of political manipulation and control, that national consciousness was able to spread and be consolidated. As a rule, the road to this national identification was and is paved with monumental narratives which do sufficient justice to the narrative ordering principles of concordance and stringency, through which they also integrate narratively heterogeneous elements and historical incongruencies.

2.2.6 Narrative Identity and National Identity

2.2.6.1 Concepts of Nations: Overview[3]

At this point we would like to define more precisely the concept of national identity we propose to use. For this purpose, however, it is first necessary to clarify the meaning of the term 'nation'.

The history of European nations as they have developed since the late Middle Ages, writes Hagen Schulze, is 'a history of many special paths, even before the curtain rose for the era of nation-states, that is, before the turn of the eighteenth to the nineteenth century' (1994, p. 126). Accordingly, there is no generally accepted definition of a 'nation', nor is there any general consensus on the time from which one can speak of a 'nation', quite apart from the exceptions that can be found for every definition of the term 'nation'. Peter Alter (1985, p. 19), for example, questions the very possibility of a systematic definition of the term.

Nevertheless, scholarly discussions revolve principally around two conceptions of the nation and the lines of argumentation connected to them: the political 'nation by an act of will' (the German *Willensnation*) and the nation defined by culture (*Kulturnation*) which is often linguistically defined and ethnically based. However, 'subjective definitions of nations ... tautologically determine in advance what is to be explained – the formation of a national idea of community' (Bauböck 1991, p. 43).

Ernest Renan, who also is credited with coining the concepts *Willensnation* and *Kulturnation* (his ambiguous concept of culture and its in part racist and sexist implications are seldom mentioned), describes a nation as a 'soul', as a 'mental principle' which is determined by the 'common possession of a rich heritage of memories' and by 'present agreement', the 'present desire to live together, the will to preserve heritage' (1995, p. 56). He sees a 'great community of solidarity' in the idea of nation (Renan 1995, p. 57). According to his characterisation, which is criticised by Bauböck (1991), Richter (1994), Silverman (1994), Euchner (1995) and others, the 'subjective will' of an association of individuals who decide voluntarily for a common past and future is decisive for the constitution of a nation: 'A large gathering of people of sound mind and warm hearts creates a moral consciousness which is called a nation' (Renan 1995, p. 58).

Borrowing from the model of a political *Staatsnation* defined by the will of its citizens, Jürgen Habermas (1993) developed the concept of a constitutional patriotism which would take the place of 'ethnic' (German) nationalism as the basis for national identification and for the political character of the polity, and would instead place in the foreground a political culture which follows universalistic principles. Such a view, in other words, sees the basis of the unity of the nation in a common state and in the rights and obligations of its citizens. Critics of this model (for example Richter 1994) find fault in the explicit equation of citizen status with national identity.

Conceptions that do not define nations by the political will of their constituent citizens refer back to so-called 'objective criteria' such as language, culture and territory. Critics of such views of a *Kulturnation* (cf. Gellner 1994, pp. 43ff., pp. 63ff., p. 74) argue that the attempt to identify a *(Kultur)nation* by its language group rests on the erroneous premise that language is an independent variable (Francis 1965, p. 115), and that the linguistic unity of a population can just as easily be the result of random intervention (on this see also Anderson 1983); that state borders do not coincide with linguistic ones; and furthermore, that there are communities to which all of these 'objective' characteristics apply but which are not (yet) nations. In addition, critics maintain that there are also 'real' nations which do not fulfil all of the criteria mentioned (cf. Hobsbawm 1990, p. 6).

In general it is extremely difficult to use such contradicting terms, which have been the focus of social scientific and historical controversy (especially in Austria) for a long time, in a very precise manner:

> The distinction between the two models is highly problematic, and it is (if they are different models at all) not easily applicable to the difference between individual countries (for example, France and Germany in the past, France and the USA or Great Britain now), but rather to differences in the countries themselves.
> (Silverman 1994, p. 34)

Nevertheless, in theoretical works the German *Kulturnation* appears mostly as an antithesis to the French concept of a *Staatsnation* and as a symbol of the attempt to depict Germany (which had no unified state) as a nation on a par with that of the French (cf. Brubaker 1992, p. 1). In numerous texts, moreover, a political value judgement is implied in the dichotomy *Staatsnation* versus *Kulturnation*, specifically between the 'bad' *Staatsnation* and the 'good' *Kulturnation* (Richter 1994, p. 312).

Bauböck (1991, p. 75) and Richter (1994, p. 315) relativise the significance of the distinction between an ethnically based and a politically based understanding of the nation in the contemporary world inasmuch as they notice a 'convergence' in the ideological patterns of these two 'paths' to becoming a 'nation'. Uri Ram (1994, p. 153) points out that some concede 'that the so-called past is a selectively perceived construction resulting from the present interpretation', while others admit 'that the so-called present has to make use of the available cultural repertoire of the collective group in question' and thus the distance between these two conceptions of nations is small. Richter (1994, p. 316) does not consider the distinction between the

Staatsnation and *Kulturnation* productive because every nation is to be thought of as a socially constructed pattern of interpretation with which the world is seen from the standpoint of the difference between 'us' and 'them'. He doubts that the category 'nation of citizens' as it is postulated in the writings of sociologists and political scientists ever existed,[4] as even the 'good' nation of citizens needs its image of an enemy in order to conceive itself as a nation. John Rex argues that even the political interpretation of a nation is not completely immune to operating with ethnic-cultural symbols: 'The problem is that, while it denies particularistic ethnic loyalties or subordinates them, it has itself to create its own sense of belonging, and it does this very often for instance to the mother country or the fatherland' (Rex 1995, p. 27).

These competing conceptions of the nation do, however, give an idea of what distinguishes a nation from other collective identities. As Rudolf Burger states:

> Every nation is the [contrived] construction of a certain pathos [*Pathetisierung*] performed by selectively historiographic means in the service of [identifiable] interests and the emotive charging [*Aufladung*] of an existing or targeted sovereign, political large-scale organisation, a mythifying formula of pathos for the state itself; and every empirical observation of a 'national consciousness' only tests the effect of propaganda.
>
> (Burger 1994a, p. 168)

Peter Alter (1985, p. 23) and Anthony D. Smith (1991, p. 14) point out that a close connection exists between nation and state.[5] A. H. Richmond (1987, p. 4) distinguishes strictly between state and nation because states can consist of several nations and nations can also be polyethnic. Alter (1985) and Smith (1991) give definitions which are problematic in that they assume the existence of a collective group preceding the nation or nation-state. Smith (1983), who perceives a nation as 'named human population sharing a historic territory, common myths and historical memories, a mass public culture, a common economy and common legal rights and duties for all members', speaks explicitly in favor of an 'ethnicist' or 'culturalist' definition of a nation and describes nations as 'cultural units'. His argument is that most nations originated historically on the basis of ethnic communities and are to a certain extent 'the heritage of older collective groups' – a viewpoint which Reiterer has described as 'primordialistic' (1988b):

> Though most latter-day nations are, in fact, polyethnic, or rather most nation-states are polyethnic, many have been formed in the first place around a dominant *ethnie* [...]. In other words nations always require 'ethnic elements'. These may, of course, be reworked; they often are.
>
> (Smith 1991, pp. 39f.)

The term 'culture', which has been mentioned several times already, should be defined in more detail in light of its central significance in the discussion of nations and national identities. Like Frank Robert Vivelo (1981, p. 55), we understand 'culture' as a system of rules and principles for 'proper' behaviour, analogous to the grammar of a language, which sets the standards for 'proper' speaking. In this sense, culture is not primarily defined by cultural products or artefacts, it is 'not the behaviour itself,' rather it 'contains the standards for behaviour' (Vivelo 1981, p. 55), or, in the words of Clifford Geertz: 'The first ... is that culture is best not seen as complexes of concrete behaviour patterns ... but as a set of control mechanisms – plans, recipes, rules, instructions (what computer engineers call "programs") for the governing of behaviour' (1973a, p. 44; cf. also Claude Lévi-Strauss 1966, p. 86, who observes that culture begins where rules appear). This view of culture contrasts with those prevalent among conceptions of a *Kulturnation,* which frequently refer to cultural artefacts (illustrated by the example of Austrian high culture) and beyond that to mentalities and everyday cultural behaviour. This interpretation of culture oscillates between the image of a homogeneous, uniform culture and the idea of heterogeneous cultural riches. All of these interpretations of culture can be found in the works we investigated.

2.2.6.2 The Nation as an Imagined Community

Nations are invented where they did not exist before, writes Benedict Anderson in a critical allusion to Gellner (Anderson 1983, pp. 14–16; cf. the critical comments by Reiterer 1993b and Holzinger 1993a and b). Anderson characterises nations – as well as all other communities that are larger than 'face-to-face groups' – as imagined communities and supports the view that communities are to be distinguished from one another 'not by their authenticity but by the way in which they are imagined' (Anderson 1983, p. 15). Nations are imagined, says Anderson:

> because the members of even the smallest nations will never know most of their fellow-members, meet them, or even hear of them; yet in the minds of each lives the image of their communion. ... The nation is imagined as *limited* because even the largest of them, ... has finite, if elastic, boundaries, beyond which lie other nations. No nation imagines itself coterminous with mankind. ... It is imagined as *sovereign* because the concept was born in an age in which Enlightenment and Revolution were destroying the legitimacy of the divinely-ordained, hierarchical dynastic realm. ... The gage and emblem of this freedom is the sovereign state.
>
> (Anderson 1983, pp. 15–16)

Anderson refers to religious communities and dynastic empires linked to each other by 'sacred languages' and by writings passed on through generations as the 'cultural roots' of nationalism, the 'miracle' of which was 'turning chance into destiny' (Anderson 1983, p. 19). As early as the seventeenth century, monarchic legitimacies, which until then had been taken for granted and defined by religious standards, began to disintegrate in Europe. State legitimacy was shifted to territories legally distinguished from one another (Anderson 1983, p. 26).

Nevertheless, nations did not simply arise from religious communities and dynastic empires. A fundamental transformation of the forms of perception of the world was also necessary in order to enable people to conceive of a 'nation' (Anderson

1983, p. 28). Anderson emphasises the significance of the fall of Latin as the 'sacred language' (analogous to Arabic and the Koran; Anderson 1983, pp. 20 ff.), the knowledge of which had previously signified privileged access to 'truth' (Anderson 1983, p. 25 and p. 40). In addition, Anderson stresses the decisive role of the connection between capitalist production methods and book printing in the sixteenth century, from which a strong impulse towards the increased significance of local languages came after the saturation of the limited market for Latin books. In the course of this development, different varieties of languages were combined into a smaller number of written languages. In this way, large new circles of readers were formed which could be mobilised for political and religious purposes (for example, Protestantism and the Reformation) and later for political and national purposes. The written languages disseminated by printing 'made it possible for rapidly growing numbers of people to think about themselves, and to relate themselves to others, in profoundly new ways' (Anderson 1983, p. 40), because they formed the basis of communication 'below' Latin and 'above' the spoken dialects and everyday language. On the other hand, printed books led to a fixation of language and thus of the images of past times (Anderson 1983, p. 47). At the same time, the market for books also created new 'languages-of-power' (Anderson 1983, p. 48), because certain dialects were 'closer' to their respective written languages and thus were able to influence their final form. At the beginning of this development, the fixation of written languages and the differentiation of their status were predominantly unconscious processes resulting from the interaction of capitalist production methods, technology and linguistic diversity. Later, these processes were able to become formal models which could be imitated and used for processes of nation-building (Anderson 1983, p. 48). Not just any language *per se*, Anderson argues, but the written language invented nationalism (Anderson 1983, p. 122).

2.2.6.3 *The Nation as a System of Cultural Representations*

If a nation is an imagined community and at the same time a mental construct, an imaginary complex of ideas containing at least the defining elements of collective unity and equality, of boundaries and autonomy, then this image is real to the extent that one is convinced of it, believes in it and identifies with it emotionally. The question of how this imaginary community reaches the minds of those who are convinced of it is easy to answer: it is constructed and conveyed in discourse, predominantly in narratives of national culture. National identity is thus the product of discourse.

In an argument similar to Anderson's, Stuart Hall describes nations not only as political formations but also as 'systems of cultural representations' (1996a, p. 612) through which an imagined community is interpreted: 'People are not only legal citizens of a nation; they participate in the *idea* of the nation as represented in its national culture. A nation is a symbolic community …' (1996a, p. 612). Hall continues:

A national culture is a *discourse* – a way of constructing meanings which influences and organises both our actions and our conception of ourselves ... National cultures construct identities by producing meanings about 'the nation' with which we can *identify*; these are contained in the stories which are told about it, memories which connect its present with its past, and imagines which are constructed of it.

(Hall 1996a, p. 613)

Or, as Uri Ram (1994, p. 153) puts it with reference to Clifford Geertz (1973b): 'Nationality is a narration, a story which people tell about themselves in order to lend meaning to their social world.' However, national narrations do not arise out of nothing, and they do not exist in a vacuum. Far more often they are brought forth, reproduced and disseminated by actors in concrete (institutional) contexts: 'The fact that nationality is a story does not challenge its reality, because myths are not mystifications' (Ram 1994, p. 154). Cultural identities can be described as 'identification points', as 'seams which arise in the discourse of history and culture. Not anything constant, but rather a positioning' (Räthzel 1994, p. 226).

According to Hall (1996a), these constructed national cultural identities and national cultures (Hall sees national identity as an example and at the same time a form of national cultural identity) are not uniform, but rather are to be thought of as a discursive sketch which represents differences between social classes, between ethnic groups or between the sexes as units 'unified' by the exertion of cultural power (Hall 1996a, p. 617; on the fragmentation of identities cf. also Gürses 1994, pp. 353–68 and Bradley 1996). They are 'the result of bringing these two halves of the national equation together [that is the modern nation-state and the ancient, nebulous *natio* as local community, domicile, family or condition of belonging] – offering both membership of the political nation-state and identification with the national culture' (Hall 1996a, p. 616). 'In the modern world,' Hall argues, 'the national cultures into which we are born are one of the principal sources of cultural identity' (Hall 1996a, p. 611). All modern nations are 'cultural hybrids' (Hall 1996a, p. 617), as, in the course of the processes of change in the modern era (for example, global homogenisation and, parallel to it, the moulding of local and particularistic identities), communities and organisations are integrated into new spatial and temporal relationships and brought into relation with each other.

2.2.6.4 *The Narration of the Nation*

According to Stuart Hall (1996a, pp. 613–15), a narration of national culture contains five fundamental aspects. He labels these 'discursive strategies' (Hall 1996a, p. 614), which is not a very fitting description, at least for the third and fifth aspects, as their relationship to the level of discourse is not immediately obvious from their names. To 'invent' a tradition, in the sense of 'to think up', is – as one can easily recognise in this synonym explicitly containing a *verbum cogitandi* – at first just as little a 'discursive phenomenon' as the 'idea' of an original people. According to their names, then, both of these aspects are related to the cognitive and mental, but not directly to the discursive sphere. Let us look at the five aspects in question:

1. Hall's first aspect is the *narrative of the nation*. It is presented in national narratives, in literature, in the media and in everyday culture and it creates a connection between stories, landscapes, scenarios, historical events, national symbols and national rituals which represent shared experiences and concerns, triumphs and destructive defeats. This narration lends meaning and security to monotonous existence and ties everyday life to a 'national destiny'.

2. The second aspect is the *emphasis on origins, continuity, tradition*, and *time-lessness*. National identity is represented in narratives of national culture as the original identity which is present in the nature of things but sometimes lies dormant and has to be awakened from this slumber. This aspect aims at an image (which manifests itself in discourses) of national character as an un-changing, unbroken and uniform being.

3. Hall takes the aspect of *invention of tradition* from Hobsbawm and Ranger (1983, p. 1). Invented traditions (mostly of a ritual or symbolic nature) make historical confusion and defeats understandable; they transform disorder into community.

4. The *foundational myth* or *myth of origin* is accorded great significance in the invention of a national culture. The origin of a nation is often set so far back in time that it is lost in the fog of time and is no longer 'real', that is, it 'exists' somewhere in 'mythical' times. Such myths not only play a role in the officially sanctioned narrations of a nation, but also in the antithetical narratives which are used as instruments to found new nations.

5. Finally, the fictitious idea of a '*pure, original people* or "*folk*"' (Hall 1996a, p. 615) is employed to support a national identity.

In Hall's view, attempts are made to cover up the real differences between people's class, gender, 'race', and so on and to construct a large 'national family' through discourse with the help of these five 'aspects'. This national unity, however, exists only as a discursive construct.

There are, certainly, some difficulties with Hall's notion of narratively constructed national identity. These arise when one tries to separate the five points from each other with some degree of clarity in order to use them for the analysis of concrete data. In our view, aspects 2, 3, 4 and 5 could easily be interpreted as subcomponents of aspect 1, once one disregards the mixing of cognitive and discursive labels in the names of the individual elements. Aspects 2, 4 and probably 5 are also rather difficult to separate if one critically analyses Hall's characterisation. Hall's definition of myths of foundation or origin – that is, those which place the origin of the nation in a mythical 'time before time' – can be found in the case of some nations but not in our material on Austria. Thus we would like to interpret and define the 'myth of origin' in a more general sense so that it can be applied to Austria as well.

Aspect 5, the idea of a 'pure original people', moreover, can be illustrated by examples from other nations, but it cannot be found in the data we investigated.

Essentialist representations of the Austrian national character and the *homo Austriacus* can be found in some of the data in question, for example in the focus groups and interviews. But this is not the same thing as Hall's 'original people'. Consequently, in our analysis we will employ the concept of the *homo Austriacus.*

By using Hall's work heuristically, we have been able to refine the category of narrative national identity and to relate it usefully to the substantive contents of our empirical data. Hall himself points out that his list is in no way exhaustive. Thus, we would like to examine the typology created by Leszek Kolakowski (1995), which to a certain extent overlaps in part with Hall's list. This should enable us to elaborate an even more comprehensive, and in our opinion more consistent, scheme with which we can analyse our body of data more systematically and completely. It should become evident from this discussion that national identity cannot be completely subsumed under the category of narrative identity.

Kolakowski believes that national identity is characterised by five elements:

1. The vague, substantialising idea of a *national spirit* or *'Volksgeist'* which expresses itself in certain cultural forms of life and particular collective manners of behaviour, especially in moments of crisis, is a metaphysical entity which does not represent an object of historical experience but still floats in the minds of many people.

2. *Historical memory* (what Kolakowski refers to as historical memory here is similar to what Maurice Halbwachs 1997 called 'collective memory'; see also Peter Burke 1989) is an indispensable prerequisite for national identity; according to Kolakowski, it is not important whether the content of historical memory is true, partly true or legendary. The further into the past the real or imaginary memories reach, the more securely national identity is supported. 'Some nationalities which have formed just recently invent an *ad hoc* artificial relation to the past without the existence of real, verifiable connections' (Kolakowski 1995, p. 33).

3. *Anticipation and future orientation* likewise form a necessary aspect of national identity. 'A nation is just as future-oriented as a person; both worry about what may become of them, both try to survive and to make preparations for potential adversity, both think of their future interests. However, there is a difference in the fact that a nation, unlike a person, does not anticipate its own death' (Kolakowski 1995, p. 54). This quote gives us the opportunity to recall Berger and Luckmann's warning (see the quotation in note 2 of the present chapter). Kolakowski, who by the way entitled his essay 'On Collective Identity', allows the nation to act as a personified actor, which is not compatible with Anderson's characterisation of a 'nation' which we have adopted. In our opinion, the idea that the themes of 'nation' and 'death' are not usually brought into connection with each other cannot be accepted. The reference (often found in discourses on national identity) to globalisation tendencies, and the resulting dangers of a loss of national autonomy and uniqueness, associates the two themes with each other indeed.

4. In contrast to Kolakowski, we would like to stress that we interpret the term '*national body*' in a purely metaphorical sense. It is linked to national identity, and it manifests itself in discussions of national territories, landscapes and nature as well as the physical artefacts which shape those elements. The metaphor of the 'national body' also plays a role in the thematic treatment of the size and limitation of a state as well as the number of its members (cf. also the criterion of boundaries in Anderson's elaboration of the concept of 'nation').

5. Finally, Kolakowski views a *nameable beginning* as another requirement for national consciousness. Legends of a founding event or of the first 'founding fathers', which are often not precisely dated, attempt to conjure up images of this beginning. In some creation myths, this beginning often marks the *exordium temporis*, or the beginning of historical time.

As problematic as parts of Kolakowski's dissection of categories of national identity seem to us, his division as such does possess a certain degree of plausibility. Consequently, we have integrated certain aspects into the categorical scheme detailing the substantive contents of (Austrian) national identity we present in section 2.3.2. When these substantive components are questioned individually regarding their ability to be integrated exhaustively into the concept of 'narrative identity', they show that national identity cannot be reduced to narrative identity. Anticipation and future orientation are not covered in narrative identity, which primarily refers to the past. Likewise, the temporal dimension of the present cannot be treated from the narrative standpoint. Both aspects, however, play a not unimportant role in the discursive production of national identity.

Summarising what has been said up to this point, we observe that the discursive construction of national identity revolves around the three temporal axes of the past, the present and the future. In this context, origin, continuity/tradition, transformation, (essentialist) timelessness and anticipation are important ordering criteria. Spatial, territorial, and local dimensions (expanse, borders, nature, landscape, physical artefacts and intervention in 'natural space') are likewise significant in this discursive construction of national identity.

Loosely speaking, the personal dimension of national identity has appeared on the one hand in relation to the themes of history and culture, and on the other hand in relation to the themes of 'selfhood', 'sameness', 'equality', 'similarity', 'difference' (or the 'other'), 'uniqueness' and 'autonomy' (the counterpart of which is 'heteronomy', which we have not yet discussed explicitly in this chapter; the term always is, however, used as an antonym when autonomy is discussed), 'unity', 'community' and 'group'. Indeed, as mentioned earlier, the primarily individual-related category of 'selfhood' cannot be applied to concepts such as 'nation' and 'national identity'. In a purely grammatical sense, it is possible to link the word 'self', traditionally described as a pronoun, to all people in the singular and plural (myself, yourself, him- or herself, ourselves, themselves). However, the nominalisation 'selfhood' would create a substantialised entity from a construct of ideas. Instead, we have introduced the term 'uniqueness', which – as we will explain presently – signifies something slightly different from the highly complex concept of selfhood. Likewise, we use the terms 'sameness/equality' and 'similarity' with a semantically looser and more undifferentiated meaning than that of Ricœur's 'sameness' for pragmatic reasons – although we keep Ricœur's theoretical considerations in the back of our minds by constantly recalling that the relational, dynamic concept of identity is tied up in a complex dialectical relationship between sameness and difference, and that narrative identity attempts to mediate in this relationship.

Like 'sameness' and 'difference', 'uniqueness' is a relational term. The *tertium comparationis* of these two terms is 'comparison'. 'Uniqueness', which on a denotative level is more or less synonymous with 'unmistakability' (which implies 'distinctiveness'), is *per se* a special form of difference. The relation of uniqueness focuses, however, on only one of the two points of comparison. The relation frequently pushes uniqueness into the center of attention and (semiotically speaking) into the foreground, while the background with the other point of comparison mostly remains completely colourless and without contours.

The process of national identification is promoted by the emphasis on 'national uniqueness'. By raising individuality, which is a prized value in modern societies, to the national level (we are aware that uniqueness and individuality are not the same, but they are closely connected and are often used synonymously), the governing representatives of a political system mostly conceal their forcible act of homogenisation and erasure of differences which is manifested in the epithet 'national'. In addition, national uniqueness, which is assigned entirely positive attributes, compensates for the unfulfilled need for individual uniqueness.

Schopenhauer (1989, p. 429) made the following overly harsh remark regarding the last aspect:

> The most inexpensive type of pride, conversely, is national pride, because it betrays in the person afflicted by it a lack of individual characteristics of which he [sic!] could be proud, so that he would not have to resort to that which he shares with so many millions of others. One who has meaningful personal characteristics will far more be able to recognise the faults of his nation most clearly, because he sees them constantly. But every miserable twit who has nothing in the world to be proud of reaches for the last resort, pride in the nation to which he belongs; this allows him to recover, and he is gratefully willing to defend all of his nation's faults and foolishness [...] with his hands and feet. For this reason, you will hardly find more than one in fifty Englishmen [sic!], for example, who will agree when you speak of the stupid and degrading bigotry of his nation with due contempt: that one, however, is wont to be a man [sic!] of mind.
>
> (Schopenhauer, 1989, p. 429)

2.2.6.5 National Identity as Habitus

Now that we have dealt with most of the conceptual basics which figure into the discursive construction of national identity, we must make a general remark on the relationship between national identity and its production. If we interpret national identities as purely discursive constructs which contain specifically developed national identity narratives as important components, how do we handle the obvious question of what motivates a person to reproduce such a discursive production? Martin gives a very enlightening answer which, however, only comments on identity narratives. Nonetheless, his points apply to the entire field of the discursive construction of national identities:

> To put it in a nutshell, the identity narrative channels political emotions so that they can fuel efforts to modify a balance of power; it transforms the perceptions of the past and of the present; it changes the organisation of human groups and creates new ones; it alters cultures by emphasising certain traits and skewing their meanings and logic. The identity narrative brings forth a new interpretation of the world in order to modify it.
>
> (Martin 1995, p. 13)

This quotation can be read as the answer to our question if we reverse the metonymic personification of the 'identity narrative' (which acts as an actor in the quotation) by putting those who bring forth the identity narrative in its place. Martin's statements, however, focus only on one area – although it is central – of the spectrum of motivating reasons for the discursive construction of national identity, specifically the area which covers the more or less conscious actions of political actors and bearers of political responsibility. One force which is likewise part of national identity, and which of course can motivate political actors as well, is not mentioned in Martin's discussion: the firm conviction in what is maintained about national identity, that is, the partly faith-related identifying bond to certain elements of the 'collective memory'.

One of the reasons why this element is left out in Martin's work, and in the work of many others who treat national identity from the viewpoint of 'narrative identity' in the sense mentioned above, is that they do not consider it from an individual-related standpoint. If the individual is taken as the object under study, then national identity can be defined heuristically as follows, borrowing loosely from Bourdieu's habitus concept (1993a, 1990, 1994b):

National identity is a complex of common or similar *beliefs or opinions* internalised in the course of socialisation – with regard to the aspects named by Hall and Kolakowski as well as to certain outgroups distinguished from the national 'we-group' – and of common or similar *emotional attitudes* with regard to these aspects and outgroups, as well as common or similar *behavioural dispositions*, including inclusive, solidarity-oriented and exclusive, distinguishing dispositions and also in many cases linguistic dispositions. Insofar as this common complex, which can also be viewed with Mead as a specific 'generalized Other', is internalised, that is individually acquired, it is also, depending on the degree of identification, more or less a part of the individual's identity complex.

The concept of habitus has been employed more and more often in recent studies on national identities, for example in Elias (1992), Blomert, Kuzmics and Treibel

(1993), Kuzmics (1993) and Paier (1996). However, in some of these studies, for example in Kuzmics' (1993) and Paier's (1996), there is a fair amount of confusion in distinguishing the habitus concept and the idea of a 'national character' or 'people's character': both terms are sometimes used as general synonyms, even by Bourdieu himself (1994c). Therefore, we see fit to clarify the matter as follows: the idea of a 'national character', or 'people's character' (in our case a *homo Austriacus*), is a mere stereotypical phantasmagoria which has no real counterpart outside of the minds of those who believe in it. This means that if we assign deceptive auto- or heterostereo-typical images (for example, Austrian *Gemütlichkeit*, intolerance, submissiveness, and so on) to one of the three components of Bourdieu's habitus concept mentioned in our description (mental level, level of emotions and attitudes, level of behavioural dispositions), then we do not assign them to the level of behavioural dispositions – which Paier (1996) does, for example – but rather primarily to the mental level, and wherever these ideas are linked to certain emotional attitudes and value judgements, then also to the second level. We do not define the third level of national identity interpreted as habitus, the level of behavioural dispositions, by means of well-known auto- and heterostereotypes, but rather far more abstractly and formally, by means of dispositions such as the willingness to take sides with the nation to which one has a feeling of belonging and to protect it when one feels threatened – right in line with the saying, 'Right or wrong, my country!'

Bourdieu describes the contribution of the state – or more specifically its administrators and officials – to the generation of national identities in his essay 'Rethinking the state' as follows:

> Through classificational systems (specially according to sex and age) inscribed in law, through bureaucratic procedures, educational structures and social rituals (particularly salient in the case of Japan and England), the state molds mental structures and imposes common principles of vision and division ... And it thereby contributes to the construction of what is commonly designated as national identity (or, in a more traditional language, national character).
>
> (Bourdieu 1994c, pp. 7f.)

Although we cannot follow Bourdieu in his conceptual equation of 'national identity' and 'national character', we do agree with his other views on identity, i.e. that the state shapes those forms of perception, of categorisation, of interpretation, and of memory which serve as the basis for a more or less immediate orchestration of the habitus which forms the basis for a kind of 'national common sense', through the school and the educational system.

In summary, we will assume the following theses: The national identity of individuals who perceive themselves as belonging to a national collectivity is manifested, *inter alia*, in their social practices, one of which is discursive practice. The respective national identity is shaped by state, political, institutional, media and everyday social practices, and the material and social conditions which emerge as their results, to which the individual is subjected. The discursive practice as a special form of social practice plays a central part both in the formation and in the expression of national identity. Some of the discursive practices condense into laws which regulate the social practices of inclusion and exclusion of individuals in the form of fixed institutional discursive practices. However, these legally prescribed practices do not always coincide with the practices actually realised. The social practices, both as actions and as discursive acts, may deviate in either negative or positive ways from the laws. In the analysis of our data we will explore how these deviations occur at the discursive level in public, political and media areas as well as in semi-private and quasi-private areas.

2.3 THE CONSTRUCTION OF NATIONAL IDENTITY IN DISCOURSE

2.3.1 Methodological Approaches

As we have discussed in the section on Critical Discourse Analysis, we are committed to an approach combining a plurality of methods. This approach, which we have refined and elaborated in several studies over many years of research (cf., for example, Wodak et al. 1990; Wodak et al. 1994; Matouschek, Wodak and Januschek 1995), distinguishes between three closely interwoven dimensions of analysis:

1. Contents
2. Strategies
3. Means and forms of realisation.

We employ further analytical methods depending on the type and size of data set we are investigating. For example, the analysis of political commemorative speeches necessitates a method which can identify the various rhetorical and argumentative features of the text, because these speeches are characterised by their rhetorical persuasive orientation. In contrast, in the study of the poster campaigns preceding the referendum on Austria's EU accession we use 'Critical Layout Analysis' which is currently being developed in research by practitioners of British Critical Discourse Analysis.

2.3.2 Contents

The matrix of thematic contents which we have devised, on the basis of a critical survey of the theoretical literature and the pilot analyses of our data, distinguishes five major thematic areas:

1. the linguistic construction of the *homo Austriacus*
2. the narration and confabulation of a common political past
3. the linguistic construction of a common culture
4. the linguistic construction of a common political present and future
5. the linguistic construction of a 'national body'.

We examine what we have termed *homo Austriacus* and *homo externus* – the latter is thematically important in the construction of inter-national and intra-national difference – in terms of emotional attachment to Austria, national mentality and supposed national behavioural dispositions; in terms of various elements of bio-graphical genesis (coincidence, fate, origin, place of birth, place of childhood and place of residence, socialisation) and in terms of the 'activation' of national identity (for example, through experiences in other countries).

The construction of a common political past revolves around founding myths and myths of origin, mythical figures, political successes, times of prosperity and stability, defeats and crises. Furthermore, we distinguish the thematic elements of the Nazi period in relation to 'Austrians as perpetrators', 'victims of National Socialism', 'Austrian victim thesis' and 'victim compensation'.[6]

In the construction of a common culture we distinguish the topics of language, religion, art (music, literature, theatre, architecture, painting, and so on), science and technology (cf. Plitzner 1995) as well as everyday culture (sport, eating and drinking habits, clothing, and so on).

The thematic contents of the construction of a common political present and future will be explored in terms of citizenship, political achievements, current and future political problems, crises and dangers, future political objectives and political virtues. Two topics which are particularly important for the construction and trans-formation of this political present and future are Austria's entry into the European Union (EU) and Austria's 'permanent neutrality'.

Finally, our analysis of the construction of the 'national body' distinguishes be-tween extension and delimitation on the one hand, and 'natural space' – landscapes as well as transformation of natural space, i.e. physical national artefacts – on the other.

We relate all these topics primarily to the discursive construction of 'national' identity which is based on the formation of sameness and difference. Wherever addi-tional linguistic constructs of 'subnational' (for example, referring to a province) or 'supranational' identities are created in our data, we relate them to the relevant topics listed above.

2.3.3 Strategies

2.3.3.1 On the Concept of Strategy

The concept of strategy derives from Greek *strategía* and, since the nineteenth cen-tury at the latest, has meant 'the art of a commander-in-chief; the art of projecting and directing the larger military movements and operations of a campaign' (Oxford English Dictionary 1988, p. 852, point 2a). A strategist (Greek *stratēgos*) is someone who is skilled in leading (Greek *àgein*) an army (Greek *stratos*).

Abstracted from a purely military context, the concept of strategy generally denotes a more or less accurate plan adopted to achieve a certain political, psychological or other kind of objective. The strategist attempts to anticipate all those factors which may have an impact on his or her actions.

Our interpretation of strategy is heavily indebted to Pierre Bourdieu's definition.

According to Bourdieu, the significance of strategies cannot be associated with a simplistic, finalistic and voluntary perspective (cf. Bourdieu 1994a, p. 90). Strategic action is oriented towards a goal but not necessarily planned to the last detail or strictly instrumentalist; strategies can also be applied automatically . As Bourdieu argues:

> I want to re-emphasise that the principle of philosophical (or literary) strategies is not cynical calculation, the conscious pursuit of maximum specific profit, but an unconscious relationship between a *habitus* and a field. The strategies I am talking about are actions objectively oriented towards goals that may not be the goals subjectively pursued.
>
> (Bourdieu 1993b, p. 90)

This quotation repudiates a simple idealistic finalism emerging from an absolute freedom of social actors, a repudiation we also adhere to. Like Bourdieu, we argue for a 'soft, relative determinism', which tries to take into account the social and material conditions as well as the fact that actors have been conditioned through the socialisation of individual acting, without, however, immediately refuting any individual space of action and thereby absolving individuals from any responsibility for their own acts. Such a perspective would be incompatible with the position of Critical Discourse Analysis, as any critical investigation would be superfluous if those criticised could skirt responsibility for their (discursive) actions by simply shifting it to discourse or a discursive formation.

Where we do not agree with Bourdieu is in his assumption that strategy and action are equivalent. We locate acts on the level of realisation: they are realisations of strategies. 'Behind' or 'within' acts we can discern specific, more or less conscious or automatised, strategies which serve certain purposes or help to achieve a particular objective. Only by looking at these – for example, discursive – acts may we draw conclusions about potential underlying strategies.

Even though Heinemann and Viehweger (1991) have applied the concept of strategy primarily in relation to text linguistics, their general definition of 'strategy' corresponds to the way we apply it to discourse:

> Thus it becomes clear that strategies mediate between communicative functions and objectives deduced from the interaction and the social conditions of inter-acting partners and, on the other hand, the realisation of linguistic (or extra-linguistic) means and their structuration.
>
> (Heinemann and Viehweger 1991, p. 215)

If we apply the concept of strategy to our different sets of data and keep in mind the varied conditions of origin of these discursive products, it may be assumed that the degree of conscious intention and finality is greatest in the political commemora-tive speeches, advertising posters and newspaper articles, and decreases in individual contributions to discussions in focus groups and even more in the individual inter-views. In other words, the quality and significance of the intentional aspect of the concept of strategy varies depending on the data examined.

2.3.3.2 An Overview of Strategies

On the macro-level we can distinguish between different types of macro-strategies employed in the discursive formation of national identity. These macro-strategies correspond to the main social macro-functions we discussed earlier, namely construction, perpetuation or justification, transformation and demontage or dismantling (see section 2.1). Although analytically distinguishable from one another, these strategies occur more or less simultaneously and are interwoven in concrete discursive acts.

Constructive strategies are the most comprehensive discursive strategies. They attempt to construct and to establish a certain national identity by promoting unification, identification and solidarity, as well as differentiation. Strategies of perpetuation attempt to maintain and to reproduce a threatened national identity, i.e. to preserve, support and protect it. A special subgroup of these strategies is the group of *strategies of justification*. These are employed primarily in relation to problematical actions or events in the past which are important in the narrative creation of national history. They attempt to justify or relativise a societal *status quo ante* by emphasising the legitimacy of past acts of the 'own' national 'we'-group which have been put into question, that is they restore, maintain and defend a common 'national self-perception' which has been 'tainted' in one way or another.

Strategies of transformation aim to transform a relatively well-established national identity and its components into another identity the contours of which the speaker has already conceptualised. This is often effected by applying subtle rhetorical persuasion. Finally, *dismantling* or *destructive strategies* aim at dismantling or disparaging parts of an existing national identity construct, but usually cannot provide any new model to replace the old one.

Serving these discursive macro-strategies are various other strategies. At this point we want to mention only those which occur most frequently, namely the strategies of emphasis or presupposition of sameness (strategies of assimilation) and the strategies of emphasis or presupposition of difference (strategies of dissimilation). *Strategies of assimilation* aim linguistically to create a temporal, interpersonal or spatial (territorial) similarity and homogeneity in reference to the various thematic dimensions we have discussed above. According to their respective social macro-functions they may be constructive, destructive, perpetuating or justifying. *Strategies of dissimilation* (cf. also Matouschek, Wodak and Januschek 1995; Matouschek and Wodak 1995; Wodak and Matouschek 1993) create a temporal, interpersonal or territorial difference and heterogeneity in reference to these same dimensions. According to their functions they may also be constructive, destructive, transformatory or justifying. Difference which is linguistically constructed through strategies of dissimilation, and which in reference to marginalised groups of others is frequently portrayed as deviance from a preferred norm, here does not usually introduce subtle distinctions, but, on the contrary, implies the affixing of undifferentiated and usually derogatory labels on the group concerned.

To elaborate all the other sub-strategies would transcend the scope of this introductory section. In place of a more detailed discussion, we have provided a condensed overview in the form of tables, which list the macro-strategies and the argumentative topoi, or formulae, and several related (but not disjunctively related) forms of realisation with which they correlate in the data. In the tables, linguistic strategies of assimilation and dissimilation are allocated to the other strategies as substrategies. If individual strategies are not self-explanatory, we discuss them in the course of our data analysis (in particular in Chapter 4).

The tables represent a summary presentation of the results we derived from the analysis of our data; they are not *a priori* categories which we imposed on the data. The relationship between strategies, schemes of argumentation (or topoi, which we understand as argumentation schemes or formulae as used in argumentation theory) and the means of realisation is not strictly exclusive, either horizontally or vertically, though the horizontal and vertical assignments indicate a preferential association or tendency. However, one and the same strategy (for example, heteronomisation) may aim at serving different functions, such as relativisation, transformation or demontage. One and the same topos (for example, the topos of danger and threat) may be employed for a relativisation, transformation or demontage, although not every strategy must necessarily draw upon a topos. Similarly, a particular trope (for example, the synecdoche) may serve many different strategies.

Finally, a last word about the relationship of strategies to topoi. As explained, we conceive strategies to be more or less 'automated' activity plans based on models of more or less comprehensive and stereotyped – in our case discursive – activities which are located on the different levels of mental, cognitive organisation and which are more or less elaborated. As such, the concept of 'strategy' is closely connected to the concepts of 'frame', 'scheme' and 'script'. However, scripts are primarily characterised in terms of representation of knowledge about prototypical action sequences. Schemes are primarily described in terms of cognitive, emotional and actional default macro-structures with respect to objects, events, situations and practices. Frames are mainly characterised in terms of memory-modelling or knowledge-organising unities of actions. In contrast to 'script', 'scheme' and 'frame', 'strategy' is mainly identified in terms of planned social (in our case, discursive) activities, of the political or socio-psychological aims or functions of these activities, and of (linguistic) means designated to help realise these aims. The aims or functions of these planned social practices can both be more general, like the four macro-functions of construction, preservation, transformation and demontage/dismantling, and more topic-related (related to the topic of 'identity'), like the different micro-functions of singularisation, autonomisation, assimilation, dissimilation and so on. In contrast to 'strategy', we conceptualise 'topoi' or 'loci' to be highly conventionalised parts of argumentation which belong to the obligatory elements of argumentation and take the form either of explicit or inferable premises. They are the more or less formal (for example *locus a minore*) or content-related (for example *topos of external constraints*) warrants or 'conclusion rules' which connect an argument or arguments with a conclusion, a claim. As such, they justify the transition from an argument or arguments to the conclusion (Kienpointner 1992, p. 194). As standard-ised argumentation schemes, topoi can become integral parts of strategic plans and serve to obtain a specific effect which has been the aim of the strategy.

The strategies presented in the tables (see pages 36–42) focus largely on specific and single elements of national identity, for example uniqueness, similarity, difference, autonomy, continuity, unity, cohesion, exclusion and inclusion. In addition, the tables contain numerous strategies and means of realisation which have been established in the course of the last decade in discourse-historical research. Finally, the means of realisation have not been grouped in the table either according to linguistic level, as for example the textual, sentence or word, or according to particular linguistic subfields such as pragmatics, semantics or syntax.

2.3.4 Means and Forms of Realisation

In this section we will look at the linguistic means involved in the discursive construction of national identity, but because of their great number we will restrict ourselves to a cursory overview (for more extensive information see Wodak et al. 1990, Nowak, Wodak and De Cillia 1990, Matouschek, Wodak and Januschek 1995 etc.).

In the current study our attention has been focused primarily on lexical units and syntactic devices which serve to construct unification, unity, sameness, difference, uniqueness, origin, continuity, gradual or abrupt change, autonomy, heteronomy and so on. The most important of these are:

1. Personal reference (anthroponymic generic terms, personal pronouns, quantifiers);
2. Spatial reference (toponyms/geonyms, adverbs of place, spatial reference through persons, by means of prepositional phrases such as 'with us', 'with them');
3. Temporal reference (temporal prepositions, adverbs of time, temporal conjunctions, temporal references by means of nouns, semi-prefixes with temporal meaning).

In addition, we will look at the phenomenon of vagueness in referential or other expressions, euphemisms, linguistic hesitation and disruptions, linguistic slips, allusions, rhetorical questions, and the mode of discourse representation (direct or indirect, or other forms of reported speech).

Another important issue in this context is the linguistic representation of those social actors who are perceived as members of a national collectivity (see also Van Leeuwen 1996), and the creation of anthropomorphised social actors. In the following section we look more closely at the ways in which agents are rendered anonymous or agency more generally is obscured by use of the passive voice, the use of the three tropes of personification, synecdoche, and metonymy, and the use of deictic 'we'.

Table 2.1: Strategies of Justification and Relativisation

Strategies	Argumentation schemes (topoi)	Means of realisation
Shift of Blame and Responsibility • strategy of emphasising the difference between 'us' and 'them'/strategy of isolation and/or singularisation • strategy of heternomisation: emphasis on extra-national dependence/heteronomy	• topos of ignorance • topos of comparison/ topos of difference • topos of external constraints and/or of external force/topos of heteronomy • topos of the force of facts	• lexical units with semantic components creating difference/singularisation ('to put into an alien uniform'), parallelisms, three-part figures • naturalising metaphors ('catastrophe')
• strategy of casting doubt • strategy of scapegoating/victim-perpetrator inversion	• topos of illustrative example	• insinuations, allusions, evocations, vagueness • metonymic causal shift, 'yes-but' figure • comparisons (including negations), analogies • stories, anecdotes, fictitious scenarios
Downplaying/Trivialisation • strategy of emphasising negative sameness or negative common features	• topos of comparison/ topos of similarity	• lexical units with levelling semantic components • sociative formations ('co-responsibility', 'take part in')
• balancing one thing against another	• topos of comparison/ *locus a minore*	• 'yes-but' figures, suggestive icons (one-sided weighting of topics manifested as detailed presentation vs. brief reference)
• strategy of discontinuation/strategy of emphasising the difference between then and now • strategy of 'squaring'/strategy of compensation (for example, postwar reconstruction work with Nazi crimes)	• topos of history as teacher	• lexical units indicating difference, personifications ('history') and metaphors ('zero hour') • *miranda* and positively connotated attributions (miranda are high-value words)
• rationalisation/harmonisation • strategy of minimisation	• topos of external threat/ topos of the superordinate aim • topos of the small number/ 'you can't just lump them all' topos	• fictitious (threatening) scenarios • quantifiers, modifying particles • suggestive-euphemistic pseudo-oppositions ('Allegiance to Austria does not mean saying no to anybody, it means only saying a definite yes to Austria')
• strategy of avoidance and strategy of euphemising (in reference to the linguistic representation of the responsible social actors and in reference to the representation of negative actions and events)		• passive (agent deletion), vague personal reference, nominalisation (agent deletion), referential transfer resulting in abstraction, depersonalisation, anonymisation (metonymy) • euphemistic verbs obscuring agents ('die/perish' instead of 'murdered by X', 'happened' instead of 'murdered')

Table 2.1: Strategies of Justification and Relativisation – continued

Strategies	Argumentation schemes (topoi)	Means of realisation
		• euphemistic denotation of actions ('he only did his duty') • systematic adverbialisation of 'Austria' in connection with something negative • discourse representation (distancing through direct/ indirect speech) • indefinite article
Legitimation/Delegitimation	• topos of appeal to authority or topos of non-legitimation: assigning authority (including *argumentum ad verecundiam*) or pointing out that a person has no right to criticise something	• quotations

Table 2.2: Constructive Strategies

Strategies	Argumentation schemes (topoi)	Means of realisation
Assimilation, Inclusion and Continuation		• lexemes with levelling components
• presupposition/emphasis on intra-national sameness/similarity, including the strategy of 'we are all in the same boat'	• topoi of comparison: topos of similarity, *locus a minore*	• referential assimilation (levelling down): spatial and personal reference (anthroponyms (personal names), toponyms (place names), personal pronoun 'we'), realisation as tropes (synecdoche, metonymy and personification)
• presupposition of/emphasis on positive political continuity (at state/ national level), negation of an alleged discontinuity	• topos of definition ('rebirth', 'zero hour')/ topos of name interpretation (*locus a nominis interpretatione*)	• temporal reference, indicating continuity: temporal prepositions, adverbs of time and adverbial constructions ('since', 'always') • referential vagueness by means of personal pronouns, adverbs of place; spatial reference through persons and toponyms ('with us', 'here', 'in this country') • proper names which are interpreted as indicating Austrian descent • ship metaphor, ship allegory, house metaphor etc. • lexemes/semiprefixes with semantic components indicating continuity (German: *wieder*/'again', *neu*/'anew')

Table 2.2: Constructive Strategies – continued

Strategies	Argumentation schemes (topoi)	Means of realisation
		• particles which construct continuity ('continuously', 'also') • indefinite article (plural forms indicating repetition etc.) implicit and explicit comparisons • parallelisms • allusions, evocations, non-distanced discourse representations which create continuity
Singularisation • presupposition of/emphasis on national (positive) uniqueness	• topos of lovely, idyllic place (*locus amoenus*)	• lexemes with semantic components, constructing singularity, individualisation ('unique') • hyperboles, *miranda* and positively connotated attributions
• strategy of simultaneous emphasis on subnational uniqueness and national model character • (tacit) transposition of subnational uniqueness onto the national level • reduction of supranational uniqueness to the national level	• explicit or implicit topos of comparison (including 'we are superior compared to them')	• parallelisms • synecdochisation (*pars pro toto* or 'part for whole')
Autonomisation • presupposition/emphasis on national autonomy and independence		• lexemes with semantic components constructing autonomy
Unification and Cohesivation • emphasis on unifying common features/shared sorrow or worries (for example, at a subnational or national level) • emphasis on the will to unify/co-operate/feel and show solidarity	• topos of comparison (for example, *locus a minore*)	• lexemes with semantic components creating unification • appeals for co-operation, pulling together and solidarity • idiomatic metaphors ('we act all in concert')
• emphasis on national model character of subnational units • unificatory warning against the loss of national autonomy and uniqueness	• topos of threat/ *argumentum ad baculum* ('threatening with the stick')	• emphasis (for example, emphatic parallelisms) • fictitious (threatening) scenarios
Dissimilation/Exclusion and Discontinuation • presupposition/emphasis on (state-internal and state-external) inter-national differences • discontinuation/emphasis on a difference between then and now	• topos of comparison/topos of difference (including 'they are inferior compared to us')	• lexemes with semantic components constructing difference • referential dissimilation and exclusion through personal and spatial reference: demonstrative and personal pronouns ('they', 'those', 'them'); synecdochical anthroponyms ('the German/s', 'the foreigner/s'); or personified toponyms often used metonymically ('Germany', Switzerland')

Table 2.2: Constructive Strategies – continued

Strategies	Argumentation schemes (topoi)	Means of realisation
	• topos of terrible place (*locus terribilis*)	• implicit and explicit comparisons • *antimiranda* (low-value words), pejorative/negatively connotated attributions, derogatory denotations (for example, '*Krowodn*' (Croats), 'Gypsies') • dissimilative sociative formations ('fellow citizens' in reference to a 'we-group') • terms denoting discontinuity/metaphors ('zero hour')
Strategy of Avoidance • suppression/backgrounding of intra-national differences • suppression/backgrounding of inter-national or supranational sameness/similarity/commonality • ignoring/downplaying of extra-national heteronomy • suppression/backgrounding of discontinuities/disruptions		• nominalisations with agent deletion ('liberation')
Vitalisation		• personifications/anthropomorphisms and other metaphors

Table 2.3: Strategies of Perpetuation

Strategies	Argumentation schemes (topoi)	Means of realisation
Positive Self-Presentation/ Strategy of Calming Down	• topos of the lovely, idyllic place (*locus amoenus*)	• referential assimilation, *miranda* and positive attributions, elative • vagueness
Portrayal in Black and White (frequently in combination with positive self-presentation)	• contrastive topos of comparison: for example, *locus amoenus* versus *locus terribilis* • topos of threat	• referential assimilation and dissimilation, antonyms, *miranda*/positive attributions and *antimiranda*/pejorative attributions, hyperboles
Continuation • presupposition of/emphasis on positive political continuity (for example, by establishing a link to the model character of the 'founding fathers')	• topos of comparison/ topos of similarity • topos of definition ('democracy')	• explicit comparisons ('as ... as'), implicit comparisons (analogies) • appeal for/demand for political continuity in the future (for example, by means of the ship allegory) • adverbs of time indicating continuity/repetition ('always') • particles creating continuity ('as well, again, continuously')

Table 2.3: Strategies of Perpetuation – continued

Strategies	Argumentation schemes (topoi)	Means of realisation
		• normative-deontic modals ('must', 'should') and normative-deontic constructions ('it is necessary')
Defence	• topos of comparison • disaster topos: rejecting an action whose consequences for Austria's future fate are depicted as negative • topos of threat (e.g. to support neutrality)	• *antimiranda*/negative attributions, comparative/superlative • negation of the necessity of a political change
Strategy of Avoidance • greatest possible suppression/circumvention of the issue of change		• resorting to referential vagueness

Table 2.4: Strategies of Transformation

Strategies	Argumentation schemes (topoi)	Means of realisation
(Possible) Positive Self-Presentation (Including Presupposition of Inter-National Difference) • emphasis on Austria's (possible) model character for Eastern Europe and/or for the whole of Europe ('to set an example')	• topos of comparison/topos of difference: presupposition of 'we are superior compared to them'	• *miranda*
Heteronomisation or Warning against Heteronomy • emphasis on extra-national dependence (for example, on the economic policies of the EU) • warning against the loss of national autonomy	• topos of (changed) circumstances/restraints or topos of the force of facts • topos of threat, *argumentum ad baculum* (to support strengthening of regional autonomy)	• metaphors (neutrality as 'price', 'tempests of the time') • vagueness • euphemisms ('80 per cent integration of the Austrian economy into the EU')
Autonomisation (as Strategy of Calming Down) • emphasis on autonomy and independence to alleviate fears of increasing heteronomy and loss of uniqueness resulting from a particular action	• topos of consequence or denial/refutation of a particular disaster topos or topos of threat	• procatalepsis (anticipatory refutation of an opponent's argument)
Discontinuating/Dissimilation • emphasis on a difference between then and now • emphasis on a necessary difference between now and the future	• topos of history as teacher • topos of a favourable time (*locus a tempore*)	• suggestive rhetorical questions • (opaque) *figura etymologica* (etymological figure) ('a crisis is also a chance in a literal sense')

Table 2.4: Strategies of Transformation – continued

Strategies	Argumentation schemes (topoi)	Means of realisation
	• topos of 'you can't have one without the other'	• metaphors ('present prosperity is prosperity partly borrowed from our children. What has been borrowed must be returned')
	• topos of consequence: 'something follows as a direct result of something else' • 'sugarcoated world' topos as special form of the topos of consequence: pointing out positive consequences of a propagated action • topos of the superordinate aim • topos of definition (*locus a nominis interpretatione*) • topos of appeal to authority, *argumentum ad verecundiam*	• emphasis • normative-deontic modals ('must', 'should') or constructions ('it is necessary') • vagueness
Devaluation/Negative Connotation of Political Continuation and Positive Connotation of Gradual or Abrupt Change/Transformation • declaring something as obsolete/ historicising (for example, neutrality) • emphasis on the model character of the 'founding generation' in regard to their courageous and spontaneous attitude to change (= at the same time a strategy of continuation)	• topos of consequence: disaster topos or 'sugar-coated world' topos	• negatively connotated metaphors ('fossilised', 'crumble', 'many well-established structures have become old and fragile under their 50-year-old patina') • positively and negatively connotated metaphors ('the hope that fresh winds from the East will blow through Western structures') • aphorisms/sayings ('If we stop growing we stop being')
Vitalisation		• positively connotated personifications ('let's turn the future into our friend') • house metaphor ('European roof') • path or crossroads metaphors ('on the way to a larger Europe', 'Austria has come to a crossroads', 'to switch the points')

Table 2.5: Strategies of Demontage (or Dismantling) and Destruction

Strategies	Argumentation schemes (topoi)	Means of realisation
Discrediting Opponents/ Certain Pillars of Identity (for example through portrayal in black and white)	• topos of comparison (*locus a maiore*) • *ad-hominem* defamation	• derogatory denotations of persons/ethnonyms • derogatory metaphors ('professional resistance fighters', 'charlatans') • insinuations by means of fictitious dialogues
Negative Presentation (of Self/Others) • disparaging the *locus amoenus*, even employing negative singularisation, i.e. emphasis on negative national uniqueness	• topos of terrible place (*locus terribilis*)	• *antimiranda*, pejorative attributions • lexical units with semantic components constructing singularity in connection with negative attributions
Heteronomisation • emphasis on extra-national dependence and/or heteronomy and emphasis on dismantling myths against one's will (for example founding myths, myth of neutrality)	• topos of external constraints/of external force	• metaphors (neutrality as 'price')
Assimilation • emphasis on inter-national sameness/similarity/communality (also serving the purpose of negation of national uniqueness)	• topos of comparison (topos of similarity)	• lexical units with semantic components constructing levelling, assimilative attributions • assimilative reference
Dissimilation/Exclusion • emphasis on intra-national differences	• topos of comparison (topos of difference)	• dissimilative reference and dissimilative and pejorative attributions/ labelling ('enemy'), 'Tito's partisans') • implicit and explicit comparisons
Discontinuation • emphasis on discontinuity/ disruptions	• *argumentum ad baculum/* topos of threat • topos of time (*locus a tempore*)	• obsolescence metaphor ('There will be a time when such historians will be out of date')
Strategy of Pronouncing Somebody/ Something 'Dead'		• assertions through derogatory metaphors as predicates ('Vranitzky is politically dead')
'Cassandra' Strategy	• disaster topos	• *antimiranda*, pejorative attributions

2.3.4.1 The Three Tropes of Metonymy, Synecdoche and Personification

Synecdoche, metonymy and personification or metaphor are employed to create sameness between people and are primarily used in connection with constructive discursive strategies. Among other things, metonymies may conceal responsible agents or move them to the background: this serves primarily to relativise. Personification attributes a human form to an abstract entity and thus constitutes a widely-used means of realising a constructive strategy, demanding, for example, identification with an anthropomorphised nation.

The metonymy (from the Greek for 'name change') replaces the name of a referent by the name of an entity which is closely associated with it in either concrete or abstract terms (on metonymy see, for example, Plett 1989, pp. 77–9, Lausberg 1990, pp. 292–5, Morier 1989, pp. 749–99, Bredin 1984 and Groddeck 1995, pp. 233–48). Metonymies can be classified into a number of groups depending on the relationship between the two involved adjacent conceptual fields. We will present a brief overview of metonymies which are involved in the linguistic representation of social actors (some of these examples are taken from the speeches studied in Chapter 4):

1. *Product for cause*; for example, 'The identity narrative channels political emotions' (Martin 1995, p. 13).
2. *Object for the user of this object*; for example, 'The buses are on strike'.
3. *Place for person*; for example, 'The whole of Vienna celebrates'; or *place/ building as seat of an institution for the (responsible) representatives of the institution*; for example, 'Washington is concerned. The White House has no solutions'.
4. *Place/building for person*; for example, 'The liberation of Mauthausen concentration camp'.
5. *Place for event/act (at this place)*; for example, 'Vienna must not become Chicago'.
6. *Country for persons*;[7] for example, 'All in all, Austria has never been so well off'; 'Austria is World Champion'.[8]
7. *Persons for country*; for example, 'We are much too small to allow disharmony in vital areas of our country'.
8. *Time for persons living during that time*; for example, 'The twentieth century has shaken Austria several times'.
9. *Institution for (responsible) representatives of the institution*; for example, 'Parliament rejected the motion'.
10. *Institution for events/actions*; for example, 'The success story of the Second Republic'.

The synecdoche (from the Greek for 'to take up with something else') replaces the name of a referent by the name of another referent which belongs to the same field of meaning and which is either semantically wider or semantically narrower (on synecdoche see, for example, Plett 1989, pp. 72–5, Lausberg 1990, pp. 295–8,

Morier 1989, pp. 1159–75, Zimmermann 1989, and Groddeck 1995, pp. 205–20). Depending on the direction of substitution it is possible to distinguish between 1) generalising synecdoches and 2) particularising synecdoches. One can further group them according to their type of relation, that is: a) the relation 'whole–part', b) the relation 'species–genus', and c) the relation 'singular–plural'.

The most important synecdoches are:

1. Generalising synecdoches, which replace a semantically narrower expression with a semantically wider one:
   a) *totum pro parte* (or *whole for part*): 'Austria is world champion'
   b) *species for genus*: 'the water [i.e. the sea] was their home'
   c) *plural for singular*: 'we' instead of 'I' (*pluralis maestatis/modestiae*, see below);
2. Particularising synecdoches, which replace a semantically wider term with a semantically narrower term:
   a) *pars pro toto* (or *part for whole*): 'He lived under my roof for two weeks'
   b) *species for genus*: 'She gave him her last penny [i.e. money]'
   c) *singular for plural*: 'The Austrian is a little bit slow'.[10]

As a special conceptual synecdoche, Lakoff and Johnson (1980, p. 38) have introduced the synecdoche of the 'controller for controlled' type, where leaders, people in power, rulers and so on replace the person who is actually carrying out an action; for example, 'Nixon bombarded Hanoi' or 'Hitler started the war'. Even if one does not assume, as do Lakoff and Johnson (1980) and many other rhetoricians, that the synecdoche is a special form of metonymy, it seems equally plausible to allocate the type 'controller for controlled' to the category of metonymy.

Personification is a special form of metaphor as it links two differing conceptual fields, i.e. a concept with the semantic feature [- human] with a concept [+ human]. The result is anthropomorphisation.

According to Lakoff and Johnson (1980, p. 34), personification is a general category which comprises a great number of metaphors which all select different aspects of a person or different perspectives from which to look at a person. Personifying metaphors have in common the fact that they can be used to give meaning to the phenomena of the world in humanised, anthropomorphised form. Such metaphors, by effecting exemplary *ponere ante oculos*, come close to what Heinrich Plett (1989, p. 27) has termed the 'stylistic principle of evidence'. Personifications possess high suggestive force. In reference to the mental construct of nation, these metaphors also imply intra-national sameness and equality. The very vividness of such metaphors, moreover, favours identification of the addressees with that of the personified collective subjects. In this way, they serve the strategy of animation.

An example of a continued personification of the Austrian nation is the following passage taken from Austrian President Thomas Klestil's speech of 27 April 1995: 'The success of this Second Republic is ultimately the success of a nation, which has learned from the terrible experiences of the First Republic … They had learned that for the life of a nation there is nothing more important than the will for self-determination.'

Ken Goodwin (1990) has examined the question of the gender of the personified nation, and concluded that most of the African and Australian authors he examined looked at nations from a clearly male perspective and consequently attributed a female persona to them. However, the issue is definitely more complex than that. For example, in Austrian dramatist Franz Grillparzer's famous play *König Ottokars Glück und Ende*, Austria is both compared to a bride, and referred to as 'blushing young man'. That even theoreticians such as Ernest Gellner are not free from androcentric bias has been demonstrated by Elisabeth List (1996, p. 106), who points to a sexist quote by George Santayana which Gellner (1994) used as the third epigraph of his book:

> Our nationality is like our relations to women: too implicated in our moral nature to be changed honorably, and too accidental to be worth changing.

2.3.4.2 'We'

There are linguistic means other than the three tropes discussed above which are also used to indicate sameness. Because of its inherent properties, the deictic expression 'we' can be very well used in the service of 'linguistic imperialism' to verbally annex and usurp. As Volmert argues:

> A speaker has at his/her disposal a whole range of (clever) options with which to present the interests and affairs of 'we-groups' in the public sphere. In a speech during an election campaign, for example, a speaker can unite himself and his audience into a single 'community sharing a common destiny' by letting fall into oblivion all differences in origin, confession, class and lifestyle with a simple 'we' (for example, a 'we Germans'). This 'community sharing a common destiny' may be bound by different degrees of intimacy and familiarity: from the common economic interests of 'society as a whole' to the emotional needs of a family-type community.
>
> (Volmert 1989, p. 123)

The first-person plural 'pronoun' 'we' is the most complex among its type and can encompass all other personal 'pronouns'. Possible references are shown in Table 2.6.

Linguistic studies usually distinguish between an *addressee-inclusive* and *addressee-exclusive* 'we', and between a *speaker-inclusive* and *speaker-exclusive* 'we'. The categorisation remains fairly broad, as in some cases the references cannot be clearly specified – as in examples e), f) and g) in the table, where the question mark implies the additional reference to a third person singular or plural.

There are also synecdochal realisations of 'we'; generalising forms such as the author's plural, the *pluralis modestiae* (modest 'we'), or the *pluralis maiestatis* (royal 'we'), which all seem to include a second person into the 'we' group; that is, they seem to be cases of addressee-inclusive 'we', whereas in fact they are addressee-exclusive.

Table 2.6: Uses of 'We'

a)	I + you	partially/totally addressee-inclusive
b)	I + he/ I + she	addressee-exclusive
c)	I + you (plural) (= I + *n* x you)	partially/totally addressee-inclusive
d)	I + they (= I + *n* x s/he)	addressee-exclusive
e)	I + you + he/ I + you + she	partially/totally addressee-inclusive + ?
f)	I + you (plural) + he I + you + she	partially/totally addressee-inclusive + ?
g)	I + you (plural) + they (= I + *n* x you + *n* x s/he)	partially/totally addressee-inclusive + ?

Another use of synecdochal 'we' is the '*paternalistic we*', which seems to be speaker-inclusive, but which actually excludes the speaker and refers solely to a 'you', more often to a singular than a plural. This usually occurs in contexts of tutelage, frequently in directives, either from parents to children ('now we'll go to bed') or from doctors and nurses to (frequently elderly) patients. In such contexts the use of 'we' instead of 'you' functions linguistically to obscure or trivialise a limited degree of self-determination on the part of the person addressed, that is, it reflects an asymmetrical power relation between the interactants which it thus tries to make more bearable.

In addition, there are metonymic realisations of 'we'; for example, if 'we' pretends to include the speaker and perhaps also the addressee as well as third persons who are not present. An example of such a use of 'we' is illustrated by the following excerpt (taken from a discussion during a Viennese workshop on the relation between Germany and Austria on 26 January 1995): 'As has been said, it is very often claimed that we are a kind of sub-variety of the Bavarians, although it's interesting in this respect that the Bavarians sometimes differentiate themselves from us and *we* from them, and actually we several times fought against them in the past'. This speaker articulates a purely *historical* '*we*', referring to Austrian soldiers and fighters long dead, to whom the speaker simply adds several people from the audience who have Austrian nationality as well as other Austrians who are absent and who could be either alive or dead. Instead of referring to the group actually involved in these fights, she includes all possible Austrians both alive and dead in order to construct a very large imaginative 'we' group of Austrians.

Another form of a usurping 'we', which, however, does not usurp as much as the 100 per cent historical 'we', is the '*historically expanding we*', which is illustrated by the following passage from a focus group discussion: 'That's really great I think that really we're such a mixed people. from the past. that we – [...] sort of have been patched together from everywhere. [...] a mixed people – that's what we are.' This kind of 'we' is a special case of the type listed in the table under g): I + you (plural)

+ they (= I + n x you + n x s/he), because the component of the third person plural which is contained in it refers not only to the living who are not present, but also – frequently or primarily – to people already dead in whose deeds and great achievements the speaker wants to participate vicariously by linguistic annexation.

Finally, the form of 'person for country' is also a metonymic form of 'we'. A statement by Austrian Vice-Chancellor and Foreign Minister Wolfgang Schüssel in his speech of 14 May 1995 – 'Co-operation is so important because we are much too small to allow disharmony in vital areas of our country' – would – literally – refer to the height of the people subsumed under 'we'; in fact it refers to the national territory conceived as the Austrian 'we-body' or 'national body', and to the number of the Austrian inhabitants.

NOTES

1. This section has gained a lot from many suggestions by Bernd Matouschek, who wrote the section on Discourse Analysis for the interim project report (cf. Wodak et al. 1995, pp. 20–52). This applies primarily to our study and treatment of the works of Hall (1996a), Martin (1995) and Ricœur (1992) as well as to the analytical distinction between the macro-topics of a common national culture, history, present and future and between several associated subtopics.
2. The term 'collective identity', which is used again and again in connection with discussions of systemic determinants of identity, is anything but unproblematic, which Berger and Luckmann (1980, p. 185, footnote 40) rightly pointed out: 'It is better not to speak of a 'collective identity', as this term can lead to a reifying hypostatisation of identity. The *exemplum horribile* of this is the German 'Hegelian' sociology of the twenties and thirties, for example the work of Othmar Spann. The same danger exists today more or less in various works of the Durkheim School and the Culture and Personality School in American anthropology.' We understand this remark as an important warning to be kept in the back of our minds, but we are not as consistent as Berger and Luckmann, who avoid the term entirely. The term does enable us to describe critically the multiple stereotypical phantasmagoric image of a 'collective identity' which is quite real in the minds of many people.
3. The sections 2.2.6.1, 2.2.6.2 and 2.2.6.3 are based on Dilek Cinar's text for the interim project report on the keyword 'nation' (Wodak et al. 1995, pp. 53–76).
4. However, Richter emphasises the importance of the typological distinction between concepts of nation, that is in the discussion about legal citizenship and the laying down of criteria for membership – an issue which is repeatedly raised in connection with the issue of national identity. Thus, in states where the principle of heredity prevails – as is also the case in Austria – the idea of a 'hereditability' of national membership occurs. In Austria, a permanent re-constitution of the members of the state through descent as well as the exclusive nature of membership to the nation-state is characteristic. Austrian legislation is still based on the principle of granting Austrian citizenship to foreign children and adolescents exclusively on the basis of descent from an Austrian parent. A precondition of granting citizenship is that the applicant's tie to the country of origin has been served by expatriation – although on a European level efforts are being made towards generally admitting dual citizenship. In comparison to other western European states, Austrian immigration laws are extremely restrictive with respect to immigrants and their descendants. Nine per cent of the population are excluded from the right to political participation and the 'foreigner status' is perpetuated across generations (cf. Faßmann and Münz 1995, p. 9). The legal basis of national membership in Austria is in direct opposition to the political concept of *Staatsnation*, which is held to be very decisive for national self-perception in Austria.
5. An extensive discussion of the various models and concepts of states and their relation to 'nation' is not possible in this context.
6. Translator's note: the German term *Wiedergutmachung* has no single, straightforward English equivalent word. It is conventionally translated as 'restitution' or 'compensation'. Following these conventions the words 'compensation' and 'restitution' will be used interchangeably for *Wiedergutmachung*.
7. This type of metonymy is simultaneously a personification. All the examples listed above, in which

something is replaced by a human being or a group of human beings, represent cases of the tropo-logical crossing of metonymy and personification. Simultaneous tropological multiple membership is ignored; if one views personificatory metonymies (which are characterised by a combination of, for example, the name of an institution plus a verb which normally describes human behaviour) exclu-sively as personifying metaphors, as does Reger (1977, 1978). His biased perspective gives the wrong impression that such personifying metonymies serve to bring something to life, making it more con-crete, whereas in fact the opposite is true: such metonymies are abstractions of concrete (responsible) actors.

8. To be more precise, this is an example of how a discursive phenomenon can be both a metonymy and a synecdoche (*totum pro parte*) at the same time.

9. At the same time this is an example of a *pars pro toto*.

Chapter 3

On Austrian Identity:
The Scholarly Literature

3.1 THE STATE OF THE ART

Academic literature on Austrian identity deals mainly with historical perspectives and attempts to prove the existence of an independent Austrian nation and a national identity as well as to document, by means of empirical quantitative surveys, how this identity is rooted in the Austrian mind (for example, Bruckmüller 1996 and 1994, Haller et al. 1996, Stourzh 1990, Reiterer 1988a, Zöllner 1988, Dusek, Pelinka and Weinzierl 1988, Kreissler 1984, Heer 1981). However, because this approach has scarcely considered social history or the history of everyday life, it has largely neglected to analyse everyday political culture or to interpret national consciousness as a manifestation of political communities.[1]

A large number of works, which concentrate mainly on the (chronological) development of European nation-states, regard the French Revolution as the beginning of the modern, plebiscitarian conception of the nation and distinguish it from the concept of a nation defined by ethnic and cultural characteristics. In this view, Austria is considered a 'belated nation' (cf. Reiterer 1988a, p. 110), which has developed from the Habsburg Monarchy (influenced by confrontation with the ideas of the Enlightenment and the French Revolution) to the First Republic (whose viability as an independent state was widely doubted and which failed largely because of ideological conflicts between its two main political camps) to the Second Republic of Austria in which the concept of *Staatsnation* has gained broad acceptance. The notion of an Austrian 'nation by consensus' after 1945 on the French model traces its national foundations to its resistance against National Socialism and its (re-)emergence as a sovereign republic.

The concept of a *Kulturnation* or a *Sprachnation* – and the resulting identification of Austria as a part of a wider German '*Kultur- and Sprachnation*' – is accepted by only a small number of scholars in Austria (for example, Höbelt 1985 and 1994). The concept itself is closely linked to ethnic interpretations of peoples and nations (which in its National Socialist version became the ideological underpinning of racist policies), and has been criticised in depth by the Austrian historian Gerald Stourzh (1990), who also points out that other language communities have no equivalent for the term *Kulturnation*, nor even a meaningful translation for it.

However, the arguments made by proponents of the Austrian *Staatsnation* frequently draw upon assumptions more traditionally identified with the idea of a *Kulturnation*, particularly when they assert or imply an inseparable complementarity between political and cultural identities. Examples of this conflation of assumptions may be found for instance in opinion polls, where 'national pride' is often linked to Austrian high culture; in the reference to the culture of the Habsburg Monarchy in the context of the debate in Austria on the meaning of Central Europe; and in Austria's promotion as a 'cultural world power' which trumpets ostensibly 'typically Austrian' cultural symbols and traditions (cf. Pelinka 1990; Haller and Gruber 1996a).

In official political contexts, the plebiscitarian concept of nation traditional in Western Europe is emphasised; in repeated opinion polls moreover, a large majority of Austrians consistently chose this definition whenever it was offered as one of the responses (cf., for example, Bruckmüller 1994a, p. 17). At the same time, views which assure or imply a culturally defined conception of nationhood may also be found both in academic publications and in everyday conversation. This usually takes the form of reference to a common language or culture but sometimes speakers refer to a common Austrian ethnic origin. Although for the most part this conceptual mélange derives from the desire to reinforce the idea of a separate Austrian state and its national identity, the use of a wide variety of Austrian cultural clichés to support these political arguments sometimes has the effect of extending the discourse to include culturally essentialist, or chauvinist and xenophobic elements (cf. Plasser and Ulram 1991, p. 41; Haller and Gruber 1996a, pp. 103ff.). This may in fact, represent one negative side effect of Austrians' clearly pronounced positive national consciousness.

3.2 THE AUSTRIAN NATION IN HISTORY

The historical birth of the Austrian nation has been interpreted in a variety of ways: Gerald Stourzh (1990), Ernst Bruckmüller (1991) and Erika Weinzierl (1993a), for example, have identified beginnings or forerunners of the Austrian nation – for example, in the tradition of various individual Austrian provinces – as early as the fifteenth and sixteenth centuries. However, most historians agree either that a separate Austrian identity developed in the nineteenth century (cf. Heer 1981)[2] or that its emergence is rooted in the resistance against the National Socialist regime and is linked to large-scale emigration after 1938 (cf. Kreissler 1984).

The toponym 'Austria', the one-thousandth anniversary of which was celebrated in 1996 by numerous ceremonies and a large historical exhibition (cf. Bruckmüller and Urbanitsch 1996), describes a variety of historical entities (cf. Zöllner 1988, Weinzinger 1990, Bruckmüller 1994, 1995 and 1996 and Plaschka, Stourz and Niederkorn 1995). The first mention of Austria as 'Ostarrichi' in a historical document on 1 November 996 referred to a region in what is today Lower Austria, then under the rule of the Babenberg margraves. In the modern period, 'Austria' designated the unifying forces of the Habsburg Monarchy as well as the House of Austria (*Casa d'Austria*), and from the nineteenth century it referred to the Austrian empire.

After the fall of the monarchy in 1918, the name Austria, which had been discredited by its association with Habsburg rule, met with strong resistance in some quarters. In addition, the Social Democrats, the Christian Socialists and the German Nationalists were unified by their desire for an *Anschluss* of this 'second German state' to the newly-founded German Republic (Pelinka 1990, p. 147). When the German-speaking deputies to the previous imperial parliament assembled in October 1918, they designated themselves the 'Provisional National Assembly for *Deutschösterreich* (German-Austria)'. In November 1918 these deputies declared the new state to be a republic and a part of the German Republic (Reiterer 1993a, p. 115). Karl Renner, a leader of the Social Democrats, favoured calling the new country, which should become an independent free state, 'Südostdeutschland' (southeast-Germany) (cf. Dusek, Pelinka and Weinzierl 1988, p. 179). In the Treaty of St. Germain, signed in 1919, Austria was obliged to maintain its independence within yet-to-be-agreed-upon borders (cf. Gutkas 1985, p. 11), and the Allies insisted that it take on the name 'Republic of Austria'. However, many members of the political élite, in particular those of the Social Democratic Party, regarded the Republic as a temporary solution and continued to adhere to the idea of an *Anschluss* with the Weimar Republic (cf. Bruckmüller 1996, pp. 303–10). In order to emphasise the German character of this newly founded state, German was set forth as the national language in the constitution.

Despite the fact that the Second Republic adopted the constitution of 1920 (as amended in 1929), and the fact that the 'social partnership' between state, industry and the unions practised in the Second Republic traces its origins to the period before 1934, the democratic First Republic of Austria (1918–34), which was forced into independence against its will, is even today still dismissed as the 'state that nobody wanted' (Andics 1962). The Social Democrats' attachment to Germany, which can be attributed essentially to the political affinity felt towards the democratic Weimar Republic, contrasted with the ambivalent Austrian patriotism of the Christian Socialist Party, to which most of the leading politicians of the authoritarian Corporatist State, which was in power between 1934 and 1938, belonged. On the one hand, these politicians promoted a Catholic and dynastic-orientated Austrian patriotism; on the other hand they tried to turn Austria into a 'better Germany'. In the Federal Constitutional Act of 1920, the coalition government formed by the the Social Democratic and Christian Socialist parties voted to adopt a strictly parliamentary form of government for the Republic of Austria. However, this coalition did not hold together for long, and domestic political tensions continued to escalate. Furthermore, the effects of the worldwide economic crisis on the economic and political situation at the end of the 1920s, and growing mass unemployment, created favourable circumstances for the radicalisation of the political climate (cf. Puntscher-Riekmann 1995, pp. 92–5).

In March 1933, Federal Chancellor Engelbert Dollfuss dissolved the National Assembly and began to rule by emergency decree, in violation of constitutional provisions. The Communist Party and the Austrian Nazi Party were banned. As a consequence of the traumatic civil war in February 1934 between the Christian Socialists, supported by the paramilitary *Heimwehr*, and the Social Democratic Party militia, the *Schutzbund*, Austrian Social Democracy was abolished, as Fascist Italy had demanded (Weinzierl 1993b, p. 58). In an attempt to unify the traditionally bourgeois parties – the Christian Socialists and other, smaller parties of the right – around the 'Austrian idea', in May 1933 Dollfuss founded the *Vaterländische Front* (Fatherland Front), which was to become the 'political monopoly of Austro-Fascists' (Tálos and Manoschek 1994, p. 122). On 1 May 1934 a constitution was promulgated for Austria. It was ideologically rooted in political Catholicism and modelled politically on Italian and Portuguese Fascism. From repeated attempts to reconcile the idea of a separate Austrian state with pan-German pretensions emerged an Austrian ideology which interpreted the Habsburg monarchy as the history of the Holy Roman Empire of the German nation. Recalling the 'greatness that Austria once was', the Dollfuss regime contrived an ideology according to which Austria, in keeping with Catholic-Austrian instead of Protestant-German or Heathen-National Socialist traditions, was to establish a true *Reich*: a federalist structure of 'central European dimensions'. However, the Austrian ideology of this Corporatist State equally assigned Austria a (privileged) place in the German(ic) *(Kultur-)nation* and thus inhibited the formation of a specific Austrian consciousness. Indeed, attempts by Ernst Karl Winters and Alfred Klahrs to provide theoretical foundations for the existence of an Austrian nation and a specifically Austrian national identity all but failed (cf. Reiterer 1993a). Historian Felix Kreissler describes this official state ideology of Austro-fascism, which promoted the desire to be simultaneously Austrian and German, as 'national schizophrenia' (1984, p. 31). After Dollfuss was murdered during a Nazi putsch attempt supported by Hitler-Germany in July 1934, his successor Kurt Schuschnigg continued his authoritarian political course as well as the 'somewhat distorted government ideology ... of Austria as a second, better German state' (Bruckmüller 1996, pp. 309 f.).

The *Anschluss* of Austria with National Socialist Germany on 11 March 1938, which was achieved by threat of military force and accompanied by euphoric celebrations by large segments of the Austrian population, marked the end of Austria's independence as a state and its integration into the German Reich. The territory of the former Austrian state was divided into seven *Reichsgaue* (administrative regions), and the name 'Austria (*Österreich*)' was replaced by *Ostmark* (meaning the Eastern border region of the Reich), a name which itself was later avoided and supplanted by '*Alpen- und Donaureichsgaue*' in 1942.

In the Moscow Declaration of 1 November 1943 (Annex 6), the Allied powers (the United Kingdom, the Soviet Union, the United States) declared the occupation of Austria by Germany null and void and expressed their desire to restore Austria as a free and independent state. In this way, the name 'Austria' (which was abbreviated to O5 as a symbol for parts of the resistance movement before 1945) regained some of its earlier importance as the prospective name of a free and independent state. After 1945, 'Austria' was the undisputed choice as the name of the Second

Republic; 'Austria' was also used politically to distinguish the Republic clearly from Germany.

Many authors (for example, Kreissler 1984 and Bruckmüller 1996, pp. 348–53) take the view that it was during the period of National Socialist rule – and in part even during the First Republic (cf., for example, Garscha 1994) – that a separate Austrian national consciousness began to distinguish itself, a consciousness which was rooted in the resistance against National Socialism and the emigration from National Socialist Austria. Hanisch (1994) has argued that a great deal of evidence for the formation of an Austrian national consciousness, in the form of resistance against Nazi rule, can be found in humorous and satirical songs. However, he also points out that poverty and deprivation resulting from the war fuelled most Austrians' resentment against the National Socialist regime and consequently raised Austrian national consciousness. Hanisch mentions a secret American report which maintained that Austrians did show a certain degree of local patriotism, but no real national consciousness in the British or French manner.

According to Stourzh (1990), 1945 was also a major historiographical caesura, for it marked the end of an Austrian *Reich* or imperial history and the beginning of an Austrian 'republican' history. Stourzh claims that the word *Reich* was still a frequently used epithet during the First Republic, but gained new negative connotations under National Socialism. It was not until 1945 that the road was paved for Austrian national consciousness which, in contrast to the Austrian ideology current in the First Republic, saw some virtue in being a small country. A more realistic, less effusive patriotism then developed as the basis for the new Austrian consciousness, one that was based on pride regarding the signing of the State Treaty in 1955, and on the myth of 'permanent Austrian neutrality'.

In most works (for example, Heer 1981; Kreissler 1984; Dusek, Pelinka and Weinzierl 1988; Stourzh 1990; and Bruckmüller 1996) there is consensus about the notion that the central pillars of Austrian identity are: neutrality and the State Treaty; the definition of Austria as a small country (cf. Pelinka 1990); social stability and the 'social partnership' (cf. Tálos and Kittel 1995, pp. 107–21; Tálos 1995, pp. 537–51, Puntscher-Riekmann 1995, p. 97 and Menasse 1991); federalism (Dachs 1994; Pernthaler 1992a and 1992b); and, to a much smaller degree, republicanism (cf. Haerpfer 1995, pp. 427–34). The political success story of the Second Republic, which (like the First Republic) emerged from the disintegration of a larger entity (Pelinka 1990), promoted the development of a stable Austrian national consciousness. The 1970s, also known as the Kreisky era after the long serving Chancellor Bruno Kreisky (cf. Eder 1995, pp. 186–99; Bischof, Pelinka and Rathkolb 1994), which were a period of reorientation for the Social Democrats, and of social reforms and modernisation attempts (in criminal law, marital law and higher education laws), are often regarded as highly influential in forging this national consciousness.

All of the opinion surveys carried out in the last few decades suggest 'that a vast majority of Austrians feel that they are a nation and do not want to be anything other than Austrians' (Kreissler 1988, p. 79). Austrian national consciousness is interpreted as a product of the Second Republic, which began to coalesce into an 'Austrian national identity' from the 1960s onwards. In 1993, for example, 80 per cent of Austrians surveyed saw Austria as a nation (cf. Bruckmüller 1994, p. 15, table 1); Haller and Gruber (1996a, p. 65) have put this figure at 85 per cent. In the study cited by Bruckmüller, only six per cent of Austrians surveyed were of the opinion that Austrians do not form a nation in its own right; Haller and Gruber (1996a) found only 4 per cent who shared this opinion.

One piece of evidence cited in support of the claim that there is an Austrian national consciousness is the relatively high rate of positive responses to opinion polls on Austrian 'national pride'. A survey conducted in 1993 found 61 per cent of those polled to be 'very proud' and 31 per cent 'fairly proud' to be Austrians. Comparative data show that while Austrians lay behind the Americans and the British, they still ranked ahead of the French, Swiss and Germans from the then Federal Republic of Germany (Bruckmüller 1994, p. 26).[3] The preferred objects of Austrian national pride include the country's landscape (97 per cent), political and social stability (96 per cent), and neutrality (87 per cent). Respondents also named Austria's (historical) cultural heritage, its tourism and its domestic security as especially important achievements (Bruckmüller 1994, p. 27f.). In response to the question of whether Austria is a *Staatsnation* based on the individual's political assent to the state in which he or she lives, or a *Sprachnation* defined by its common language, approximately three-fourths chose the *Staatsnation* idea (cf. Bruckmüller 1994, see also Reiterer 1988a).

3.3 (SELF-)STEREOTYPING

Statements attesting to a typical Austrian character are found above all in literary texts. These take the form both of positive self-representations (in the works by such authors as Grillparzer, Raimund, Wildgans, Waggerl, Doderer, Hofmannsthal, Roth und Csokor) and of critical negative images, for example in Kraus's work or in the figure of Merz and Qualtinger's 'Herr Karl'.[4] Stereotypical images antithetical to the image of the comfortable, (self-)satisfied (Eastern) Austrian can also be found in the essays of Erwin Ringel (1984). Ringel characterises the Austrians as typically neurotic, hostile to children and having an above-average level of suicidal tendencies.

The stereotypical image of a *homo Austriacus* is connected to the belief that there is a 'typical Austrian character', 'typically Austrian' behaviour, and an 'Austrian mentality', and in the end also connected to the fantasy of 'Austrian ancestry'.[5] It has also served as a kind of avatar of 'essentialist' notions of what is specifically Austrian. According to Bruckmüller, such stereotypes, which correspond to the idea of a *Kulturnation*, have been instrumental in the reconstruction of what is 'Austrian' after 1945. Both the Catholic camp and the Communists used all available old stereotypes of the 'typical Austrian' in order to construct an agreeable Austrian self-image: the opposition to Prussia, the 'Phaeacian' stereotype, the 'mixed' ancestry, Austria's 'heyday' at the time of the 'Wars against the Turks' and the 'Wars against the Prussians', as well as the Austrians' supposed tolerance and musical talent (Bruckmüller 1994, p. 123).

The 'Phaeacian' stereotype – which depicts Austrians as happy, comfortable, friendly people who enjoy life and place great value on enjoyment, especially eating and drinking – plays an especially important role in the definition of 'typical Austrians' (cf. Reiterer 1988a, pp. 101ff.), and in the Austrians' self-image, as well as in how they are viewed from abroad (cf. also Paier 1996, pp. 171–3). At the same time this stereotype is often associated with Austrians' supposed placidity (cf. Breuss et al. 1995; Bruckmüller 1994 and 1996). Characteristics which actually carry negative connotations, such as a lack of diligence, sluggishness or sloppiness are frequently re-interpreted as positive traits and described as 'endearing' human weaknesses which serve to make Austrians even more likeable. A study carried out by the Paul Lazarsfeld Society, in which the Austrian national character is compared with that of the Germans, comes to similar conclusions. In the study, the 'character traits' of 'typical Austrians' were not generally considered to be 'cleverness', 'perseverance', 'success-orientation', 'elegance' and 'quickness', but noticeably high values were assigned to the Austrians 'with regard to the characteristics happy, generous, sociable, quiet and tolerant' (quoted in Reiterer 1988a, p. 103).

The scholarly literature on Austrian identity has repeatedly called attention to a relatively strong regional consciousness (cf. Bruckmüller 1994, pp. 68f.), especially in the provinces of Tyrol, Vorarlberg and Carinthia (cf. Bruckmüller 1994, pp. 18ff., and 1996, pp. 67ff.). A study performed by the Social Science Research Society (*Sozialwissenschaftliche Studiengesellschaft*) suggests that the Austrian population regards itself to be very heterogeneous: 68 per cent of the Austrians surveyed maintained that there are large regional differences within the Austrian population (cf. SWS 2, p. 221). Historian Moritz Csáky (1991, p. 46) has emphasised the historically developed ethnic-linguistic and cultural plurality of Austria, while Ernst Bruckmüller has argued that in Austria's current territory, regional and provincial identities can be seen at an earlier time than any references to a national identity (1991, p. 51 and 1996, pp. 155–99).[6] Indeed, Austrian federalism and the federal provinces were decisive factors in the foundation of the Austrian state at the beginning of both the First and Second Republics (cf. Dachs 1994, p. 76).

3.4 THE 'GERMAN QUESTION'

The question of the relationship between Austria and Germany and the discussion of whether Austrians belong to any kind of (larger) 'German nation' represents, in the words of Albert F. Reiterer, the 'touchstone' of Austrian national identity'; 'more than a century of recent Austrian history has been characterised by this question.' (Reiterer 1988a, p. 121; cf. also Bruckmüller 1996, pp. 276–16 and Botz and Sprengnagel 1994).[7] The origin of such discussions is the ('pan-German' orientated) conception of a German *Kulturnation* (cf. Erdmann 1989 and 1994), which is supported by Fellner (1985 and 1994), Höbelt (1985 and 1994) and Mölzer (1988 and 1991), among others. According to this interpretation, there are three German countries (including East Germany at the time) and two nations, but only one German people and one German cultural community, to which the Austrians also belong: 'belonging to the German people' is linked in this context to the German language. Erdmann says that 'this Austrian *Staatsnation* is a part of the German people' (Erdmann: '*Das Ende des Reiches*', quoted in Ardelt 1994). Höbelt (1994) sees most Austrians, German Swiss and Southern Tyroleans as Germans because of their mother tongue. For his part Höbelt has argued that 'Austrian' and 'German' are not mutually exclusive identities but different components of *one* identity.

As mentioned earlier, the majority of Austrian historians are critical of this view. According to Reiterer (1993a, pp. 113 and 116), the idea that a 'German Austria' once belonged to a larger German nation is a logical error which confuses the state construction of the German Reich before 1806 with national unity. Bruckmüller (1996) maintains that a nation of German-speaking Austrians began to distinguish itself in the nineteenth century, at first as a way of coming to terms with the non-German-speaking subjects of the monarchy. The *Deutschösterreicher* or 'German-Austrians', who were excluded from the nation formed in Germany, felt like an actual *Staatsnation* under the monarchy, and in this way two 'German' nations came about, the 'German German' (*reichsdeutsche*) and the 'Austrian German' (*deutschöster-reichische*); the latter oriented itself politically primarily towards the Austrian state but identified culturally with 'everything German' (pp. 77f.). Haas (1994) also stresses the point that Austrian consciousness developed more in confrontation with Slavic peoples than in identification with Germany (p. 203).

The political hopes that were articulated by the antidynastic, middle-class political, intellectual and journalistic élites (including the leading Austrian Social Democrats Victor Adler, Engelbert Pernerstorfer and Karl Renner) during the later part of the nineteenth and the early twentieth centuries – in particular, the hopes for the completion of a pan-German national-democratic revolution that the 1848 revolutions had inspired – do indeed convey a strong impression of a German national identity on the part of the Austrians.

However, after 1945 at the latest, whatever residual 'German' identification Austrians still retained was removed. The Austrian *Willensnation* ('nation by an act of will') was at first conceived in opposition to German nationalism in Austria, at least in the form that had made ideological accomodations to National Socialism. Academic discourse – which has always been politicised – on distinguishing identities developed along the lines of the dichotomy 'German' versus 'Austrian' (cf. Pelinka 1990, pp. 17ff.). In the construction of new means of identification that could express Austrian national feeling in the Second Republic, recourse was frequently made to Austrian music, from Viennese classical music to *Schrammelmusik* (popular Viennese entertainment music); to Austrian films with the Austrian landscape as their backdrop; to Habsburg nostalgia; to the New Year's Concert in Vienna, the Opera Ball and the Salzburg Festival as representative events of 'high culture'; and to great events in cultural history. All were found to be very helpful in the search for what is 'typically Austrian' (cf. Zoitl 1991, p. 35).

According to Reiterer (1993a, p. 117), the majority of the Austrian population still saw themselves as belonging to the German people after 1945, and as mentioned earlier a broader Austrian national consciousness took time to develop. In contrast, Austrian political élites referred to their common experiences in concentration camps and in prison, which had brought out a desire to do away with National Socialist rule and had given rise to a 'longing for [their] lost independence as a state' (Gutkas 1985, p. 13) (cf. also Kreissler 1991, pp. 156f.). Reiterer also maintains that the resulting Austrian patriotism had a decisive influence on the political culture of the Second Republic of Austria. Kreissler (1993, p. 6) writes: 'It was not until after the (long dark) night of the Third Reich that Austrian identity was brought back to consciousness by resistance and exile'.

However, Austrians still retain strong but ambivalent feelings towards the Germans (cf. Coudenhove-Kalergi 1990, p. 56), which is frequently expressed in anti-German resentment.[8] Since we assume that language plays an important, some-times even central role in the formation and consolidation of nations, we need to investigate the significance of the German language, or the Austrian variety of German, in the construction of an Austrian national identity. The constitutional stipulation of German as Austria's official language, the policy of assimilation regard-ing autochtonous and immigrant minorities, language policy, and the everyday discursive practices of many Austrians – for example, prejudiced discourse against minorities – all suggest that language and belonging to a linguistic group have been and are significant factors contributing to the construction of Austrian national identity. The fact that language is also seen as significant in distinguishing Austria from Germany strongly suggests that the specific Austrian variety of the German language is one constitutive feature of Austrian identity.[9]

References to Austrian German and the linguistic distinction between Austria and Germany can be found in essays as early as the 1960s in works by Kurt Kahl (1966) and later in Georg Schmid (1990). Others, such as Rudolf Muhr (1989 and 1993), Muhr, Schrodt and Wiesinger (1995) and Wolfgang Pollak (1992, 1994a and 1994b), also assign Austrian German an essential role in the construction of Austrian national identity.[10]

For linguistic minorities living in Austria, the relationship between language and identity frequently gives rise to 'dual', or multiple identities. One's interactions in different situations, or linguistic domains (family, friends, public life, and so on) may result in a variety of possible identification scenarios for the individual concerned. Members of local, regional, ethnic and national minorities are subject to a far more complicated interplay of situation-specific, multiple identity constructions than are those who belong exclusively to the unilingual majority. In this context, ethnic background may play an especially important role on the primary level of self-identification.

The constitutional status of minorities in Austria is specified in Article 7 of the Austrian State Treaty of 15 May 1955; however, of the five paragraphs in this Article, only three (Articles 2 to 4, regarding the right to elementary education in Slovenian or Croatian and the right to a proportional number of secondary schools; recognition of Slovenian and Croatian as official languages in addition to German in mixed-language regions; and the regulation of bilingual topographical signs and labels, and of rights to equal participation in cultural, administrative and judicial institutions respectively) were enshrined in constitutional laws.

The application of a numerical principle in granting minority rights was consciously avoided in Article 7. This principle was first introduced in the Ethnic Groups Act (*Volksgruppengesetz*) of 7 July 1976, which the federal government viewed as an executive directive implementing Article 7. Representatives of the minorities concerned rejected the government's interpretation of the constitutionality of the Act. According to the Ethnic Groups Act, bilingual signs are to be provided only in areas in which 25 per cent or more of the population are members of the given ethnic group. According to the Ethnic Groups Act, bilingual signs are required to be erected only in areas in which 25 per cent or more of the population are members of the given ethnic group. The provision for use of the minority language is, however, somewhat less restrictive. According to this provision of the Act, in areas where at least 20 per cent of the population are native speakers of an officially recognised minority language, such inhabitants are granted the right to use their mother tongue in all official dealings with state authorities. The Ethnic Groups Act defines 'ethnic group' as groups of Austrian citizens with a mother tongue other than German and with their own ethnic identity (*Volkstum*) in all parts of the republic (cf. Bamberger et al. 1995, p. 562) and guarantees these groups legal protection. It also provides for the establishment of representative bodies for ethnic groups in the Federal Chancellery as well as measures to promote minority cultures and activities in Austria. The Ethnic Groups Act extends rights for ethnic groups not only to the Slovenes and Croatians whose names appear in the State Treaty, but also to the Hungarian and Czech populations and, in an amendment in 1993, to the Slovak, Roma and Sinti populations as well. No institutional form of separate political representation at the level of regional or provincial governments (as is the case in Italy or in Schleswig-Holstein in Northern Germany) is provided for under Austrian law. With regard to school language policy, which is especially important to such minorities, to date regulations have been established for Slovenes in Carinthia and Croatians and Hungarians in Burgenland. However, these regulations only authorise bilingual education for the first three years of primary school, and then only under certain conditions (such as that parents specifically register their children for education in their native language). Only in extremely rare cases is it possible for minority children to receive their entire primary and secondary education in their native language.[11]

For members of ethnic minorities in Austria, language is the most important element of their ethnic identity, both in their perception of themselves and in others' perception of them. However, their native language hardly has a real function in public speaking; the diglossic situation only involves the minorities themselves. Bilingual members of the ethnic minorities with relatively well established linguistic double identities are thus constantly confronted with the problem that unilingual majority groups generally do not view bilingualism as a positive characteristic.

3.5 AUSTRIA'S NATIONAL SOCIALIST PAST

Until the 1980s, the crimes of the Austrian National Socialists (cf. Manoschek 1995, pp. 95f.) were not an issue in public discourse. The official self-perception of the political élites after 1945, which was based on a theory which viewed Austria as an 'occupied state' with no international legal status, found expression in the thesis which held that (almost) the whole Austrian population had fallen victim to National Socialism – and subsequently to the Allied occupying forces. This 'collective manufacturing of myth' regarded the Nazi era as an 'accident of history' (Münz 1991, p. 10; Wodak et al. 1990). The myth of a new beginning, the *Stunde Null* (zero hour) (cf. Haslinger 1988, p. 69), coupled with a self-pitying attitude and collective denial of responsibility,[12] became an essential element of the political culture of the Second Republic and paved the way for the genesis of the so-called 'victim thesis', which many scholars regard as the *Lebenslüge* ('grand delusion') of the Second Republic (cf. Gruber 1988, pp. 58f.).[13]

The Moscow Declaration of 1 November 1943, which was decisive for the country's future fate and declared Austria's re-establishment as one of the Allies' postwar aims, described Austria as the first victim of Hitler's Germany but at the same time pointed out Austria's responsibility for having fought on the German side. In contrast to this balanced assessment, Austrian postwar governments deliberately cultivated the victim aspect, manœuvering not only to achieve the State Treaty and Austria's complete sovereignty, but also to reject any legitimate demands for compensation of Nazi victims (Neugebauer 1994, p. 898). The inconsistent and half-hearted approach to the denazification process in Austria (cf. Stiefel 1981; Meissl, Mulley and Rathkolb 1986; and Sternfeld 1990) corresponded to this attitude. The Denazification Act of 1947 had been preceded by a number of milder drafts, which had been rejected by the Allied powers and which resulted in mass amnesty of the so-called *Minderbelasteten* – that is, Nazi officials, party members and sympathisers found guilty of relatively minor crimes (Haslinger 1987, p. 55f.).[14] Austrian national governments between 1945 and 1952 thus acted in contradiction to the declarations of intent given to the Allies and blocked the restitution of so-called 'Aryanised' property and the compensation claims of Austrian Jews, as well as the return of Austrians who had been forced out of their homes or businesses by the Nazis (cf. Knight 1988; Bailer 1993; Reinprecht 1992). However, former SS members' pension entitlements were fully recognised, including their years of service in the SS (cf. Manoschek 1995, p. 102).

For opportunistic political reasons, in other words, in order to emphasise the acts of the Austrian resistance movement, only persons who had been 'politically persecuted' were eligible for official victim status in postwar Austria. Jews were ineligible for these claims if they were not defined as 'politically persecuted'. Parts of the Roma and Sinti minority, homosexuals or others classified by the Nazis as 'antisocial' people received no compensation payments, and many of them are still waiting today. Compensation payments were frequently interpreted as acts of mercy and were accompanied by parallel measures in favour of former Austrian National

Socialists (cf. Bailer 1993, pp. 255ff.). Frequently, they were only granted in response to great pressure exerted by Allies. As the first victim of National Socialism, Austria was not legally obliged to pay 'compensations' (cf. Manoschek 1995, p. 100).

The collective shift of responsibility for the Nazi crimes to Germany, conducted with 'patriotic complacency', 'created a political culture of unawareness' in Austria (Ziegler and Kannonier-Finster 1993, p. 33). The acceptance of the Nazi experience as a (negative) normative standard for self-reflection came very late (cf. Pelinka and Mayr 1998). Thus, 'skirting responsibility' became an essential element of the political culture of the Second Republic (Ziegler and Kannonier-Finster 1993, pp. 35f.), which found its expression in ignoring those who were politically and racially persecuted (cf. Manoschek 1995, p. 103).[15]

Austria's former President Kurt Waldheim – 'a true Austrian' (Pelinka 1988, p. 16) – and his ideas about 'doing one's duty' under the Nazis ultimately came to symbolise this trivialising, unreflecting attitude towards Austria's Nazi past. In this context, openly expressed antisemitism once again became acceptable,[16] as Waldheim campaign slogans such as 'Now more than ever' and 'We Austrians will vote for whom we want', as well as antisemitic statements of various political officials in the course of the electoral campaign, demonstrated. In addition, the tenor and language of other episodes during the Second Republic involving 'Jewish' themes (such as the controversy between Bruno Kreisky, Friedrich Peter and Simon Wiesenthal) likewise suggest the presence of 'the antisemitic structures which underlie Austrian political culture' (cf. Wodak et al. 1990).[17]

Obscuring problematic historical events is also a characteristic of Austrian memorial culture (cf. Seiter 1995, pp. 684–705; Uhl 1994, pp. 111–96). Throughout the Second Republic, there has been a tendency to separate the events of the Second World War from the political objectives of the Nazi regime and to glorify the soldiers who died at the front as heroes fighting for their home land (cf. Gärtner and Rosenberger 1991, Heer and Naumann 1995, Gärtner 1996, Manoschek 1993 and 1996b). The initiative 'Stalingrad: Fifty Years Later' taken by a non-partisan and interdenominational committee, which included the then Federal Chancellor, federal ministers, provincial governors, mayors, and church representatives, is characteristic of this kind of historical perspective. To justify the erection of a memorial commemorating all soldiers who died at the battle of Stalingrad, its proponents argued that all the soldiers – including *Wehrmacht* soldiers – who died at the front also be accorded victim status. Thanks to the efforts of the committee, this monument was dedicated in 1996, notwithstanding the fact that the *Wehrmacht* soldiers the monument commemorated had taken part in a war which was devised as a racist war of extermination by Hitler Germany (cf. Huemer and Manoschek 1996, pp. 9f.).

Until the early 1990s, Erika Weinzierl has argued, Austria's 'co-responsibility [for Nazi crimes] was officially tabooed despite the fact that more than half a million Austrians had had to be denazified' (1993a, pp. 5f.). In the meantime, the 'state doctrine' of Austria as Hitler's first victim had become fragile: in an address delivered in the Austrian parliament in 1992, Austrian Chancellor Franz Vranitzky became the first official to declare explicitly that Austria had been both a victim and a perpetrator of National Socialism. Two years later, in a speech of similar content, Vranitzky conceded that Austria had been slow to recognise its moral responsibility, and apologised to the victims of the Austrian Nazis (cf. Bunzl 1993, p. 49; Neugebauer 1994, p. 898). Thomas Klestil, who succeeded Kurt Waldheim as President, delivered a similar speech before the Knesset in Israel in November 1994.

In 1991, in a speech to the parliament on 7 August, Franz Vranitzky had vaguely initiated support for Nazi victims 'who had so far not been considered at all or not adequately by these measures or who had not been taken into consideration with respect to moral or material claims'. But it was not until 1994 that the Sozial-demokratische Partei Österreichs or Austrian Social Democratic Party (SPÖ), the Österreichische Volkspartei or Austrian People's Party (ÖVP), the Greens and the Liberal Forum introduced a binding resolution in Parliament calling for the establishment of an aid fund. The resolution was not adopted until 1995, the year which marked the fiftieth anniversary of the foundation of the Second Republic. The National Aid Fund for Nazi Victims was endowed with a sum of ATS 500 million, which although intended to deal primarily with 'hardship cases' among the victims was ultimately designed to pay compensation to persons persecuted by the Nazi regime for their 'political, ethnic, religious, national, or sexual orientation; for reasons of health; or for so-called asocial behaviour' (cf. *Der Falter*, 15 June 1995, p. 9). The fund, however, was not to start its work before the official celebrations were over.[18]

In the discussions and parliamentary debates on the Nazi victim fund, the views expressed by several politicians were quite revealing. Restitution, which ultimately remains a symbolic act (cf. Goschler 1992, p. 222), was characterised by the leader of the Social Democratic parliamentary caucus as 'a gesture ... accompanied by concrete help ... towards those who really need it ... that is, for those who are really in need of support' (Stenographic protocols of the 40th session of the National Assembly of the Republic of Austria, p. 62). The leader of the ÖVP caucus considered old-age pensions to which victims were entitled anyway as part of the 'restitution' (cf. Bailer 1995). In the session of the National Assembly of 1 June 1995, the FPÖ MP Harald Ofner demanded 'restitution' not only for the 'millions of immediate victims', by which he meant 'primarily our Jewish fellow citizens', but also for 'those Austrians from areas previously belonging to the Austro-Hungarian monarchy' (Stenographic protocols of the 40th session of the National Assembly of the Republic of Austria, p. 56), since 'from the victim's perspective, a victim is always a victim, and it is of no significance who, when, and where the harm was inflicted upon this person' (ibid., p. 57). The FPÖ (Freiheitliche Partei Österreichs or Austrian Freedom Party, Austria's far-right party) submitted a corresponding amendment proposing 'that all persons of good will should at last join hands, across all trenches and graves' (ibid., p. 69).

This example illustrates the renewed denial of the Republic of Austria's basic responsibility for the victims of Nazi crimes in two respects. On the discursive level, numerous politicians and other official speakers continue to exclude many victims, restricting entitlement of 'victims' to economic need. As a consequence, the late and relatively low financial payments of ATS 70,000 are made to seem more like 'generous donations'. The institutional practice of actual payments out of the fund corresponds to the discriminatory and exclusionary attitudes towards many Nazi victims that were evident in the legislative debate. Thus the number of people even eligible to receive compensation is already low at a time when hardly any survivors remain; the number of eligible victims is then further reduced by adding the additional requirement of economic need (Beckermann 1995a).

The real significance which Austrian politicians have accorded victims of Nazi crimes may be inferred from the fact that those persons who were to administer the aid fund were only able to begin their work much later, because guidelines for the implementation of their work had not been produced in time. An administrative director for the fund was appointed by the responsible parliamentary committee in the autumn of 1995. Although incoming applications for compensation are considered according to the applicants' age, many die before their application has been processed.[19] In May 1996, the board of trustees of the fund, including representatives of religious groups, political parties and academics' decided on a 'hereditary arrangement': since most of the victims were old and could possibly die before their application is settled, their potential claims could be bequeathed to their descendants. Nonetheless, 'restitution' was reserved for 'the needy' only.

3.6 EUROPEAN INTEGRATION AND 'PERMANENT NEUTRALITY'[20]

The signing of the Austrian State Treaty[21] in May 1955, on the basis of which Austria was finally 'resurrected' as an independent state, has a close political connection to Austria's declaration of permanent neutrality.[22] However, Austria did not legally oblige itself to remain neutral in the State Treaty; neutrality was purposefully not mentioned in the State Treaty to prevent the Allied signatories to the Treaty from being able to interpret neutrality as they wished (cf. Nick and Pelinka 1993, p. 22). However, neutrality is one of the political foundations of the State Treaty, which – instead of a peace treaty – forms the basis in international law of the sovereign Second Republic, and in which Austria guarantees that all traces of National Socialism will be removed and accepts the stipulation prohibiting another *Anschluss* to Germany (cf. Strejcek 1992, p. 9 and Koja 1991, p. 62).[23] This document and the declaration of Austrian neutrality have been raised to the status of 'sacred texts' by Austrian historians and are considered to be the consummation of the striving for independence by the Second Republic.[24]

Austria's neutrality is set forth in the Federal Constitutional Law of 26 October 1955. This law was expressly acknowledged by the signatory states and informally acknowledged by most countries with which Austria had diplomatic relations. Among other things, this law states: 'For the purpose of maintaining its independence over the long term and for the purpose of promoting the inviolability of its territory, Austria declares its permanent neutrality by its own will. Austria will maintain and defend this neutrality by all available means. In order to secure these purposes, Austria will not join any military alliances, nor will it allow the establishment of foreign states' military bases in its territory.'

Permanent neutrality became one of the most important identity-promoting characteristics of the Second Republic. As a prominent part of the 'Austrian way' promoted by Federal Chancellor Bruno Kreisky in the 1970s (cf. Reiterer 1988a, pp. 172f.), it played an essential role in the 'success story' of Austrian politics and moulded the image of the Second Republic as an 'island of the blessed' and as a diplomatic meeting place (cf. Khol 1990, p. 34).

Until the mid-1980s, there was a general consensus in Austria that Austrian neutrality and Austria's resulting role in international politics could not be reconciled with full membership in the EC, which had always seen itself as a political community and was closely connected to NATO (cf. Falkner 1995, pp. 331–3; Nick and Pelinka 1993, p. 24): as a neutral state, Austria was obliged not to enter into such supranational alliances of states (cf. Luif 1982).

For a long time governments defined the country's foreign policy as active neutrality. This implied a certain degree of distance from both power-blocs (though with a clear ideological orientation towards the West). Austria saw itself as an intermediary in the conflicts between East and West as well as in those between North and South. Permanent neutrality was understood as constant impartiality (cf. Rotter 1990, p. 10). By the mid-1980s, however, changing geopolitical surroundings and the threat of decline in the Austrian economy caused by the introduction of the European Common Market (cf. Falkner 1995, p. 333; Nick and Pelinka 1993, p. 24) had begun to raise questions about the meaning and function of permanent neutrality.

In 1987, a legal opinion commissioned by the Austrian Federation of Industry disrupted this basic political consensus concerning the incompatibility of permanent neutrality and membership in the EC (cf. Falkner 1995, p. 333; Pelinka, Schaller and Luif 1994, p. 152). According to this opinion, they became reconcilable if Austria asserted its neutrality in an appropriate clause in the relevant documents (cf. Noll 1993). After 1987, the internal debate was thus defined primarily in terms of Austria's political will to accede to the EC or not. By the late 1980s, Austria's efforts to integrate itself into the Western European community politically and economically had led to an upheaval in the continuity of the political interpretation of neutrality. In fact, Austria had always interpreted its obligations under the policy of neutrality more narrowly than Switzerland, particularly in regard to military neutrality (cf. Pelinka et al. 1994, p. 26). Moreover, there had never been an official binding declaration specifying the details of neutrality: none of the documents related to neutrality (the Moscow Declaration of 1 November 1943, the Moscow Memorandum of 15 April 1955, the State Treaty of 15 May 1955, and the Neutrality Act of 26 October 1955) contained a precise definition of Austria's rights and obligations as a neutral state.[25]

The 'new dynamic of the EC' (Pelinka et al. 1994, p. 285), including the idea of the European Common Market, which was a factor of uncertainty for the Austrian economy (since approximately two thirds of Austria's exports went to EC countries), and the intensification of European (political) integration, coincided with Austrian domestic party politics. On the one hand, the ÖVP and later the SPÖ attempted to use their pro-Europe orientation to fashion themselves as 'European parties' (cf. Falkner 1995, p. 334); on the other hand, Austria was in an image crisis due to recent scandals (cf. Gehler and Sickinger 1995, pp. 671–83). After the wine scandal (in which some Austrian wines were found to contain glycolalcohol, an ingredient in anti-freeze), the public exposure of Austrian nationalised industrial companies' arms shipment to warring countries (in violation of Austrian Law) and the Waldheim affair, Austria was searching for a (Western) European identity which would enjoy a wider acceptance internationally (cf. Kramer 1991, p. 192). Yet another reason for the decision to apply for membership in the EC, according to Schaller (1991, p. 500), was the government expectation of domestic political modernisation and liberalisation that such a move would engender. Schneider (1994, pp. 8f.) maintains that accession to the EC also served as a 'back door' through which unpopular decisions in economic and social policy (like turning away form 'Austro-Keynesianism') (cf. also Kaiser et al. 1994) could be introduced.

In a report to the National Assembly in 1989, the federal government proposed that Austria apply for membership in the EC, but with certain conditions (preservation of permanent neutrality, of the federal state principles, of the Austrian social system, of its strongly progressive environmental policy, and of its large-scale rural agriculture and forestry, and with a solution to the problem of transit before accession, cf. Falkner 1995, p. 334). The National Assembly voted by a large majority to empower the federal government to begin negotiations with Brussels (cf. Falkner 1995, p. 334), which in fact began in 1993 after the Commission's application evaluation, or 'avis',[26] which was generally positive because of Austria's economic and political stability. The EEA (European Economic Area) Treaty, which allowed Austria to participate in the European Common Market but gave it no decision-making rights at European Union level, also provided the Austrian federal government with an additional argument in favour of membership in the European Union (cf. Falkner 1995, p. 335) after it went into effect in 1994. Because joining the EU entailed altering the Austrian constitution in ways that impinged upon several of Austria's constitutional principles, a referendum on membership had to be held.

The discussions preceding the EU referendum mainly revolved around the issues of the economic consequences of accession,[27] the transit issue, questions of increased immigration and property ownership by foreigners, problems of democratic policy, and the question of the effects of membership on the individual provinces of Austria (cf. Laireiter et al. 1994).[28] The referendum had been preceded by a massive pro-EU advertising campaign in politics and the media.[29] It was held on 12 June 1994 and resulted in a surprisingly high proportion of 'yes' votes (66 per cent).

Despite the 'neutrality clause' that had been included in its application for membership, Austria's permanent neutrality was in fact not the subject of negotiations. In the treaty of membership itself, Austria, along with the other applicants Norway, Finland and Sweden, declared its readiness to co-operate 'completely and actively' in the EU's common foreign and security policy from the time of entry (Falkner 1995, p. 337).

During the war in former Yugoslavia in the early 1990s, even though the number of its proponents had already declined, most Austrians still remained advocates of neutrality (cf. *SWS-Rundschau* 1999/2, pp. 231–8, and 4, pp. 535–42, as well as the survey carried out by *Profil* on 13 January 1992). In an opinion poll in May 1993, 51 per cent of Austrians agreed that 'the goal of negotiations has to be to prevent Austria's membership in the EU from endangering neutrality' (*Dokumentation market-Archiv* M25, 1993). Nevertheless, concern about the future of Austrian neutrality was not among the main motives of the EU opponents; they were far more concerned about the decline of Austrian environmental standards or special problems in individual sectors of agriculture (cf. Kaiser et al. 1994, p. 8).

Despite extensive discussion of European policy and security policy, for a long time the advisability of Austrian neutrality as such did not become an important subject of debate. Most politicians rejected statements against neutrality out of hand in ritualised obligatory fashion. Austria's neutral status, which to many connoted peace, security and the political continuity of the Second Republic, had become a symbol of what is Austrian and a synonym for Austrian sovereignty (cf. Brünner 1993, p. 20); as such an effective taboo had attached itself to it. Neutrality as a central symbol of Austria, and the mythification of neutrality in the determinate political context of the Second Republic, are both firmly anchored in the 'collective' memory of the Austrians. To this day, the close connection of neutrality to the origin of independence makes a dispassionate discussion of the political facts impossible. The passion which characterises discussions of whether neutrality and EU membership are compatible betrays neutrality's mythical character (as the taboo-laden 'central concept of the Austrians of the Second Republic', Bruckmüller 1994, p. 135). Consequently, the debate on neutrality in recent years has concentrated more on the symbolic than on the political meaning of neutrality. As Rudolf Burger has observed, neutrality as a foreign policy matter is actually about a domestic political phenomenon in which the social psychological nature of the Austrians manifests itself: 'The more Austrian neutrality becomes a mere silhouette in foreign policy, the more it becomes a fetish in domestic politics ... a relative term has become a term of substance', a 'change in essence of the concept of national character' (Burger 1994b, p. 364, cf. also Menasse 1995, p. 86).

Nevertheless, the meaning of Austrian neutrality is in the process of transformation. Not only have changes in the political landscape required a rethinking of the concept of neutrality and its functions (cf. Unterberger 1992, pp. 11f.; Thalberg 1993, p. 31; Brünner 1993, pp. 20ff.). Increasingly neutrality seems to be becoming a meaningless symbol, the content of which can be defined at will. Indeed, the ideas of neutrality range from a role as intermediary in the North-South conflict and in southeastern Central Europe, to a part as good-faith arbitrator in international conflicts, to the role of advisor to the EU in matters touching on Austria's presumed expertise. At present (1996), there is very little discussion about whether Austrian neutrality is in principle compatible with participation in the European integration process. The current frame of reference is rather the (supposed) necessity of a 'collective security policy' due to supranational threats in the new geopolitical situation and the compatibility of such a security policy with neutrality.[30] The 'new' security needs of Europe – and especially those of Austria at the external border of the EU – also form the most important argument in the present political discourse on neutrality. Threats from the 'population explosion' in developing countries and from the consequences of global disturbances in climate, the problems of food supply worldwide, extreme economic discrepancies between the industrialised countries of the North and the developing countries of the South, the danger of an energy shortage as well as an increase in terrorism and violent domestic confrontations in the countries of the West – all these themes have been presented as reasons necessitating a re-evaluation of European security policy as a whole, including of course, the question of the continued relevance of Austria's neutrality (cf. Hagen 1994, and also a critical view by Matzner 1995, p. 40–4). Because of its proximity to the former Yugoslavian region, moreover, the argument goes, Austria would be especially interested in the construction of such a security system (cf. Schneider 1994, p. 17). Austria's 'special intermediate situation' (neutral and independent, belonging to the West but without being completely obligated to its institutions' and (according to Reinprecht 1995, p. 341) 'under the lee of the ever-dominant East-West conflict') came to an end at the latest in 1989 with the fall of the Iron Curtain. 'Without a doubt, Austria has moved a bit closer to the West since 1989' (Reinprecht 1995, p. 341).

The developments and debates mentioned above could conceivably increase support for the view that any such traditional neutral foreign policy would diminish in significance or even become dysfunctional; such debates could also cause chip away at neutrality's symbolic power among Austrians.[31] Similar to the way in which Austrian identity in the Second Republic was given its particular political inflection by the élites of the two large political camps, the decision to join the EU and the political measures which membership has entailed can also be interpreted as an élite phenomena, which diffused into public opinion by the 'trickle-down effect' (Pelinka 1994, p. 150).

Even before the time of Austria's entry into the EU, Reiterer (1993a, p. 118) spoke of Austria's 'European identity'. Increasingly, references have been (and are) made to the European aspects of Austrian history: on the one hand, Austria has traditionally served as a bridge to the East; on the other hand – with allusions to the 'wars against the Turks' and references to the Baroque era – it is often emphasised that Austria has also on occasion served as a 'bulwark' against the East. Similar ideas can also be found in current discussions of Austria's function as country on the EU's eastern border, and especially in the debate on migration.

NOTES

1. However, several authors (for example, Bruckmüller 1994 and 1996, Breuss et al. 1995 or Pelinka 1985 and 1990) point out the significance of patterns of symbolic identification and interpretation.
2. Although 'conscious Austrianness' in the nineteenth and at the beginning of the twentieth century primarily implied orientation towards the House of Habsburg and a pronounced Catholic attitude

(Münz 1991, p. 8), some authors, for example Heer (1981), assume cultural Austrian traditions going back to the time of the monarchy as the basis for the genesis of an independent Austrian nation.

3. See also Haller and Gruber (1996c, pp. 455–94, table p. 490), who ranked Austrians in first place (1995) and in second place (1990) regarding national pride in comparison to the citizens of other countries on the basis of two series of surveys (International Social Survey, 1995 and World Value Survey, 1990) in various European countries. Furthermore Hallet et al. (1996) present findings which suggest that 51 per cent of Austrians feel a very strong and 31 per cent a strong connection to Austria.

4. Examples of anthologies in which texts on this subject are compiled include Jung (1988), Walter (1992) or Jung (1995). Reiterer (1988a), Bruckmüller (1994a and 1996) and Breuss et al. (1995) include social scientific findings on this subject in their works.

5. The question of the existence and origin of an 'Austrian people' is answered by two different myths of ancestry, the 'Germanic' and the 'multicultural' (cf. Coudenhove-Kalergi 1990).The idea that present-day Austrians are primarily of German descent is opposed by the multicultural myth, 'according to which the Austrians brought elements from all sides and thus unified German orderliness, the Slavic soul, Hungarian cuisine and Italian musicality in an inimitable way' (Bruckmüller 1994, p. 142, cf. also Csáky 1991). This multicultural myth emphasises Austria's ethnic, linguistic and cultural plurality. See also André Tibal (1936), who describes the Austrian mentality as decisively influenced by the Reformation and Counter-Reformation and a 'baroque' approach to life. According to Ernst Fischer (1945), the Austrian 'national character' has been shaped by centuries of fights for liberty. On the Austrian person as an 'artefact of the Habsburg monarchy' see Bruckmüller (1996, pp. 234–6).

6. The historical origin of regional consciousness must primarily be assumed to be rooted in the resistance to Habsburg centralism. After 1848 and 1861, regional consciousness represented a conservative counterbalance to liberalism (cf., for example, the Catholic-oriented Tyrolean provincial consciousness).

7. In Austrian everyday language, 'national' means *'Deutschnational'* ('German-national'); an Austrian-national attitude would be called 'patriotic'.

8. See the survey conducted by the Paul Lazarsfeld Society (1980/1981, pp. 27 and 29), which found that the Austrians think the Germans to be the by far most likeable nation with whom they feel the closest affinity (70 per cent). However, Plasser and Ulram (1991, pp. 145f.) have found a decreasing percentage of such felt emotional affinity to Germany (1980: 70 per cent, 1987: 64 per cent; 1990: 60 per cent). See also Weninger (1991, p. 491) and the IMAS-Survey of June/July 1993 (*Der Standard*, 23 July 1993), according to which four out of five Austrians think that close and good relations to Germany are important for Austria (see also Bruckmüller 1996, pp. 146–8, Haller and Gruber 1996b, pp. 406, 408f., 425f; and Haller 1996b, pp. 516–18).

9. A discussion among German studies scholars of the complex issue of the relation between the different varieties of German spoken in different states has yielded the concept of 'pluricentric' (or 'plurinational') languages. This concept seems helpful in understanding the connection between language and national identity in Austria. Its proponents argue that German, like other world languages, is spoken in several states with several centres of linguistic development, where so-called 'national varieties'- the German in the Federal Republic, the Swiss and Austrian – with their own specific norms and forms have developed (cf., for example, Wiesinger 1988; Muhr, Schrodt and Wiesinger, 1995; Clyne 1995 and Ammon 1995).

10. Today, German is the language spoken by 92 per cent of the people living in Austria (Austrian Central Statistical Office 1993, p. 23).

11. Since the end of the monarchy and, above all, since the foundation of the Second Republic, there has been a drastic decrease in minority languages.

12. 'National Socialism was also a local Austrian political movement with old traditions,' writes Wolfgang Neugebauer (1994, p. 896). Thus, in 1938, at the time of the *Anschluss*, the NSDAP (Nationalsozialistiche Deutsche Arbeiterpartei) had about 90,000 illegal members in Austria. By March 1938, the first pogroms against the Jewish population were carried out by the Austrian population, already resulting in such a high degree of excesses during the lootings and 'Aryanisations' that the NSDAP felt the need to interfere in order to moderate the Austrians. Furthermore, Austrians such as Eichmann, Kaltenbrunner, Globocnik, Seyss-Inquart and Murer occupied central positions in the murderous system of National Socialism (cf. Manoschek 1995, p. 97).

13. This is reflected by the willingness on the part of top politicians to be guest of honour at celebrations

of former soldiers' leagues and similar associations as well as by the fact that streets and public buildings are named after Nazi criminals and officials of the Nazi system. It is reflected most clearly by the fact that many people who were influential in public life during the Third Reich continue to be so in the Second Republic.

14. Universities and law courts, some areas of art, of the media and of administration were examples of insufficient handling of the denazification process (cf. Kaindl-Widhalm 1990, p. 31). Former Nazis and Nazi sympathisers were soon wooed by both major political camps as they constituted a large potential of voters. In the general elections of 1949 the (former) Nazis were already allowed to vote.

15. For many decades, 'restitution' was not an issue for the political élites of the Second Republic (Bailer 1993; cf. also Pelinka and Mayr 1998). Austria's portrayal as Hitler's 'first victim' and as a victim of National Socialist aggression, as well as the problematical and broad definition of the concept of victim, which, for example, equated the former inmates of the 'Austro-fascist' detention camp Wöllersdorf with the victims of National Socialism in the first Victims' Welfare Law in 1945 (cf. Bailer 1993, p. 275), resulted in the fact that financial compensation payments to the victims of racist and political persecution were limited to charitable donations of the amount of ATS 6,000 (cf. Traxler 1995) or to the granting to victims of favourable conditions with respect to pension entitlement.

16. Thus, Ilse Leitenberger wrote in an article in *Die Presse* about 'World Jewry' and accused this construct of 'profiting from a dark past' (*Die Presse*, 25 March 1986). Cf. also Gruber (1991, pp. 214–21).

17. That Austria's Nazi past has not been adequately dealt with to this day was also suggested by the trial of the Neo-Nazi Gerhard Honsik, who had publically denied Nazi crimes. The trial judge demanded expert testimony by historians about the National Socialist mass murder of Jews, although this is not doubted by any serious historian and although in Austria the mere denial of Nazi crimes is defined as a criminal act.

Throughout this book we have chosen to use 'antisemitism' and its derivatives rather than the more conventional 'anti-Semitic', and would like to explain why. There seems to be no obvious compelling orthographic reason why the German words *Antisemitismus, antisemitisch, Antisemit,* and so on, should be spelled anti-Semitism, etc., rather than antisemitism (or vice-versa), but there is no denying that 'anti-Semitism' is the usage most frequently encountered, and suggested, for example by the *Chicago Manual of Style* (CMS). According to the CMS, the word anti-Semitism falls into the category of 'Exceptions to the Closed Style for Prefixed Compounds'. The CMS's reasoning (but not its alone) is that when adding prefixes to a word that is capitalised, the resulting word should retain the capital letter. Since Semite and Semitic are capitalised, the CMS argues by analogy that anti-Semite and anti-Semitic should also be capitalised. By extension, the noun form for anti-Semitic, that is anti-Semitism, should also be capitalised.

We have nothing against these arguments as general editorial guidelines. However, in the case of anti-Semitism vs. antisemitism it is a question of the purported semantic significance of a specific orthography. Specifically, the Israeli historian Shmuel Almog has forcefully maintained that the words 'Semite' and 'Semitic', though originally used with reference to a language group, came to be used as racial categories when employed by völkisch ideologues in the nineteenth century and 'anti-Semites' thenceforward. Almog's point (somewhat oversimplified) is that these terms have become so loaded by their Nazi usage that merely rendering the term 'Antisemitismus' as 'anti-Semitism' concedes the essential (racial) proposition that there are 'Semites' or that there is something called 'Semitism'. It is true that in common usage the term 'Semite' refers either to people speaking a Semitic language or descendants of Shem, and most dictionary entries would record at least these two usages. And while we are not completely convinced by Almog's argument, at least in the categorical way in which he states it ('So the hyphen, or rather its omission, conveys a message; if you hyphenate your "anti-Semitism", you attach some credence to the very foundation on which the whole thing rests. Strike out the hyphen and you will treat antisemitism for what it really is – a generic name for modern Jew-hatred which now embraces this phenomenon as a whole, past, present and – I am afraid – future as well'), we do see his point in the comparison between, say, anti-Feminism and anti-Semitism.

Manuals such as the CMS are, of course, written to provide guidelines and promote consistency, but the usages they prescribe are, of course, both historically bounded and somewhat arbitrary. Thus, if there were compelling semantic reasons to choose one spelling over another, then an appeal to the CMS authority alone would have little weight. However, one need not personally be convinced of Almog's arguments to note that people like Almog do feel quite strongly about this issue. In the end it seems really to come down to weighing the authority of the CMS or similar manuals against the alleged possibility of unwittingly reinforcing racialist categories. Since there appears to be no compelling orthographical reason to retain the preferred CWS usage, we prefer to use 'antisemitism' and so on, rather than 'anti-Semitism'. See Shmuel Almog, 'What is a Hyphen?' *SICSA Report* 2 (Summer 1989), pp. 1–2. We would like to thank Richard Mitten for calling our attention to this issue and for contributing this extensive explanation of it.

18. The resolution was adopted with the votes of all parties represented in Parliament, with the exception of the Greens, who felt its content to be humiliating and disgraceful, as it contained no legal claim for the victims to compensation. The same opinion was expressed by Paul Grosz, then President of the Jewish Community. The law establishing the aid fund in effect amended the Victims' Welfare Law to include handicapped people as victims. However, neither homosexuals nor those people designated as 'asocial' by the Nazis were included, because members of the ÖVP and FPÖ all voted against it.

19. By the middle of May 1996, the claims of 3,280 persons had been settled by the fund. The majority of applications are from the United States, Israel, Austria and England (*Wiener Zeitung*, 19 June 1996).

20. This chapter is partly based on Dilek Cinar's interim project report on 'EU accession, neutrality and Austrian identity' (Wodak et al. 1995, pp. 108–19).

21. On the history of the genesis, the content, the legal context, etc. of the State Treaty see Rotter (1995, pp. 122ff.).

22. This is already expressed in the Moscow Memorandum of 15 April 1955, which presents the 'political foundation' of Austrian neutrality as the result of the Austro-Soviet negotiations.

23. In 1964, these provisions were given the status of constitutional provisions.

24. Prisching (1995, p. 71) describes Austrian neutrality as 'part of a political campaign aimed at developing consciousness of the state'. See also Haller and Gruber (1996a, pp. 89 and 115) and Haller 1996, 2nd thesis on p. 503 as well as pp. 508–10). In 1965, the National Assembly declared 26 October the Austrian national holiday, as this day was connected with the law of neutrality which 'completed a period of Austrian history and formed the basis which enabled Austria to regain a safe place among the European states' (Gutkas 1985, p. 82).

25. On the debate over the qualification of neutrality and Austria's UN membership cf. Noll (1993, p. 193) and Teuber (1993, p. 23).

26. Because of Austria's status as a permanently neutral country, difficulties in implementing collective foreign and defence policies were feared and discussed.

27. On the attitudes towards the European Union see the statistics in *SWS Rundschau* 1995/4: The 'New European Union' (pp. 453–60).

28. Slogans such as 'Together, not alone' (*Gemeinsam statt einsam*), 'Moving forward or staying still' (*Fortschritt oder Stillstand*) 'Who if not we' (*Wer, wenn nicht wir?*), or 'At the centre of Europe or just outside?' (*Mitten in Europa oder knapp daneben*).

29. For 39 per cent of EU sympathisers, general economic advantage was the most important reason for voting in favour of EU accession.

30. 13 per cent of those people who had voted in favour of Austria's joining the EU regarded domestic and foreign security as the most important criterion (cf. Plasser and Ulram 1994, p. 110).

31. See Prisching (1995, p. 72), who thinks that it is not possible to stop discussing Austrian neutrality because it has become part of Austrian identity. One would have to limit oneself instead to suggesting possible ways of slowly weaning people away from the feeling of neutrality (see also Pelinka et al. 1994, p. 473). Höll (1995, p. 466) predicts a decrease in the importance of neutrality and demands a re-definition of Austrian foreign policy. See also recent opinion polls on the issue of 'neutrality'. Haller et al. (1996) take the view that for the majority of Austrians, neutrality is still something very precious. The statistical results provided by the authors must, however, be criticised as they do not distinguish between the 'past' and 'present' meaning of neutrality.

Chapter 4

The Public Arena: Commemorative Speeches and Addresses

4.1 RHETORIC AND THE CONSTITUTIVE CONDITIONS OF POLITICAL ORATORY

4.1.1 The Commemorative Address as a Special Genre of Oratory

Classical rhetoric distinguishes three classes of genre: the judicial (*genus iudiciale*), the deliberative (*genus deliberativum*) and the epideictic (*genus demonstrativum*). According to the ideal-typical classification scheme, judicial oratory is focused temporally on the past, and thematically on justice or injustice, and its function is to accuse or defend. Deliberative rhetoric is associated with the future, thematically with expediency or harmfulness, and functionally with exhorting or dissuading. Finally, epideictic oratory is linked to the present, thematically to honor and disgrace and functionally to praise or blame (cf. Plett 1989, pp. 15f.).

With the exception of Friedhelm Frischenschlager's lecture 'Austria in a Europe of Solidarity', delivered before the SPÖ's *Zukunftswerkstätte* ('Workshop for the Future'),[1] all the political addresses we analyse in this study were concerned with commemoration and may therefore be attributed to epideictic oratory in a broader sense. However, none of the three classes mentioned above occurs in pure form: the diversity of topics and temporal references usually results in the simultaneous presence of elements from all three oratorical categories within one and the same speech (on the close relationship between epideictic oratory and political speech, see Ottmers 1996, pp. 18–30).

Commemorative speeches are normally delivered on public days of remembrance, which are usually associated with the 'magic of numbers' (Huter 1994), and primarily serve to retrieve the past for the present. 'In many instances,' writes Anton Staudinger, 'this special aura of anniversaries tends to legitimate ways of dealing with the past, by selecting affirmative elements from the past which seem useful for justifying present interests' (1994, p. 21). The commemorative addresses we have analysed were all highly epideictic in nature, that is, they assigned praise or blame to certain moments of Austria's past or present which were selected in accordance with a particular occasion. However, epideictic oratory does not exclusively serve as vehicle for the linguistic self-presentation and self-promotion of the speakers, as has been assumed by many rhetoricians (for example, by Matuschek 1994, pp. 1258ff.);

it also has an 'educational' function, that is it seeks to convey certain political values and beliefs, to construct common characteristics and identities and to create consensus and a spirit of community, which in turn is intended to serve as a model for the future political actions of the addressees (cf. Perelman 1980, pp. 28f.).

In addition, the speeches in our study contained many deliberative elements and/or argumentative insertions. They sometimes even exhibited traces of judicial rhetoric, in that they sought to justify problematic actions and events. This was the case, for example, with the issue of guilt in reference to the Nazi past, or in cases where future political decisions were being justified.

Obviously, an analysis in rhetorical terms seems the most adequate method for our purpose, as the selected speeches contained a wide range of rhetorical elements. We will investigate the more subtle forms of persuasive, identity-constituting rhetoric, and will also explore how the authors of these speeches drew upon the repertoire of classical rhetorical topoi.

4.1.2 On the Authors of Political Speeches

The reason we treat the authors of speeches as a separate category is that it cannot be assumed that the 'animator' – to use Goffman's (1981) term – that is, the politician who delivers a speech – is also the person who actually wrote it. Ultimately it may not be of great importance whether the speakers actually write the texts of their speeches themselves – which is highly unlikely considering the workload of current politicians, especially the highest political representatives of a state – or merely take part in its composition, because the person who delivers the speech is always solely responsible for its content. Therefore politicians are also the 'principals' of their statements (cf. Goffman 1981).

One of the determining conditions of contemporary public political oratory, according to Kammerer (1995), is the increasing influence of the media on leading politicians, which sometimes results in something like rhetorical omnipresence. Kammerer writes: 'Chancellor Helmut Kohl delivers between 120 and 150 speeches a year. This number doubles during election campaigns. In addition, there are salutations, contributions to newspapers and journals and several hundred personal letters. Writers of speeches contribute considerably to the production of all these texts' (Kammerer 1995, p. 20).

In Austria, the situation is very similar. In 1995, Austrian President Thomas Klestil alone delivered about 160 addresses and speeches.[2] No one with even a vague knowledge of the workload of the president would seriously believe that Klestil had written all these speeches himself. However, the increasing personalisation of politics forces politicians to conceal the origin of their speeches from the public and to obscure the fact that top political offices, such as those of the President, the Chancellor, or cabinet ministers, necessitate large teams with corporate identity status, of which speechwriters are important members (this has been shown by Campell and Jamieson 1990, p. 11 regarding the office of the President of the United States). In this chapter, the question of authorship will concern us only marginally and we will no longer distinguish between the politicians as speakers and the authors of the speeches.

Traditionally, the production of a speech consists of five phases: *inventio* (selection of topics), *dispositio* (arrangement of topics), *elocutio* (linguistic development of the arranged topic), *memoria* (memorising) and *actio* (delivery). Kammerer (1995, p. 27) claims that ghost speechwriters are primarily involved with elocution, that is the linguistic development of the topic, and in part also with the thematic arrangement of individual speech sections. Together with political advisors, they are also responsible for the selection of content. Memorising and delivery are the sole responsibility of the speaker, with memorising depending on whether a speech is read out or delivered without notes.

4.1.3 The Speaker's Political Position and the Contents of a Speech: a Few Hypotheses

We have formulated a number of hypotheses, based on the assumption that a relation exists between the political office which a speaker holds at the time he or she delivers his or her speech and the 'construction of Austrian identity'.

The Federal President is the head of state and hence the supreme representative of the Austrian collective, both internally and abroad (Heinrich and Welan 1992, p. 134 and Welan 1995/96, pp. 34ff.). As national 'preacher' and a kind of voice of the nation, the president is expected to address moral issues deemed important to the state in a solemn, dignified manner on relevant occasions (Welan 1995/96, p. 137) and, ideally, to act as an integrative authority to promote harmony and to defuse potential conflicts. However, the president's authority appropriates that of a 'passive king' (Welan 1995/96, p. 138), that is, his or her actions primarily consist of talking and he or she is therefore evaluated mainly by his or her words (Kammerer 1995, p. 28). Thus we assumed that in comparison to all other speakers we examined, Klestil's speeches would most strongly aim at creating identity and unity and would neglect intra-national differences as much as possible, or would present them in such a way as not to inhibit the generation of a feeling of national identification. We assumed that for this purpose Klestil would primarily select and favour those linguistic means of realisation which implicitly or explicitly expressed sameness, similarity, unity and solidarity. This hypothesis was tested on our data, while other factors which might have influenced his performance, such as the audience, the occasion and Klestil's party political affiliation (prior to this election: upon his election he resigned from the ÖVP) were also taken into consideration.

The Federal Chancellor, the supreme governmental authority in Austria's political system and the 'active king' of the constitution (Heinrich and Welan 1992, p. 138), also represents official Austria. While the Chancellor is not confined to being a purely ceremonial speaker, he or she also acts as another voice of the nation on appropriate occasions, appearing as a person generating identity and integration inside Austria, and as a representative of the country, a human national *pars pro toto*, outside Austria. However, we assumed that as the head of the majority party the

Chancellor would not ignore intra-national differences as much as the President, particularly differences between the political parties, and that in his or her speeches the Chancellor would generally employ those constructive and perpetuating strategies which served to support his or her political position of power and consequently maintain the political status quo. Accordingly, we assumed that the chancellor would primarily stress continuity and stability for the future – an essential component of sameness – and, where changes seemed necessary, cautious strategies of transformation would be used. We tested this assumption on several speeches delivered by Chancellor Franz Vranitzky.

In addition, we analysed two speeches by representatives of the majority party, the SPÖ: an address given by Heinz Fischer, the First President of the National Assembly, during the joint session of the National Assembly, and the Federal Council (*Bundesrat*) on 27 April 1995; and the speech of Interior Minister Caspar Einem on 7 May 1995, the anniversary of the liberation of the Nazi victims imprisoned in the Mauthausen concentration camp.

We assumed that the representatives of the political opposition, and also to a somewhat lesser extent the members of the smaller coalition party, would employ different strategies. These politicians would, we believed, attempt to present readings of history and visions of the political present and future that would contrast, and in some ways compete, with the quasi-official views articulated by the majority parliamentary and governmental party. The models of identification these politicians enunciated would thus support alternative images of national identity, images shaped by their respective political, historical and ideological perspectives. They would employ certain constructive strategies that corresponded to these perspectives, but above all they would adopt various strategies of disparagement (of the official version) or transformation. This hypothesis was tested on speeches by various politicians from the ÖVP (Erhard Busek, Wolfgang Schüssel, Heinrich Neisser, Werner Fasslabend and Jürgen Weiss); by Jörg Haider, the leader of the largest opposition party, the FPÖ; by three members of the Green Party – Madeleine Petrovic, Terezija Stoisits and Hannes Tretter – and by two politicians from the Liberal Forum, Heide Schmidt and Friedhelm Frischenschlager. The respective political positions of these speakers at the time of their speeches were also considered.

4.1.4 How the Occasion and Audience Influence the Contents of a Speech

Undeniably, the occasion of a speech and the audience which is being addressed – both the immediate audience and that implied by mediation of the mass media, that is the Austrian population as a whole – considerably influence the contents, strategy selection and forms of realisation chosen by the speaker. Journalists sometimes assume that politicians adapt their speeches to a given audience to such a degree that they may with some justification be compared to the proverbial chameleon. Whether this is a correct observation or must be dismissed as hyperbole will be only touched upon in the course of our analysis, since only a small number of speakers in our data addressed different audiences on different occasions; these were Thomas Klestil, Franz Vranitzky and Jörg Haider.

In addition, we will explore how the speeches' rhetorical elements reflected awareness of, and response to, the problem confronting all speeches addressed to the general public, namely, that their audiences comprise different political groups, and are, of course, also potential voters. Of particular interest in this connection are cases where speakers attempt to address multiple publics (Kühn 1992 and 1995). These attempts may result in what Utz Maas (1984) calls 'polyphony of interpretations', and in the deliberate use of allusions and ambivalent expressions as well as unintentional slips.

4.2 THE DATA

Our data consists of 22 commemorative speeches, major policy addresses or declarations, and one lecture. These are listed in full in Appendix 1.

4.3 ANALYSIS

4.3.1 Introductory Remarks

Our analysis focuses on content. Consequently, individual speeches are not analysed separately, sequence by sequence, as this would considerably extend the scope of our study. Moreover, not everything in a speech is equally relevant. Therefore our analysis is largely thematic, and compares and contrasts the statements of different politicians on one and the same topic (cf. section 2.3.2) following the thematic areas outlined in Chapter 2. This approach will enable us to identify the most important aspects and the main strategies and forms of linguistic realisation, as well as the overall strategic profile or pattern of politicians, parties or speech occasions.

Of the five main thematic areas discussed in our theoretical considerations, the construction of a common culture and of a 'national body' hardly occurred in the political commemorative speeches, in contrast to the focus groups and interviews. There were scarcely any attempts to construct an 'Austrian person' or *homo Austriacus*. The thematic texture centres almost exclusively on the narration of a common political past and on the discursive construction of a common political present and future. However, we would first like to examine briefly how individual speakers perceived the concept of nation. We will do this by identifying the small number of references in their speeches to a common culture, to the *homo Austriacus*, and to the relation between Austrian national and regional self-perception.

4.3.2 On the Understanding of Nation, National and Regional Consciousness, and Identity

In the speeches we analysed, the term 'nation' seldom occurred, although the majority of speakers had no doubts about the existence of a separate Austrian nation. Austria's sovereignty as well as Austrian identity were portrayed by most speakers as

already strongly pronounced. Whenever politicians referred to regional consciousness in a particular province (Vorarlberg, Carinthia), it mostly served simultaneously
to reinforce Austrian national self-perception. *Kulturnation* was never mentioned in
the speeches, at least not explicitly, but this may be explained by the fact that culture
itself was not actually addressed in these speeches. The concept of nation which
was articulated in the commemorative speeches on the fiftieth anniversary of the
foundation of the Second Republic was predominantly embodied in those features
identified with the concept of *Staatsnation*. The only exceptions were the speeches
by the then Carinthian Provincial Governor Jörg Haider and by Defence Minister
Werner Fasslabend. However, these might have been influenced by the specific
audience these two speakers were addressing.

The concept of a 'Greater German' *Kulturnation* lay behind Fasslabend's speech
at Ulrichsberg, as became particularly evident at one point in the speech. This may
be explained by the large number of Germans who were in attendance at this 'European celebration', that is it may be interpreted as an attempt at multiple addressing.
Nowhere in his speech, however, did Fasslabend use the term 'nation'. Instead, he
preferred the collective noun *Volk* (people), which he used extremely often and even
decorated with the epithet *eigenes* ('own') several times, without, however, clarifying
the referential ambiguity of whether the 'Austrians' also belonged to this 'own people'
or not. The fact that he mentioned several Austrian composers suggests this interpretation (although we will not comment on the question of Rainer Maria Rilke's
nationality here), which may be seen from the following excerpt from his address:

> For most members of the present generation it is actually unthinkable that a
> people which produced outstanding and sensitive persons of world renown such
> as Goethe and Schiller, Lessing, Hölderlin or Rilke, Bach and Beethoven, Mozart,
> Haydn and Wagner, Kant, Schopenhauer, Hegel and Nietzsche during the eigh-
> teenth and nineteenth centuries, that such a people in the second third of the
> twentieth century used its power in a dictatorial system which not only caused the
> Shoah, the Holocaust, but, moreover, was the reason why the whole of Europe
> was covered by war: from the polar sea to the deserts of Northern Africa and from
> the Atlantic to the Caucasus.
>
> In this war, millions of human beings, soldiers and civilians, lost their lives,
> there was terrible misery and distress and ultimately the own people and the own
> country [*sic*] were drowned in utter misery and utter suffering. A people and a
> country were dismembered and destroyed, raped and expelled.
>
> (*Fasslabend*)

In this passage, the two-part conjunction 'not only … but moreover' functioned
to highlight and emphasise the contents of the second part of the sentence, which
follows the conjunction ('… but moreover'). By means of this conjunction, Fasslabend implied a weighting of the contents. This allows Fasslabend's expressed need to
remember also the Nazi mass murder of Jews to be turned into a clear concession
to the immediate audience present at Ulrichsberg, which included former soldiers of
the Wehrmacht and the Waffen-SS and members of right-wing student fraternities.

His addressee-oriented weighting of contents was also reflected iconically by the contrast he created between the Holocaust, which was only mentioned in passing, and the detailed portrayal of the 'suffering caused by the war', which concealed the responsible actors by means of passive voice constructions and the employment of 'quasi-natural' allusions and metaphors. In addition, the phraseology used to describe the geographical location of the combat area ('from the polar sea to the deserts of Northern Africa') evoked Nazi diction, which was well-known to the major part of the audience.

Klestil used the term 'nation' in connection with the topos of 'history teaching lessons' (cf. section 4.3.3.2.1) in several of his speeches. He frequently anthropo-morphised the nation and compared its development to the stages in the life of a human being. However, he personified not only the nation and Austria, but also the provinces[3] and various national constituent institutions of the Second Republic which were founded in 1945, for example the ÖVP. In one passage, *Klestil 26* did come quite close to the concept of a *homo Austriacus* when he used an essentialist attribute 'our industrious people' in an attempt to allay potential fears concerning Austria's economic development in connection with its membership in the EU:

> Austria's big and important institutions will succeed in making the right decisions by their own efforts, and then we will not have to worry about the stability of our society. Then we can also be sure that our industrious people will be able to keep up with European economic competition.

> (*Klestil 26*)

Although the President used none of the terms *Staatsnation, Willensnation* or *Kulturnation* in his speech commemorating the founding of the Second Republic, the concept of nation which is implicit in his remarks resembles most that of the *Staatsnation*. Klestil explicitly endorsed the concept of *Staatsnation* or *Willensnation* in his speech during the Ostarrichi ceremony at Neuhofen on 19 May 1996 (for a detailed analysis see Reisigl 1998 and Reisigl 1999), although his statement remained unclear because of its vague deictic and phoric references (the following passage is a transcription and translation of what Klestil actually said, rather than the official written version of his speech, which deviates from his spoken remarks in a number of points):

> According to the experts, we Austrians are a *Willensnation*, which means that it is not a common language, culture, or ancestry which determines our Austrianness, but only the determination to have this community. And I think this is an excellent foundation, because it distinguishes itself from no one automatically and it excludes no one. Allegiance to Austria does not mean saying no to anybody, it means only saying a definite yes to Austria.

> (Klestil, speech during Ostarrichi ceremony, 19 May 1996)

The impression that the politically desirable characterisation of the collective of Austrians as *Willensnation* did not completely reflect Klestil's understanding of nation was confirmed by the analysis of those speeches which primarily dealt with the topic of culture. Thus, in his opening address at the Bregenz Festival on 20 July 1996, Klestil explicitly spoke of 'our charisma as a *Kulturnation*'. And in the year before, in his opening address at the Bregenz Festival on 20 July 1995, the President stated:

> Nobody will seriously deny that year after year Austria has made huge efforts in terms of money and effort at the federal, provincial and municipal level in order to meet the great goals of a *Kulturnation*. There are not many countries which succeed in setting up such a tremendous cultural budget ... It is certainly not sufficient for a *Kulturnation* to limit itself to tremble with respect before the artistic heritage of past centuries. ... And I mention this because I know that particularly now it is absolutely crucial to take a stand as a *Kulturnation*. Culture was for a long time a neglected and unpopular topic in the integration process – but not any longer ...
>
> (Klestil, opening address at Bregenz Festival, 20 July 1995)

These comments corresponded entirely to the program of the ÖVP, adopted on 22 April 1995, which states that 'if Austria wants to maintain its position as an eminent *Kulturnation*, it must support and activate its precious resources and talents' (ÖVP 1996, p. 141).

'Austrian consciousness', 'patriotism', 'positive attitude towards the state', 'allegiance to, love of and pride in the republic and for the homeland (*Heimat*)', or even 'belief in Austria' were topics repeatedly addressed by Klestil and ÖVP politicians using strategies of unification which serve to construct identity. On the whole, they lent a 'national' patriotic note to Klestil's speeches. In contrast to the First Republic, Klestil stated, the commitment to the Second Republic is undisputed and the Austrians are proud of their commitment to their homeland (*Klestil 27*). Never before, he argued, had the belief in Austria been more justified than today (*Klestil 27*). The overwhelming majority of Austrians, he noted, appreciate the democratic foundations and the traditions of the Austrian state, love their country and care about its fate (*Klestil 21*). But although he was full of praise for the national pride of the Austrians, Klestil demanded 'an even more stable Austrian consciousness on the way towards a larger Europe' (*Klestil 27*), a 'patriotism understood in the right way', which did not differentiate from and exclude anyone, but which brought people together. This latter, however, is actually a *contradictio in adjecto*, because of the close link between Austrian self-confidence and national chauvinism (confirmed in the findings of Haller and Gruber, 1996a, pp. 61–147).

One form of realising the unification strategy, which frequently occurred in Klestil's speeches, was his explicit appeals for co-operation or for efforts for the benefit of Austria. Though usually formulated as a hope or wish, they could sometimes be formulated as assertions. Interestingly, these appeals were at the same time always appeals for continuity. This connection was expressed by particles such as 'also in future (*Weiterhin*)' or 'also', for example at the end of *Klestil 27*, where the President explicitly appealed to his audience: 'And so I ask you on this public holiday:

let us also in future work together for our beloved country, the Republic of Austria.'

Whenever he spoke at an event related to a particular province, Klestil addressed the issue of the relationship between Austrian national and regional consciousness. From all his speeches commemorating the fiftieth anniversary of the foundation of the Second Republic delivered in Austrian provinces, we have selected as an exemplification of this *Klestil 24*, delivered on the fiftieth anniversary of the restoration of the independence of Vorarlberg, Austria's westernmost province. On the whole, Klestil employed two main strategies in this speech which attempted to mediate between Austria and the province and aimed at combining them. The first strategy had a unifying function and emphasised the features common to both the national and subnational, as follows:

> From its first hour the growth and development of this province have been closely intertwined with Austria's fate, because:
> 1. It was only when Vorarlberg joined the Republic in 1918 that it started to be a political unit.
> 2. It lost its independence again when independent Austria disappeared from the map in 1938.
> 3. With the rebirth of Austria in the spring of 1945 Vorarlberg also regained its independence.

The creation of a parallelism between Vorarlberg and Austria's past by means of the criteria 'unity', 'autonomy' and 'shared suffering' was preceded by an explicit linguistic unification ('closely intertwined with Austria's fate'). The second unification strategy which the President extensively employed here coupled emphasis on subnational (province-related) uniqueness with highlighting the model character of the province for the whole nation. Thus Klestil paid his tribute to regional pride and at the same time used it to enhance identification at a national level.

Vranitzky avoided the simplex 'nation' when he referred to the imagined group of Austrians. In numerous instances he referred to the Austrians metonymically using the toponym 'Austria'. Only in compound nouns did he employ 'nation' as second element – as in *Wirtschaftsnation* (economic nation) and *Industrienation* (industrial nation). This particular use of the collective noun 'nation' indicates that, in Vranitzky's worldview, the concept of nation was closely associated with economics, which suggests in turn that Vranitzky favoured the concept of *Staatsnation* rather than *Kulturnation* (as economic criteria are normally not essential characteristics of the latter). In addition, the reconstruction of Austria after the war was for Vranitzky primarily an economic achievement, which he called a 'national *tour de force*' (*Vranitzky 7*), again an indication that 'economy' and 'nation' are in a relation of lexical solidarity in Vranitzky's speeches. At the same time, the economic orientation of the Chancellor's thinking was even observable in those speeches where he referred to culture and the 'national body' (there was only one incidence of this in his two 1995 speeches). For example, Vranitzky praised Austria as a 'country which every year attracts millions of citizens from many different countries to pay homage to its cultural achievements and beautiful landscape' (*Vranitzky 7*). In this passage,

Vranitzky implicitly regards culture and landscape from an economic point of view, i.e. as profitable touristic capital. However, his statement may also be interpreted as serving to construct identity by means of a concealed argumentation *a minore*, that is, as a comparative topos of argumentation that proceeds 'from the smaller' (cf. Kienpointner 1992, pp. 121 and 287f. and Kienpointner 1996, p. 113) as follows: If millions of non-Austrians feel so attracted to the Austrian culture and the Austrian countryside, then the Austrians are all the more called upon to appreciate their landscape and to identify with their culture.

Twice in his speeches, Vranitzky explicitly referred to Austrian self-confidence. In Israel (*Vranitzky 1993*) he presented himself as the representative of a new, modern, self-assertive, independent and democratic state which had been founded in antithesis to National Socialism. In *Vranitzky 7*, the Chancellor portrayed the self-confidence, autonomy and identity of contemporary Austrians as arguments against the denial of the Austrian National Socialist past: 'Today our self-confidence, our independence and identity are without any question strong enough to face the truth in a clear and objective way.' As this statement also contained a reference to the denial policy of the postwar generation, it suggests a slight attempt at justification, for it implied that this attitude of denial may at least partly be explained by the lack of independence and self-confidence during the postwar years.

In contrast to Klestil and ÖVP politicians, Vranitzky described the relationship between Austrians and their country much less frequently in terms of emotions such as love, pride or loyalty. Whenever Vranitzky mentioned feelings of pride, it was in connection to something more tangible, for example, to particular persons or accomplishments. At one point, Vranitzky raised Austria to the status of an acting subject, which was justifiably proud of 'its' position as an economic nation, 'its' high standard of living, and 'its' social status. In contrast to Klestil, there was no trace of a para-religious relation to Austria: Vranitzky never mentioned a 'belief' in Austria.

An interesting characteristic of Vranitzky's language was a syntactic choice that may in fact have a significance transcending the purely syntactic dimension: Vranitzky used 'Austria' in the subject position only in connection with something positive – frequently even metonymically or as personification. If something negative was said about Austria, it never occurred in the subject position in any of Vranitzky's four speeches, but underwent subject demotion and appeared in adverbialised form, i.e. as adverbial of place, as circumstance of space. Thus, anthropomorphised Austria remained 'clean', as the following quotation from *Vranitzky 7* illustrates: 'We know what negative things are possible in Austria, but we also know what Austria is capable of accomplishing in a positive sense.' This subtly modifying strategy of avoidance on the one hand and the strategy of elevation to promote identification on the other is connected to Vranitzky's function as representative of official Austria. In contrast, opposition politicians, such as Jörg Haider, also associated Austria in subject position with something negative, though preferably in those cases where they spoke about 'official Austria', that is where the aim was disparagement or devaluation of political opponents. In Klestil's speeches, Austria also appeared as a personified subject in connection with something negative, although in these cases its role was not that of an actor but of a 'patient' or 'learning' subject (see section 4.3.3.2.1).

Closely connected with Vranitzky's trivialising preference to adverbalise Austria in connection with negative aspects of its past were his repeated statements that it was not Austria which had brought great suffering for many people between 1938 and 1945, 'because the state no longer existed' (*Vranitzky 93*), but that it was 'citizens of this country' who 'shared in the responsibility' for causing this suffering (*Vranitzky 91*) (see also Menasse's critical remarks, 1995, p. 17). For Vranitzky, Austria primarily meant 'the state'. In an abstract way, he perceived the nation-state as being subjected to the pull of both globalisation and isolation, and consequently to rapid changes (*Vranitzky 27*): 'Although we observe globalisation and the inter-connection of all problems, society is at the same time more fragmented and de-centralised than ever before. The character of the nation-states between supranational union and regional needs changes rapidly.' What the consequences of these changes are or will be for Austria, the Chancellor, who presented himself as a political guarantor of continuity, did not say.

Deputy Chancellor Wolfgang Schüssel also commented on the role of nation-states by quoting Germany's President Roman Herzog. Herzog had argued for the independence of nation-states from the economy and had largely repudiated the nineteenth-century concept of nation-state, as it inhibited international economic co-operation: 'We have learned that a free market is more useful than the most sophisticated customs barriers and protectionism, that one can continue to live within the context of a nation without perpetuating the nation-state of the nineteenth century, and that it is wiser to co-operate than to insist on the idea of sovereignty of past generations.'

In contrast to Vranitzky, the Green minority spokeswoman for minority issues Terezija Stoisits emphasised cultural, linguistic and ethnic diversity as a 'constituent characteristic' of the Austrian identity at a press conference held on 15 May 1995. In her press release issued on 26 October 1995, the national holiday, she stressed that through their language, their culture and their self-conception 'our ethnic groups … have contributed considerably to the unity of the Austrian nation' (*Stoisits 26*). In the same press release, Stoisits argued in line with the Green Party's 'Programme for Co-existence'[4] adopted in April 1990, which states that 'Austria's cultural identity and uniqueness is the result of centuries of social and cultural communication between the numerous cultures of the Danube area; due to its development and its cultural and intellectual character, the modern Austrian nation is a multiethnic nation'. Stoisits continued the unifying strategy underlying her statement by claiming that members of ethnic groups had reason to be particularly proud of their contribution to Austria. She concluded her press release by recommending a change in the Austrian constitution in favour of Austrian ethnic groups: 'What is still missing in Austria is a commitment on the part of the Republic to its linguistic and cultural diversity and to actively preserving these special values, which should be laid down in the constitution as one of the state's objectives.'

Madeleine Petrovic, parliamentary leader of the Greens, openly challenged the official founding myth of 1945: she described the genesis of Austrian national consciousness and pride as having been initially imposed from outside, but which since then had turned into a virtue. Quoting Jean Améry, she stressed the difference in origin between Austrian and French national consciousness:

> Austrian national consciousness is not simply something which was wrung from history, as had been the French national consciousness, which originated in the Revolution of 1789. As Austrian national consciousness was imposed on the Austrians by the course of world events, 'as initially *homo Austriacus* suffered it, but then transformed it into an honorary title', as Jean Améry put it, it is for many survivors of the Nazi horror 'something fundamentally unbelievable'.
>
> (*Petrovic*)

Jörg Haider's conception of the nation was generally well-known, at least since his statement on Austrian television in 1988: 'Well, you know as well as I do that the Austrian nation is an ideological deformity. Because belonging to a people (*Volk*) is the one thing, belonging to a state, the other' (quoted in Bailer and Neugebauer 1993, p. 373). On the same ideological grounds, in November 1990, Haider demanded the abolition of Article 4 of the State Treaty, which embodies the *Anschlussverbot* with Germany, justifying his claim by saying that it would restrict Austria's sovereignty.

Were things different in 1995, five years later? Had the FPÖ, which from its inception in 1956 had always had a German nationalist orientation, suddenly turned into a 'classic Austrian patriotic party'?

Despite the patriotic turn Haider took in the summer of 1995, for example, in an interview with the Austrian weekly *Wirtschaftswoche* on 17 August, in actual fact he had not altered his interpretation of Austria as a *Kulturnation* nor had the FPÖ as a party; the turn only represented a tactical, pragmatic shift of emphasis, a reprioritising of party political linguistic guidelines, devised in reaction to the particularly marked national consciousness of the Austrians.

But what exactly did the two speeches we analysed reveal about Haider's conception of the nation? At Ulrichsberg (*Haider 90*), before an audience coming from different European states, Haider spoke of the loyalty, courage and love which the 'generation of soldiers' had brought back to their fatherland (*Vaterland*) after the Second World War. Haider left to his audience the meaning they should assign to this vague and empty term *Vaterland*. That the war veterans of the Second World War did not fight for Austria, but rather under the National Socialist banner, was not mentioned in his speech. This attitude was also reflected in Haider's refusal to award in his function as Carinthian Governor the cross of honour for 'Contributions to the Liberation of the Republic' to former Austrian members of the resistance. In a discriminatory account he justified this by claiming that as former partisans they had opposed Austria's unification and had even been 'enemies of this country' (cf. Gärtner 1996, p. 211). Of the two occurrences of the *mirandum* (or high-value word) *Heimat* (homeland) in *Haider 90*, the first referred to Carinthia, the second was somewhat ambivalent as it undoubtedly referred to Carinthia and probably also to Austria. In this speech extract, the terms of 'self-confidence' and 'patriotism' also occurred, which Haider attributed descriptively to Carinthia and normatively postu- lated for Austria:

> We have every reason to demand self-confidence and patriotism as they have evolved in Carinthia for the whole of the Republic as well. Because ultimately only a shared conviction that our home (*Heimat*) needs and deserves to be protected engenders the climate and the spirit which enable the country to steer safely through times of crisis and situations of danger on its own.
>
> (*Haider 90*)

Haider's main strategy, which underlies this statement and which he used several times at Ulrichsberg, was a strategy also used by Klestil in Vorarlberg: the simul- taneous emphasis on subnational uniqueness and on a province's model character for the nation as a whole. This strategy constructs intra-national difference without threatening national unity – at least as long as the Austrians from other provinces do not feel devalued, which can best be ensured by appropriate audience segregation.

At the beginning of his speech at the ceremony to celebrate fifty years of the Second Republic (*Haider 1995*), Haider claimed that the Austrians had every reason to be proud of their achievements, which transformed the ruins of 1945 into a flourishing country. Speaking of the 'identity of contemporary Austria' Haider stated:

> Our Austria of today actually has its own identity, but it is an identity which has been acquired the hard way by all; it is not a decreed identity, or one that needs to be based on half-truths; [it is] an identity which is strong enough to live with the truth and with its past.
>
> (*Haider 1995*)

Whether this identity must be understood as national identity was not clear from Haider's statement. His reference to its acquisition 'the hard way' may be interpreted as subtle change of direction away from Pan-Germanism, that is as a strategy of transformation. The idea that this identity was 'strong enough' also occurred in *Vranitzky 7*. For the Chancellor, Austrian identity was strong enough to face the historical truth, but of course, Haider and the Chancellor had strongly divergent notions of what this truth was.

At the time of his speech at Ulrichsberg, Haider was still Governor of Carinthia, that is, the supreme political representative of the province. However, this political office by no means caused him to mediate in a conciliatory and integrative manner between the different ethnic groups living in Carinthia. On the contrary: Haider aimed at internal subnational differentiation from and exclusion of the Carinthian Slovenes. As was mentioned above, this attitude was directed against Slovene resist- ance fighters, as well as against people such as the Carinthian poet Janko Messner, a critic of National Socialism and of the Austrian form of pan-Germanism.

Intra-national exclusion inside state boundaries – in this case towards the Slovene minority – has a long tradition in Carinthia and has been particularly strongly connected to the festivities celebrating the 'Carinthian Referendum'[5] (cf. Stuhlpfarrer 1981, pp. 14f. and Staudinger 1994, p. 19). Fasslabend also excluded Slovenian Carinthians in his speech at Ulrichsberg. In contrast to Haider, however, his approach was very subtle, as is demonstrated by his concluding words thanking all those who contributed to the unification of Carinthia in 1920. Only after thanking 'all others', did he turn to the 'Slovenian fellow citizens':

> And I would like to thank all those who have contributed towards it. Not only those who fought, but of course also all others, who, no matter where, made their contribution. And of course I would also like to thank our Slovenian fellow citizens, who with their vote in the then 'Area A' ensured that the outcome of the referendum was an unambiguous 'yes' and thus ensured the unity of the province.
>
> (*Fasslabend*)

In summary, we can say that the context – the occasion, the topic and the audience – decisively influenced whether in their commemorative speeches politicians characterised the Austrian nation as *Staatsnation* or as *Kulturnation*. In the context of commemorating the founding of the Second Republic – and, of course, the signing of the State Treaty – politicians portrayed Austria as a *Staatsnation* or a *Willensnation*. At cultural events such as the openings of cultural festivals, they tended to present Austria as a *Kulturnation*. Yet although they did not have a greater German *Kulturnation* in mind, they seemed unaware of the essentially problematic character of this polysemic buzzword. Occasions which transcended the state level such as the Ulrichsberg 'Celebration of Peace and Europe' finally tempted speakers to evoke greater German overtones – especially if a certain Austrian public was brought together with a certain German one.

4.3.3 The Construction of a Common Political Past

4.3.3.1 Austria's Origins

As has been already demonstrated in the chapter on the discursive construction of national identity, we understand 'narrative', in the context of presenting a history of a community imagining itself as nation, not strictly as a linguistic text-type with particular structural features, but as a somewhat wider, more abstract category. Narratives about nations portray concepts of history which, through certain linguistic means, identify and designate particular historical events and facts which are deemed relevant for a large number of human beings and establish chronological and causal relations.

One component which is normally not missing from any narrative of a nation's history is that of a nation's origin or foundation. There seem to be no 'typical' myths of origin available for the 'belated' Austrian nation (on the issue of possible Austrian myths of origin and founding myths, which we cannot consider here, see Reisigl 1999 and Wodak et al. 1998).

The millennium myth of one thousand years of Austrian existence, which in ironical contrast to its nationalist temporal dilation (Burger 1996 [1993]) has been circulated for only a relatively short time, does not feature in the political speeches of our study, and is not even alluded to. First, this seems to indicate that in 1995 it was not yet part of the repertoire of the Austrian 'collective national consciousness' and therefore did not yet fulfil an identity-constitutive function. Another reason may be that the spell evoked by the number '1000 years' did not take effect until 1996. How broad the acceptance of this new foundation myth will ultimately be, whether the thousandth anniversary of the 'Ostarrichi' document will eventually establish itself as *the* Austrian myth of origin and whether it will in retrospect essentialise and rationalise, as well as accommodate, the desire for national self-inflation and the glossing-over of the myth of small size, is at the moment open to speculation.

As to the frequently quoted 'rebirth' of Austria in 1945, an underlying consensus seems to pervade all political speeches that the year 1945 is not a particularly suitable date for the creation of an original founding myth. Although 'beginning', 'birth' and 'origin' are often mentioned in this context, the 'beginning' in 1945 is only a relative one. This is manifested across all political camps by the use of linguistic expressions which refer temporally to a – non-specific – 'before'. References to the historical events surrounding the end of the Second World War and the foundation of the Second Republic can be distinguished by their linguistic designations, which correspond to party political differences. In any case, the concept of a 'zero hour' in connection with 1945 is used primarily by ÖVP politicians. It is clearly repudiated by Vranitzky several times, although even he presupposes it at one point in con- tradictory fashion. The speakers distance themselves from this usage, at least by marking it with inverted commas in the written form of their speeches (*Klestil 23*) or by using the indefinite article. Whenever it appears, the 'zero hour' is co-textually relativised through expressions such as 'again' or 'new'. The birth metaphor in reference to the foundation of the Second Republic occurs only in Klestil's and Vranitzky's speeches. 'Liberation' is used by politicians across all parties, although Haider distances himself from this term. The ambiguous designation of the military defeat in 1945 as 'liberation' largely corresponds to a strategy of trivialisation, as it implies that a large majority of Austrians did not side with Hitler Germany or fight for the Third Reich and therefore are not accountable. The official guideline con- cerning this usage is an essential precondition for the victim thesis.

Finally, 1955, the *annus mirabilis* of the Second Republic, which brought the signing of the State Treaty on 15 May, marks a decisive caesura and is more or less unanimously celebrated as the culmination of the 'success story of the Second Republic' (*Klestil 27*), which has decisively contributed to the genesis of a national perception of the Austrian state on the part of the Austrians and whose contents have 'become flesh and blood', according to Schüssel, who uses this somatising, metabolic metaphor when commemorating the fortieth anniversary of the signing of the State Treaty (*Schüssel*). No doubts can be cast on the integrative, identity-constitutive force of the State Treaty as one of the cornerstones of the Second Republic (*Stoisits*), and the importance of this year is also evidenced by the fact that it is much more strongly present in the memory of the focus group participants and interviewees than, for example, the year 996 or the year 1945. However, the State Treaty seems not particularly suitable for the construction of a truly 'classic' nationalist foundation myth, probably because it primarily accommodates constitutional and state-patriotic national consciousness rather than a culturally-oriented perspective.

4.3.3.2 Austria and National Socialism

Today, no public 'national memory', especially not that of Austria or Germany, is possible without confronting the darkest aspects of the national past. In the following sections we want to look more closely at how these dark chapters were commemorated in the context of the official celebrations surrounding the fiftieth anniversary of the Second Republic.

Common to all the speakers was their belief that there could be neither an account of nor a judgement on history which would be definitive by some universally valid standard. All political parties pointed out that the negative aspects of the past had to be confronted and worked through, though with varying emphasis. Both ÖVP and SPÖ politicians – with the exception of Caspar Einem – as well as the FPÖ's Jörg Haider, more or less explicitly propagated moderation in this process so as not to inhibit tackling the challenges of the future. Incidentally, this view corresponded with the beliefs of many of our focus group participants.

On the whole, Austrian resistance to National Socialism was hardly present as a topic in the commemorative speeches. The resistance fighters as a group of victims were only mentioned in the speeches of Einem, Schmidt, Fasslabend, Klestil, Vranitzky and Haider, although in different ways. Einem talked about the resistance movement in the greatest detail: he pointed to some of the obstacles that impeded resistance at that time, for example, the strategic compartmentalisation of responsibility in the Nazi system which made it easier for people within that system to perpetrate inhumanity, and the diverse experiences and backgrounds of people living at that time (he referred to the latter by quoting from a published lecture by the historian Ernst Hanisch., cf. Hanisch 1988, p. 198). In addition, Einem criticised indifference and emotional illiteracy vis-à-vis cases of systematic mass murder, which, he suggested, may be partly explained by the sheer abstraction of the large number of murdered victims, which not only posed a problem to the resistance movement, but which made it more difficult to cope with the past even decades later.

4.3.3.2.1 The Topos of 'History Teaching Lessons' as a Strategy of Transformation and Trivialisation in the Construction of a Common Past

In addition to the above-mentioned similarities, there were clearly different modes of interpreting the Nazi past which corresponded to different political mentalities. For example, the Ciceronian topos of '*historia magistra vitae*' (cf. Koselleck 1989, pp. 38–66) is a specific, for the most part strongly enthymematic, argumentative scheme which is used as a strategy of transformation and refers to a change situated in the past. This topos was used principally by Klestil and the ÖVP politicians as *ceterum censeo* in their commemorative speeches, and established a collective cognitive-emotional buffer zone by which people were comfortably cushioned from confrontation with the horrendous facts of the past. It lessened people's susceptibility when confronted with this topic – it immunised them against feelings of empathy and on the whole inhibited their facing the negative aspects of their past. The assumption of a self-referential point of view, which this topos promoted – the focus of attention was 'we' who have supposedly learned from history – meant that the victims afflicted by these wrongful acts were lost from sight. Empathic concern about the victims was therefore not very likely, the more so as 'our' actions were frequently alluded to in a very vague and abstract way.

Heide Schmidt and Caspar Einem adopted a fairly sceptical stance towards the topos of history as a teacher of lessons. Schmidt essentially called the topos itself into question by quoting Primo Levi, who stated about the crimes in *Auschwitz*: 'It happened, and therefore it may happen again. It can happen, anywhere.' Einem regretted that although much had been said about this issue, very little had entered the hearts and minds of the people. He also criticised the tendency to remember the past as if it were something completed, something which was over, overcome, no longer part of us, which did not affect us any longer.

The strategic topos of history as teacher of lessons to the nation formed the argumentative frame of Thomas Klestil's speech of 27 April 1995. Klestil first introduced the topos in a general way, and then related it to Austrian history in the twentieth century, in order to outline Austria's route to successful catharsis. This catharsis had convincingly led Austria from the shattering of its self-confidence, via a process full of sacrifices, to freedom and independence, to democracy and prosperity. Klestil's realisation of this topos combined several strategies simultaneously. By implicitly referring to the idea of 'common sorrow' he assumed a collective 'suffering value' which evoked feelings of identification and solidarity in his audience and encouraged them to activate the victim thesis, which, as we have shown, operates to trivialise the negative aspects of the past (*Klestil 27*). In his speech of 21 April on the occasion of the fiftieth anniversary of the foundation of the ÖVP, Klestil employed the same topos, one which personified history:

> Even before [April 1945], history had proved a relentless teacher, using the most drastic means to teach the political camps a new and more peaceful form of dealing with conflicts – and those politically responsible have understood this terrible lesson.

> (*Klestil 21*)

4.3.3.2.2 Austrians as Perpetrators in the National Socialist Period

Although the Nazi crimes committed by Austrian perpetrators were mentioned by representatives of all political parties, they were also, in one way or other, trivialised by means of depersonalisation, abstraction, metonymisation, the use of passive constructions, or by the representation of the social actors responsible for these crimes through formation of sociatives. Causal explanations which shifted responsibility to external circumstances occurred in most speeches across all political parties. Favourite linguistic means of trivialisation were sociative formations formed with the prefix 'co-' (*Mit-*), for example, 'co-responsibility' (*Mitverantwortung*), which clearly had a mitigating, relativising function in two respects. Firstly, since 'co-' refers to an activity carried out jointly with others, it exonerates the individual by pointing to negative sameness or commonality. Secondly, 'co-' implies that those 'co-responsible' were only peripheral actors.

Of all speakers, FPÖ leader Jörg Haider went furthest in relativising Austrian perpetrators. He was the only one who explicitly adopted the strategy of balancing one crime with another, a form of *tu quoque* ('you too') argument.

In his Ulrichsberg speech, Defence Minister Fasslabend argued against collective accusation and against collective exoneration. He quoted from the letter of a former, unnamed soldier who emphasised his involuntary participation 'in a merciless, murderous power struggle'. The soldier had employed the trivialising emphasis of heteronomy, and this shift of guilt culminated in the construction of 'innocent perpetrators': 'The burden we had to carry was even heavier because we had to share in the burden of guilt which had been caused by a criminally deluded political regime' (*Fasslabend*).

The extent to which the audience influenced the decision of a speaker to address 'sensitive' issues such as the Nazi crimes committed by Austrians may be illustrated by the speeches of Thomas Klestil. In a speech to the Israeli parliament, the Knesset, on 15 November 1994, he regretted 'that some of the worst perpetrators of the Nazi dictatorship were Austrians', and added, referring to Austrian restitution policy:

> We know that for a long time we did not do enough and we did not always do the right thing to ease the fate of survivors of the Jewish tragedy and that of the victims' descendants; and that we have omitted for much too long to commit ourselves to those Jewish Austrians who at that time had to leave the country humiliated and embittered.
>
> (Klestil, speech to the Knesset, 15 November 1994)

However, such clear words were entirely missing from his speeches before a primarily Austrian public in 1995. Only in his commemorative speech of 27 April did he briefly touch upon this aspect of Austria's past, which was undoubtedly due to the fact that people who were expelled from Austria in March 1938 were in the audience. In none of his other speeches was this topic addressed. If the National Socialist period was addressed at all, it was only done from the perspective of the Austrian victim thesis.

Klestil 27 introduced the topic of Austrian perpetuation of Nazi crimes during the Nazi period by quoting from the Moscow Declaration of 1 November 1943, which in its second part laid down in written form an external assignment of guilt, stating that Austria had 'a responsibility which it cannot evade for participation in the war at the side of Hitlerite Germany' (see section 3.5). This type of discourse representation could be interpreted as a slight form of distancing (cf. Wodak 1997), although later in his speech Klestil pointed to the belated confrontation by posing the following questions: a) why did National Socialism enjoy so much popularity 'also among us', b) why were 200,000 Jewish fellow citizens persecuted and expelled and why were 65,000 of them murdered, c) why did so many Roma and Sinti suffer the same fate, d) why was there no military and only limited political resistance, and e) how could tens of thousands of Austrian political opponents of National Socialist dictatorship disappear without a trace in prisons and concentration camps, from where much too many did not return. The language in which Klestil addressed the issue of Austrians as perpetrators, however, concealed the perpetrators and mitigated their actions. He obscured the actors by means of passive constructions, with the effect that the victims themselves faded into the background (see Van Leeuwen 1995a); in addition, he used metonymic and personifying abstraction as well as a highly problematic qualifier ('much too many').

After Klestil had raised the above-mentioned questions about the way Austria had dealt with its Nazi past, he moved on to criticise some of the belated answers to these questions and 'packaged' a number of implicit answers and half-answers to the questions into this critique. Thus, Klestil criticised the fact that some of these belated answers had been:

> distorted and without an understanding of the forces and constraints of a dictatorship. Without an understanding of the countless Austrians who were put into an alien uniform against their will. And also without an understanding of the determination of postwar politicians not again to tear apart the republic at the time of reconstruction.
>
> (*Klestil 27*)

The adverbial construction 'at the time of reconstruction' in the last sentence had an argumentative, justifying impact. As a component of the implicit topos of the superordinate aim (Kindt 1992, p. 199), such a construction suggests that reconstruction work had had priority over the necessity of coming to terms with the past, which would have led to friction and the formation of antagonistic political blocs and therefore would have threatened the reconstruction process. The way Klestil talked about the 'forces of a dictatorship' suggests a *locus a circumstantia*, that is he argued from external circumstances. Strategically, it also had a justifying quality and its function was to trivialise in a twofold way: it exonerated individual actors from responsibility for their actions by denying that they had had freedom and autonomy of action, and by shifting the responsibility to external forces. It further trivialised National Socialism by generalising its negative historical uniqueness through the use of the indefinite article ('a dictatorship'). Klestil's metaphorical-synecdochal second answer to the question of Austria's entanglement in Nazi crimes was also based on this general topos of external force: according to Klestil, of more than 1.2 million Austrian soldiers in the Wehrmacht (cf. Manoschek 1996a, p. 14), 'countless Austrians ... were put into an alien uniform against their will' (*Klestil 27*). The culprits, therefore, were the German soldiers. In this passage Klestil constructed an inter-national difference within a strategy of justification which was designed to shift guilt to external forces. In connection with the emphasis on heteronomy, this presentation was a clear allusion to the victim thesis.

Differentiating Austria from Germany frequently served to support a strategy of trivialisation. In our data, differentiation from Germany usually occurred only in connection with the common past in order to relativise Austria's own responsibility and guilt. However, in some cases where something was imposed from outside, for example, the Allied *Anschlussverbot*, this differentiation was turned into a self-acquired virtue. Differentiation from Germany played a role in the speeches of Busek, Fasslabend, Schüssel and Frischenschlager, and in *Klestil 27, Vranitzky 27* and *Haider 95*, though in this latter case a very unusual one. Busek praised the founders of the ÖVP for their unwavering commitment to Austria and their renunciation of the 'flighty *Anschluss* dream' (*Busek*). Fasslabend juxtaposed 'Austrian' and 'German': 'Victims were those Austrian soldiers who were conscripted into the German *Wehrmacht* and lost their lives in battle' (*Fasslabend*). As demonstrated above, *Klestil 27* relativised the responsibility of former Austrian soldiers in the *Wehrmacht* through the topos of external constraints (*Klestil 27*). Schüssel stressed Austria's strong sovereignty vis-à-vis Germany and ridiculed the *Anschlussverbot* (*Schüssel*). In his lecture, Frischenschlager claimed that in 1945 the Austrians began to feel and present themselves as a negation of the German nation for strategic reasons, i.e. in order to legitimate their independence; Frischenschlager referred here to theses by Rudolf Burger (*Frischenschlager*). *Vranitzky 27* praised 27 April 1945 as the day of the declaration of 'independence from the *Anschluss* to Germany'.

We have already pointed out Vranitzky's way of dealing with Austrian Nazi perpetrators in the context of discussing his understanding of the nation. We have stated that Vranitzky attempted to mobilise the autonomy, self-confidence and identity of contemporary Austrians as counter-arguments against the denial of their National Socialist past (*Vranitzky 7*). Although *Vranitzky 27* partly criticised the denial policy of postwar politicians, he demonstrated considerable understanding for their attitude and generally seemed to favour moderation in the process of coming to terms with the Nazi past. An important linguistic characteristic we have noted in Vranitzky's speeches is that whenever he referred to something negative from Austria's past, he tried to keep 'the Austrians' clean by rendering the *designatum* 'Austria' adverbially, whereas in positive contexts 'Austria' was allowed to appear in the subject position, even as personification. Moreover, we have observed that Vranitzky, in contrast to Klestil, used the expressions 'commit' and 'commitment' only in those contexts where the political admission of guilt was addressed. On the whole, the instances selected from the four speeches delivered by the Chancellor suggest that even Vranitzky's dealings with the dark side of the Austrian past was a linguistically mitigated attempt to 'come to terms with the past'. Although this global impression was confirmed by a more refined analysis, the latter enabled a far more complex longitudinal analysis which revealed that between 1991 and 1995 Vranitzky may perhaps have changed not his attitude, but rather the ghost writers of his speeches.

Vranitzky's declaration of 8 July 1991 before the National Assembly in Vienna

(*Vranitzky 1991*) marked a positive turning point in Austrian political culture in respect to Austria's Nazi past, because it included sentences such as the following:

> We admit to all dates of our past and to the acts of all parts of our people, to the good and the bad; and just as we claim the good, we have to apologise for the bad – to the survivors and to the dead. Austrian politicians have repeatedly made this avowal.
>
> (*Vranitzky 1991*)

Above all, it was this admission of guilt arguing with the topos 'you can't have one without the other' which led to Vranitzky's being awarded an honorary doctorate by the Hebrew University in Jerusalem on 9 June 1993. In his speech during the ceremony (*Vranitzky 93*), the Chancellor repeated this admission of guilt word for word. In *Vranitzky 91*, he was even more outspoken about the perpetrator aspect in regard to many Austrians, for example, when he explicitly stated that some Austrians in the Nazi system 'rose through its ranks to be among the most brutal, hideous perpetrators'. At the same time, there were also passages in this speech which contained elements of justification. For example, he outlined in a condensed, abbreviated way Austria's historical development between 1918 and 1938 by using the topos of external circumstances: 'Impoverished and without hopes for the future of their country, many Austrians turned to the Nazis and indeed supported the *Anschluss* that eradicated Austria from the map' (*Vranitzky 91*). Here, the linguistic representation of the responsible actors was similar to that in Vranitzky's speech before the Austrian Parliament (*Vranitzky 27*).

The specific occasion at Mauthausen required Vranitzky to talk in great detail about the National Socialist past (*Vranitzky 7*), although a major part of his speech was dedicated to a detailed positive self-presentation of contemporary Austria as a contrast to National Socialist Austria. The perpetrator aspect was mentioned several times. About the systematic mass murder of six million Jews Vranitzky stated:

> Although only a minute percentage of Germans and Austrians were directly involved in the cynically termed 'Final Solution', it could, however, only be implemented because at least in the beginning the majority of the people living in the Third Reich supported a system which, step by step, was preparing for the Holocaust.
>
> (*Vranitzky 7*)

In the passage which followed, which is similar to *Vranitzky 93*, the Chancellor argued that the economic crises after the First World War were the cause for the rise of National Socialism – a condensed, too mono-causal attempt at explanation. In clear dissociation from Jörg Haider, whom *Vranitzky 7* repeatedly attacked without, however, even once mentioning his name, the Chancellor alluded to Haider's infamous quip about the 'orderly employment policy' of the Third Reich at a session of the Carinthian Provincial Assembly on 13 June 1991. In the course of a verbal exchange, Haider turned towards the Social Democratic fraction in the Provincial Assembly, and said: 'In the Third Reich they had an orderly employment policy, something the federal government in Vienna is not even able to achieve' (quoted in Bailer and Neugebauer 1993, p. 378). In answer to this assessment of Nazi employment policy, which led to Haider's losing his position as Provincial Governor on a vote of no-confidence by the Carinthian Provincial Assembly on 21 June 1991, Vranitzky directed the following words:

> There were only a few who anticipated that the employment policy of the Third Reich, which even today is assessed as a successful policy by some ideological reactionaries [*Ewiggestrigen*], only served one purpose: to implicate an entire people in the preparation of a war which was unleashed by the National Socialists consciously and single-mindedly.
>
> (*Vranitzky 7*)

At another point of his speech, Vranitzky explicitly pointed to the Austrian crimes of the Nazi period. He preceded it by rejecting the collective guilt thesis – which he had also done in his 1993 speech:

> There is no collective guilt, but from this horror and this shame we must learn to understand that such things must never happen again. Mauthausen, as a symbol for a cynical system where not only countless Austrians became victims, but also many of our fellow citizens had leading positions in the unscrupulous planning and organisation of deportations and ultimately mass murder, must never be forgotten.
>
> Because today we know only too well that only through the active participation of numerous offices, organisations and enterprises could the machinery of the extermination apparatus, which extended far beyond the actual places of extermination, operate until the last days of the war.
>
> (*Vranitzky 7*)

Thus, *Vranitzky 7* explicitly rejected the trivialising strategy of (negative) moral equivalence (*Aufrechnung*). He stressed that there was no point in weighing the suffering of Austrians and Germans caused by Allied troops against the injustice committed by the Nazis.

Madeleine Petrovic also argued against the trivialising strategy of (negative) moral equivalence. She explained that in every war injustice occurred on all sides, and although there was also unneccesary damage caused by the Allies, this did not rescind the historical truth 'that a very clear aggression was initiated by Germany.' On 8 May 1945, she continued, a political power was defeated which, in the name of a *Volksgemeinschaft*, had begun and relentlessly continued the aggression internally and externally. Arguing against the Austrian victim thesis, Petrovic stated:

> The millions of murdered, imprisoned and humiliated victims of the Hitler regime are opposite the countless murderers, facilitators, informers and executors of the Nazi movement, who knew very well what they were doing and who yet took part in it.

Today we know that there was a collective complicity of perpetrators in the Third Reich! What has later often been presented as the rape of our country was in fact all too often a willingness to take part in every step towards the 'final solution of the Jewish Question', in which some Austrians were active at the front line.

(*Petrovic*)

Using a strategy of relativisation, *Haider 90* referred to the glorious postwar reconstruction work. The strategy of guilt-shifting frequently employed by the FPÖ leader may be aptly illustrated with the following example from *Haider 90*, which was preceded by the critique of history, which, he argued, continuously evoked the impression of collective guilt on the part of the soldiers. At the same time, this passage exemplifies the victim thesis as propagated by Haider:

Our soldiers were not perpetrators, they were at the most victims, for the perpetrators were sitting somewhere else and at no time in the historical development of the twentieth century did they have to muster the courage, or the honor which the soldiers serving in their grey uniform had to prove every day at the front (attempt at applause). This generation of soldiers truly brought back loyalty, courage and love to their fatherland, as is laid down at Ulrichsberg. This generation of soldiers need not blame themselves for anything, for ultimately the only thing they can blame themselves for is having been born into an era in which they lost their best time, the youth, to a catastrophe, in which they mostly turned from young men into men having grown old and grey in captivity.

(*Haider 90*)

In *Haider 90*, criticism of the collective guilt thesis turned, at least implicitly, into its antithesis, collective innocence. Haider attempted to account for this by using pseudo-arguments, by supporting it with the strategy of (negative) moral equivalence, even turning the military defeat of the Nazis to his rhetorical advantage:

For their generation personally had to endure much even after the end of the Second World War. And it is perhaps time to clarify here that in future also the young generation and those who are responsible in Europe would be well advised not to make a distinction between good and bad soldiers of the older generation. For it cannot be that those who stood at the side of the victors are celebrated as heroes, whereas those who stood at the side of the losers are labelled as criminals.

(*Haider 90*)

4.3.3.2.3 The Victims of National Socialism, the Austrian Victim Thesis and the 'Restitution'

There are a number of factors which determined the way in which the victims of National Socialism were referred to, and which groups of victims received detailed attention. These were the speaker's affiliation to a given political party, the place where the speech was delivered, the occasion, and the composition of the primary targeted audience. ÖVP politicians and the FPÖ leader, for example, did not explicitly commemorate the homosexuals as a group of victims, but referred to them through allusions: 'for racial or other reasons victims who were forced to emigrate or to die in concentration camps' (*Fasslabend*). That Vranitzky talked about the Jewish victims in more detail in Israel than in his Austrian speeches may also be explained by the location and addressees of the speech.

The Austrian victim thesis, which was deduced from the first part of the Moscow Declaration, seemed to underlie at least implicitly most of the speeches we analysed. Haider and the ÖVP politicians continued to propound the victim thesis most blatantly, but the President and, to a somewhat lesser extent, the Chancellor also presented it to their audiences, even if, as we have demonstrated in the previous section (*Klestil 27*), they also included the second part of the Moscow Declaration.

In several speeches that referred to the Austrian 'restitution policy' vis-à-vis the victims of Austrian Nazi crimes (for example in several speeches by the Chancellor), the subject was glossed over. Even though all the speeches seemed to imply a consensus that financial 'compensation' was an obligation which had to be met, various speeches (for example *Schmidt* and *Haider 95*) suggested that the political parties were not at all of one mind on which groups of victims were to be 'compensated'.

Heide Schmidt, the leader of the Liberal Forum in parliament, who of all politicians was most precise in her treatment of victims,[6] argued against weighing the claims of one victim group against those of another and referred to the polemical political debate over the Victims' Welfare Law. She argued that all victims should be recognised as equals and critically remarks in her speech of 26 January 1995 that 'even today homosexuals are hardly ever mentioned, let alone materially compensated' (*Schmidt*).

In his opening remarks to the joint session of the National Assembly and the Federal Council on 27 April 1995, National Assembly President Heinz Fischer reminded his audience of the 'noble task and obligation to keep the collective promise of establishing a national aid fund for the Nazi victims in the forthcoming weeks or months' (*Fischer*).

Explicitly denying that 'coming to terms with the past' was possible in a literal sense, President Thomas Klestil briefly but emphatically referred to the issue of 'compensation': 'And therefore I think that the past can never be mastered, but that it can be worked through adequately – if the facts are made clear, the victims are compensated at last – at last! – and misanthropic ideologies are recognised for what they are and overcome!' (*Klestil 27*). The stress, which was indicated by repetition and emphasis in the speech and by two exclamation marks in the written form, together with modalisation ('can'), conditionality ('if') and indirect reference to the future gave Klestil's statement a postulational meaning, which clearly showed that the supreme national 'preacher of the state' had put his finger on something which had been a sore point for fifty years in the political life of the Austrian Second Republic.

Of all politicians, Vranitzky addressed this 'sore point' of Austrian postwar policies in the most detailed way. The term 'compensation' (*Wiedergutmachung*), in itself an exaggerated and cynical euphemism, which ostensibly promises to restore what it is impossible to restore, often serves as a kind of rhetorical sedative for a bad conscience. In his remarks to the Austrian Parliament, however, Vranitzky only partially acknowledges the ambiguous nature of the issue of *Wiedergutmachung* with a parenthetical remark ('to the extent possible'):

> Much has been done in the past years in order to compensate, to the extent possible, for the damage which has been caused, to alleviate the suffering which has been caused. Much remains to be done, and the Federal government will continue to do everything in their power to support those who have so far not, or not sufficiently, benefitted from the measures or whose moral and material claims have up to now been neglected.
>
> (*Vranitzky 91*)

This entirely positive presentation of the issue suggests only very subtly that the Austrian restitution policy since 1945 had left (and still leaves) much to be desired. This was expressed somewhat more clearly in *Vranitzky 93*, although in that address Vranitzky became entangled in a partial attempt at justification. He argued that because many of the Second Republic's 'founding fathers' had been deported to concentration camps, the Moscow Declaration was interpreted one-sidedly, which in turn was one of the reasons for 'so many misunderstandings surrounding Austria's record in caring for the victims of the Holocaust'. In the German translation issued by the Federal Press Office, however, Vranitzky again spoke of 'compensation' without any qualification, although later in the speech, he stated explicitly: 'We know that all the tragic losses, the suffering and the pain cannot be undone.' Although Vranitzky partly criticised political cowardice, this speech was also characterised by positive presentation in connection with 'restitution'. The Chancellor announced there would be continuity between present and future policy; moreover, he mentioned as a positive achievement that the acquisition of dual citizenship had recently been made possible for the victims of the Nazi terror, and that Austria had initiated many visiting programs for those expelled and for their children and grandchildren (*Vranitzky 93*). Here, too, the German translation deviated negatively from the English text. The German text spoke about people expelled 'from *our* country', whereas the English original as well as the French translation did without the first person plural possessive deictic ('those who had been driven out of *the* country'). This usage finalised the victims' expulsion linguistically by excluding them from the 'we-group' – they were, in fact, expelled from their (!) country.

While in his address before the expatriate Austrians expelled in 1938 (*Vranitzky 27*) the Chancellor did not consider the issue of compensation, *Vranitzky 7* dealt with it in great detail: in this speech Vranitzky stated that the fiftieth anniversary of the Second Republic was also an occasion to reach out to all Austrians who had become victims of National Socialism, in order to show them with a clear gesture not only that they had not been forgotten, but that they were still an important part of Austria. To this end, he stated, the government had initiated various measures in recent years, and the Government and Parliament had jointly decided to establish an aid fund for the victims of National Socialism. This fund, according to Vranitzky, would demonstrate that after 50 years the younger generation had not forgotten the injustice which had taken place at that time. 'This is meant to be a sign of reminder (*Mahnung*), awareness and of conciliation' (*Vranitzky 7*).

Haider 95 spoke about 'compensation policy' and the victim thesis very ambivalently and vaguely. He exploited both topics polemically in order to discredit his political opponents – above all, Vranitzky and the SPÖ – as 'Socialist realists' who conspired against him and the FPÖ. He introduced the passage excerpted below with the strategy of 'pronouncing something dead', which had as its aim disparagement and change, a strategy directed against Haider's main political opponent:

> The left in Austria is not dead. What is dead is its integrative social force which was responsible for its power from Victor Adler to Bruno Kreisky. Vranitzky is politically dead because he no longer represents anything social. What is very much alive, however, is the real-socialist element – and its ideologists are currently constructing a joint majority excluding bourgeois forces.
>
> In order to achieve this aim, they use whatever means they can and above all, the following: because the ghost of the Eastern Bloc is no longer there to frighten the Austrians in their determination to be free, the Nazi skeleton is resurrected without any scruples. The pragmatic half-truths of the founders of the Second Republic now become very helpful: from the Austrian victim thesis to the missing compensation of persecuted Jews under the Nazi regime. What are they making of it? Fear that Austria could again become a 'victim'; the supposed proof that antisemitism has always been there, today more than ever, and, of course, it is strongest within the democratically successful competitor, the FPÖ.

> (*Haider 95*)

In this passage, Haider disparaged the founding fathers of the Second Republic by criticising the 'victim thesis' and the 'non-existent' compensation of Jews who had been persecuted by the Nazis as pragmatic half-truths, even though he himself had used the victim thesis again and again, as several examples have shown. Haider insinuated further that his opponents would take up and continue these two half-truths and create a new victim thesis in order to produce fears that Austria could again fall victim to the Nazi terror, which was associated with the FPÖ. At the same time, these same opponents wished to use the issue of unsettled compensation claims to prove that Austrian postwar history had been and still was pervaded by anti-semitism which was also concentrated in the party of the FPÖ. Haider's characterisation of 'missing compensation' as a pragmatic half-truth, however, was extremely ambiguous, because it could suggest that it is only half true that compensation of the victims had not been sufficient.

There was broad consensus concerning the victim thesis among Klestil, Fasslabend and Schüssel. Motifs such as the 'injustice of collective suffering', and 'the external compulsion' occurred repeatedly in Fasslabend's speech and Klestil's addresses, frequently coupled with the topos of external constraints and the topos of history teaching lessons. Schüssel emphasised in his speech that it had been:

correct, of course, correct and necessary to remember all the victims whom National Socialism sacrificed [*alle Opfer die der Nationalsozialismus bitter gebracht hat*], which has brought immense sorrow and also guilt upon us. But it is also correct and necessary these days to remember those hundreds of thousands – young people – who were sent to war by a criminal regime, which cost them the best years of their lives – and afterwards often also years of imprisonment, years of health, maybe also limbs, maybe even their lives.

(*Schüssel*)

In this passage, Schüssel referred to the victims very one-sidedly: 'all the victims' were mentioned in passing, whereas the young soldiers' fate was portrayed in great detail. This has iconic relevance. In this excerpt, National Socialism was represented as an abstract, external, personified agent which had brought guilt 'upon us'. As the expression '*der Nationalsozialismus hat Opfer gebracht*' is ambivalent in German and could also mean that it was National Socialism that had to make sacrifices, it is left to the reader to decide whether Schüssel's formulation was a linguistic mistake or must be understood as a Freudian slip. The synsemantic environment does seem to suggest an interpretation as a Freudian slip.

In her statement, Petrovic devoted much more time to the National Socialist perpetrators than to the victims. Although she explicitly argued against the victim thesis, she continued it through her choice of words, shifting it to an abstract level by means of metonymy and personification; however, she went on to speak about the issue in a much less trivialising way:

Separating fascism from the war as was done later has helped one generation to forget very quickly that they had not only been victims of air-raids and shell fire, but primarily victims of a mass delusion and incitement which they followed. It was, in all probability, the biggest success of the National Socialists to plant the fixed idea of a superior *Volksgemeinschaft* into the heads for decades to come.

(*Petrovic*)

In this passage, Petrovic offers one explanation of the strong attraction of the victim thesis and the resistance to confronting the Nazi past, namely the distinction made between fascism, which was largely denied, and the war, whose victims 'the Austrians' had supposedly been.

In her speech, Petrovic also addressed financial 'compensation' and stressed that only out of concrete compensation and conscious political counteraction could something like a 'new greatness' evolve, without, however, explaining what she meant by 'new greatness' or 'old greatness'.

In Vranitzky's speeches, the victim thesis was addressed particularly at those points where he showed sympathy for the 'soldiers who were ... abused in a grinding, brutal war', who 'simply wanted to forget this time' (*Vranitzky 7*). Moreover, the victim thesis was also discernible in a passage where the Chancellor thanked the 'war generation' for their reconstruction work and reminded his audience of the experiences of this generation in the war:

This generation, these women and men, also, however, deserve respect because they had to endure National Socialism, because they were in many ways suppressed by a dictatorship, because the men of this generation were, for the most part innocently, many thousand kilometres away from their home and the women of this generation overcame these days of hardship with great courage and commitment.

(Vranitzky 7)

In summary we can say that the 'victim thesis' and 'perpetrator thesis' were 'naturally' interwoven in the commemorative speeches of the President and the Chancellor as well as in most of the other speeches we investigated. Speakers showed no embarrassment whatsoever in respect to the contradictory nature of the two theses. Where the Austrian perpetrators during the Nazi period were mentioned, the speakers drew primarily upon strategies of justification and relativisation, even if the frequency of these instances of justification or relativisation, as well as the choice of specific strategies and means of realisation, were related to the speakers' respective party political affiliation.

4.3.4 The Construction of a Common Political Present and Future

The images of Austrian current political culture which individual speakers described, and the evaluation of the current political and economic situation which they presented, were also highly dependent on party political affiliation and the kind of public that was being addressed. The more responsible the politicians were for the political climate and the more interested they were in the perpetuation of the status quo (which, of course, held largely true for SPÖ politicians), the more idyllic and positive the verbally constructed image would be and the more it would resemble a *locus amoenus*. We do not view the *locus amoenus*, however, as a literary topos in a narrow sense, as one which paints an Arcadian idyllic landscape with green, lush meadows, cool forests, clear brooks, melodious twittering of birds etc., but rather as a 'beautiful landscape' often mentioned in a more general sense to refer to the common national territory or serving to depict a rather abstract ideal political place where human beings live together happily, in affluence, in harmony and without conflicts. The phrase 'island of the lucky', coined by Pope Paul VI in 1971 and soon renamed 'island of the blessed' (Bruckmüller 1996, p. 125), rhetorically points to this idyllic place, the *locus amoenus*. Where it occurs in the political speeches, it frequently not only serves the purpose of mere self-presentation but is part of a comparative scheme by means of which the strategy of emphasis of inter-national difference is realised. We can say that, on the whole, this strategy, which aims at promoting national identification and emphasises differences between Austria and other states, was rare in the commemorative speeches; if it occurred it was usually in connection with the mention of positive achievements such as prosperity, freedom, democracy and social stability. However, the less speakers were interested in perpetuating the status quo and the more they were interested in a radical political change – of course to their own advantage – the less positive were their assessments of the current political situation and the more they tended to present the political achievements they viewed positively as being in danger. Thus they might have warned of a *locus terribilis* or portrayed certain political continuities in a negative light, that is, presented them as ancient and fossilised structures. This held true for the opposition parties (the FPÖ, the Greens and the Liberal Forum) as well as for the smaller party of the coalition government, the ÖVP.

In contrast to the other data of our study, in the commemorative addresses a great deal of space was devoted to the subject of the political future. This may be partly explained by the fact that politicians are by definition the custodians of the future of a collective. Since they are at the same time custodians of their own personal political career as well as of the future of their party, they frequently make reference to common worries and problems, to common opponents and enemies as well as to common aims – in regard both to the present and to the future – in order to stimulate those forms of identification, solidarity and union among their listeners which seem most advantageous for their parties and themselves. Therefore the presentation of the political present and future in the speeches oscillates primarily between the strategies of perpetuation, of transformation and of disparagement, depending on the party-political affiliation of the speaker.

4.3.4.2 Austria, the European Union and Europe

Of all the speakers in our analysis, Jürgen Weiss, President of the Federal Council, was the only politician who openly expressed fear that the European integration might threaten Austrian identity in certain ways. Austria joined the EU from a position of power, Weiss argued, and believed that concerns expressed about a possible loss of significance of the provincial legislative bodies in Austria had been largely, but not completely, dispersed by hopes that more civic-oriented regional units would be established to balance centralisation and counter the trend towards uniformity:

> The common, large European roof erected above the nation states will only weather the tempests of the time if its broad, regionally anchored foundations are strengthened, not weakened. By joining the European Union, Austria has executed a state reform from outside which must be complemented by a reform from within to ensure that the redistribution of competencies and the division of powers will again be in balance.
>
> (*Weiss*)

In this excerpt, Weiss utilised Austria's EU membership itself as an argument in favour of extended and civic-oriented regional competencies by linking the topos of threatened national autonomy with the necessity to strengthen subnational, regional autonomy. Drawing upon the tropes of allegory and metaphor to illustrate his claim, he compared Europe to the house's roof, the European nation states to its individual rooms and the European regions to its strong foundations. This 'European house' was, among other things, responsible for protecting its inhabitants against the 'tempests of the time'. In the second part of the speech extract, Weiss used a topos of consequences, implying that a foreign policy reform had to be followed by a domestic adjustment process.

Friedhelm Frischenschlager emphasised that European and Austrian identities did not exclude each other. On the contrary: especially for ethnic groups and national minorities, a constitutional and an ethnic consciousness can combine in a meaningful way if based on fundamental rights. Frischenschlager demanded a democratic-constitutional state for western Europe which would create loyalty towards, and consciousness of, the constitution instead of the elevation of the nation. The European Union offered the chance 'to solve the problems existing in Europe collectively instead of solving them in the too narrow context of the individual state' (*Frischenschlager*). Frischenschlager remarked critically that although integration was accepted as an abstract phenomenon, the practical steps necessary for its implementation were evaluated too critically or were rejected entirely because they were viewed from the narrow perspective of the nation-state. On the issue of geographical expansion and the economic-ideological orientation of the EU, Frischenschlager argued, as did Leggewie (1995, p. 33), that 'Europe must remain Western and become more Eastern'. The 'supernational heritage' of Austria could, according to Frischenschlager, be advantageous both in the ongoing process of integration of the EU member states and for the geographical eastern enlargement of the EU.

As a convinced proponent of Austria's EU membership, Thomas Klestil used all the strategies and persuasive devices at his disposal in his television address two days before the EU referendum on 10 June 1994 (his speech is quoted in Kettemann, Grilz and Landsiedler 1995, pp. 82–3). Referring to his personal conviction, his experiences in life, and his responsibility 'to save Austria from damage and to secure its future', he threw the entire weight of his person and office behind the proponents of membership. Moreover, he strategically employed a vaguely formulated topos of threat, which almost took on the quality of an *argumentum ad baculum*[7] ('Wars in contemporary Europe are only imaginable between those peoples who are not taking part in the integration process'). As additional arguments in favour of EU membership, Klestil used positive self-presentation, culminating in a *locus amoenus* (in terms of Austrian prosperity, its high social and environmental standards and the stable currency), Austria's ability to serve as a model for the 'young democracies in our neighborhood', and Austria's economic integration in the EU, which, in his view, was already about eighty per cent complete.

How did the President treat the topic 'Austria and Europe' after Austria had officially joined the EU on 1 January 1995? In *Klestil 27*, but also in *Klestil 26* and in *Klestil 23*, he addressed the topic 'Europe' in the context of a transformation strategy, more precisely the 'topos of changed external circumstances', on which he based his justification of and demand for change in Austria. With political change in mind, *Klestil 27* claimed metaphorically that Austria had reached a 'crossroad' because, in view of European transformation, Austria too needed to take leave of postwar policies. Alluding to Austria's role-model function, Klestil stated in a positive self-presentation towards the end of his speech that contemporary Austria possessed all the prerequisites for becoming a model of a future worth living in the new Europe as well. As so often, the particle 'as well' served to construct continuity.

As might be expected, the issue of 'Europe' was an important topic in *Klestil 25* due to the specific occasion and audience: after praising the contribution of Alois Mock (the former Minister for Foreign Affairs) to Austria's EU membership, Klestil said of Austria's role in Europe:

> If one day the history of the great European transformation, which began with the Helsinki process and reached its climax with the fall of the Iron Curtain, is written, then Austria's eminent role as a motivating but also a stabilising force will be evident – and the great merits the former Foreign Ministers of our republic have earned [in this respect].
>
> (*Klestil 25*)

Vranitzky 27 addressed the issue of the EU in the context of a positive self-presentation, strategically using the emphasis on inter-national difference in order to portray the status quo in Austria as particularly praiseworthy. Using the years 1945 and 1955 as points of contrast, Vranitzky said about the EU-member Austria: 'Who in 1945 would have imagined an Austria as it presents itself today, in 1995? A well respected, appreciated member of the international community of states, a social and stable community, the youngest member of the European Union.' Referring to the statement made in the *Neue Zürcher Zeitung* that Austria had reached a turning point and that domestic adjustment had to follow the external change of EU entry (cf. the statement by Weiss at the beginning of this section), *Vranitzky 27* countered rhetorically by means of positive self-presentation and an allegorically decorated demand for continuity: 'In Austria no turnabouts are necessary, and neither are turncoats, by the way; what is necessary is to keep on course, to steer safely past rapids and maelstroms, use the winds and currents and, where necessary, make course corrections, but no abrupt manoeuvres.' Apart from the fact that Vranitzky overstretched the ship allegory, this passage is interesting in that it contained a strategy of perpetuation, that is a demand for political continuity, as well as the 'we are all in the same boat' strategy, which has a unifying and solidarity-enhancing function (Kienpointner 1983, p. 151). It suggested to the audience that Austria was a boat and that the Austrians, who were on that boat, were all moving in the same direction, at least for part of the way, and that they all had the same destination. In other, less figurative, words: that they were in the same position in many ways and had the same future before them. The rhetorical manoeuvre of this Austrian state-captain was designed to alleviate the fears prompted by Austria's joining the EU and to signal that EU membership would not entail drastic changes, but only the most marginal course corrections. In a party-political context, the demand for continuity must be interpreted as a message to the electorate that the SPÖ wished to continue to steer the boat in the future (on the ship metaphor see also Münkler 1994).

Haider 95's comments on the topic can be subsumed under three points. Firstly, he presented the situation in terms of a black-and-white topos of comparison, in which a reform-happy eastern Europe faced a European Union characterised by 'enormous persistence' and an Austrian state characterised by 'particular inertia'. Thus, Haider attempted to portray the comparatively uniform, gradual political developments in Austria and western Europe as particularly old and negative. Behind the Treaty of Maastricht, for example, Haider detected the intention 'to immediately divide Europe anew, in order that those who call the shots in Brussels will not have to share their power.' This, he said, was not the way to a large free Europe; that way, in his view, would be dangerous. In order to support his claim, as he does so often, with an *argumentum ad verecundiam*, Haider quoted the 'eminent liberal Ralph Dahrendorf'. On the whole, Haider adopted the strategy of negative connotation of continuity in order to sell a political change – in the sense of a radical change – to his addressees.

Secondly, as former proponent of Austria's membership in the EU, Haider turned opponent, interpreted Austria's entry as an attempt to run away from its own problems and went on to warn that the achievements of the postwar period were in danger:

> Fifty years of the Second Republic: wouldn't it be nice if, looking back with pride, we could celebrate with confidence and optimism in the sense of continuity. But we have reached a crossroads. The reconstruction period is long over. The achievements have become fragile. Rushing into the European Union, as we can see ever more clearly, did not solve any of our problems.
>
> (*Haider 95*)

In this passage, Haider chipped away at the *locus amoenus* circulated by the SPÖ and, though to a lesser extent, by the ÖVP. He attempted to dismantle it by pessimistic forebodings in order to pull the rug from under its feet rhetorically, and in order to propagate a change.

Thirdly, Haider contended that the government had not kept its promise about taxation given prior to the EU referendum. He presented himself as the more socially conscious politician and complained that 'the most basic social considerations ... no longer [count]'.

In commemorative speeches, the topics 'EU' and 'Austria's accession to the European Union' primarily served as an argumentative reservoir, whose elements were used by the speakers to make political capital, depending on their party-political affiliation. On the one hand, because of the tension between nation-state and supranational community and the fears this tension engendered, an appeal for transformation and change was contrived, although the explicit warning of a threatened national identity was on the whole rather played down. At the same time, the majority party and its top representatives primarily attempted to alleviate these fears and to call for the greatest possible continuity and the maintenance of the status quo.

4.3.4.3 Austria's 'Permanent' Neutrality: the Transformation of a Fiction Lived as Reality?

After listening to the politicians, no one in good faith could have prognosticated that Austrian neutrality would be 'permanent'. Above all, the ÖVP politicians, Haider, and Frischenschlager all emphasised that the concept of Austrian neutrality was obsolete, frequently without even explicitly mentioning neutrality (for example, Busek and Fasslabend, who both employed the topos of changed external circumstances for their security policy argumentation). The attempt was made, more or less cautiously, to prepare the Austrian population for the impending renunciation of neutrality. Preferably, the issue of neutrality was subsumed under the topic 'joining the EU'. The SPÖ largely dodged this sensitive issue, and one senses that the ÖVP had taken on the task of convincing and persuading the population. In any event, this ploy seems to have worked with their own voters (see the focus group data in 5.2.1.4).

Vice-chancellor Schüssel distinguished between the function of neutrality at the time of the Cold War and the function neutrality had today. Neutrality 'then' was a 'window of history'. Ironically, Schüssel alluded to the attitude of the SPÖ, which originally had opposed neutrality: 'At that time neutrality was a very controversial issue and some who today act as if they were the guardians of the Holy Grail, would in the past have found themselves in a party which by no means cared much for neutrality.' Thus Schüssel wanted to signal to the SPÖ that it should not brag too much in reference to neutrality. Schüssel pleaded for co-determination in all EU institutions in the future. 'We rightly demand participation in all institutions which deal with supranational protection of the environment. Consequently, is it not necessary to take part in decision-making processes and in the responsibility in all matters pertaining to European foreign and security policy?' (Schüssel) This argumentative scheme constituted a particular variant of the topos 'you can't have one without the other'. European foreign and security policy was mentioned and the future role of Austrian neutrality was implicitly addressed; the fact that Schüssel disguised his answer in the form of a suggestive rhetorical question pointed to a strategy of transformation which aimed to change the attitude of his addressees.

Klestil 27 commented on the historical function of neutrality at the time of its declaration and during the time of the Cold War in the following way: 'The price of neutrality which we then paid for independence secured us the privileged place of peace and stability in the Cold War and in the process of détente of the superpowers for decades to come.' This formulation again contained a historically expanded deictic 'we' of which there are two realisations, by means of which a temporally transcending imaginative collective was constructed. By relating the metaphor of being a price that had to be paid to neutrality, Klestil stressed its involuntary, heteronomic character of origin; in contrast to Haider, however, he did not mention those to whom the alleged price had been paid. Klestil balanced the negative evaluative labelling of neutrality by describing neutrality as a safeguard for decades of stability and peace – a designation which, interestingly, no longer extended temporally to the time of Klestil's remarks. Although in this speech Klestil evaded any explicit evaluation of the present role of neutrality, he implicitly evaluated it by praising the 'founding fathers' for their exemplary courage, spontaneity and creativity in regard to change. Klestil, too, called for an open discussion about issues of security policy. In this linguistically indirect demand a subtle strategy of transformation was at work.

Klestil did not touch upon the sensitive topic of neutrality in the other speeches of our study. In other speeches, however, Klestil has made it very clear that he regards neutrality as obsolete, for example in his televised address of 8 June 1994 or in his speech on the national holiday on 26 October 1994, whose contents will be discussed in Chapter 5.

Vranitzky 27 did not even bring up neutrality. On the subject of the political present and future, *Vranitzky* said:

> Austria is situated in the centre of a world which, without the balance of the great blocs, is more unstable than ever before. Migrations, fundamentalism, nationalism and international power struggles contribute to this uncertainty. Austria must contribute to stabilising, transnational security structures as a neutral and new member-state of the European Union.
>
> (*Vranitzky 27*)

Although *Vranitzky 7* talked about the need to continue to work on the idea of the European peace order, he did not explain what this meant for Austrian neutrality.

Frischenschlager pointed out that the political advantages of integration for Austria that had played such a prominent role in the pro-membership campaign were scarcely mentioned any more; indeed, he added, discussions about the EU were largely evaded. The absurdity of the 'Austria first' or 'Austria alone' approach, according to Frischenschlager, was demonstrated most clearly by the problematic issue of security. Frischenschlager distinguished between the past and present roles of neutrality more explicitly than all the other politicians:

> As security concept for a single state embedded in the security architecture which was created after 1945, neutrality has been truly meaningful (it has, however, thank God, never been really challenged). But it cannot count as a suitable security policy recipe for the future.
>
> The best protection for Austria is a more fully developed Western European Union: a security system which comprises all democratic states of Europe (instead of mere collective defence) on the basis of the Charter of the United Nations and the General Declaration of Human Rights.
>
> (*Frischenschlager*)

In contrast to NATO, which guaranteed protection only to its members, Frischenschlager argued, a European reworked Western Union could, as a united community, turn collectively against an aggressor. Military action by a collective army with shared command structures, he concluded, would be imaginable only as a last resort.

Like *Klestil 27*, *Haider 95* regarded neutrality as the price Austria paid for its independence in 1955:

> Then we were really [free]. Of course not of 'our own free will', as it says in the Constitution, but neutrality was declared the price for the signature of the Soviets. The most pragmatic party in this was the ÖVP. The Socialists, even when they were in Moscow for the negotiations, still threatened to leave. The ÖVP exerted pressure on them and at the last minute they were given the go-ahead. Until the last minute, neutrality imposed as a prohibition to any international solidarity seemed to the Socialists a price too high to pay. For exactly this reason, the VdU was the only party to vote against the law in the National Assembly. Today it is the Socialists who have turned their former disavowal of international solidarity into a virtue, who block a sincere discussion on neutrality and who do not want to admit that in 1989 the Soviet empire collapsed and with it also the justification for the former price of freedom.
>
> (*Haider 95*)

Haider 95 mentioned the origin of neutrality in detail, in contrast to the other speakers, which may also have been due to the length of the press released address. The above extract contained a historically expanded 'we' in the first sentence. Although Haider did not explicitly say that he was willing to renounce neutrality, this fact was clearly visible in his tirades against the SPÖ. Haider not only reminded the SPÖ politicians that their party once opposed neutrality, he also accused them of inhibiting an 'honest' discussion of neutrality and of being unaware that 'the reason for paying' the price was no longer valid. Beyond the specific counter-arguments Haider adduced, his attack on the SPÖ also contained a spurious attempt at justification. Haider claimed that the rejection of neutrality by the predecessor party of the FPÖ, the VdU (*Verband der Unabhängigen*, or League of Independents), which, incidentally, was notorious for having been a 'haven for old Nazis, Neo-nazis, sympathizers of greater German ideology and a small number of liberals' (Bailer and Neuigebauer 1993, p. 328), was traceable to a Socialist-inspired feeling of solidarity.

If one looks at the status of the neutrality debate as reflected in the selected speeches from 1995 we examined, one can summarise it thus: the former, extensively used 'national buzzword', which had helped in the construction of a single common national self-portrayal, has long since become a party-political one. Even if the former meaning of neutrality was still appreciated by a majority – though the strategies of heteronomisation and historicisation had long since resulted in the fading of the mythical splendor of neutrality – three Austrian political parties the (the ÖVP, the FPÖ and the Liberal Forum) have abandoned the present and future role of neutrality as obsolete. Only the Greens continue to cling unwaveringly to the concept of neutrality.

NOTES

1. The lecture was included because its contents fitted very well into our study and we were thus able to form a more complete picture of the various political views on Austrian national identity, as we were unable to locate any full-length speeches by Liberal Forum representatives.
2. We were not able to discover how many speeches were delivered by Franz Vranitzky in 1995, as the Federal Chancellery refused to provide us with a list of titles.
3. For example, in *Klestil 24* he talked about the 'biography' of the province of Vorarlberg, while in a speech on 19 May 1996 about Austria's 'millennium' he stated: 'Austria is a family with nine family members'.
4. This Programme advocates a multicultural Austria and vehemently rejects 'ethno-political exclusionary strategies vis-à-vis the minorities' as is propagated by Austrian Pan-Germanism. Such strategies, the Programme argues, would jeopardise and defame Austrian cultural identity as a whole.
5. Resistance to the provisions of the Treaty of St Germain in regard to Carinthian territory resulted in the 'Carinthian Referendum' of 28 October 1920, where a majority of the Carinthian population opted to remain with Austria.
6. 'Auschwitz is the symbol and synonym of a technically and strategically perfectly planned and systematic mass murder of Jews, Roma, Sinti, homosexuals, differently abled people, critics, opponents and so-called "asocial" people' (*Schmidt*).
7. An *argumentum ad baculum* (see, for example, Eemeren, Grootendorst and Kruiger 1987, p. 89) is a rhetorical-pragmatic fallacy, in which a threat is used as a persuasive device ('*with the rod*'), and which may contain external threatening scenarios which are intended to evoke irrational fears.

Chapter 5

Semi-Public Discussions:
The Focus Group Interviews

5.1 DATA

5.1.1 Focus Group Interviews in Social Science Research

A focus group, also called a group interview or group discussion, is in essence 'a discussion among a number of participants on a certain topic predetermined by a moderator …, which serves to collect information' (Lamnek 1989, p. 121). Whereas this method has not been widely used in social science, group interviews are common in market research to investigate consumer motivation and behaviour. In the German-speaking countries, this method was occasionally employed by the Frankfurt Institute of Social Research in the 1950s, and in Austria it has recently been used in the reception analysis of tabloid print media by Bruck and Stocker (1996).

In the following paragraphs this method will be outlined as far as it is relevant for the purpose of our study (for more information on the subject see, for example, Bruck and Stocker 1996, Morgan 1993, Lamnek 1989, Greenbaum 1988, Morgan 1988, Friedrichs 1985).

The focus group method, according to Bruck and Stocker, entails interviewing a group of, ideally, five to twelve persons selected according to certain theoretically predetermined criteria ('theoretical sampling') on a particular subject, using a guided discussion technique. The discussion is conducted by a moderator, who structures, summarises and attempts to ensure balanced participation, raises specific topics in an informal way, and above all encourages the participants to contribute to the discussion (Bruck and Stocker 1996, p. 46).

The discussions are videotaped and/or taped, transcribed and subsequently analysed according to various qualitative procedures.

The objectives of group interviews are defined by the focus of the respective investigations, which may differ widely (cf. Lamnek 1989, p. 127). They range from ascertaining beliefs and attitudes of individual participants to the analysis of group processes leading to the formation of specific individual or group opinions. In any case, it is a method which can 'be adapted very flexibly to serve a particular topic, issue, purpose of study and target population' (Lamnek 1989, p. 128). Information can be obtained from a relatively large number of people in a reasonably economic way. Other advantages of group interviews include a greater vividness of individual opinions, a more realistic communicative situation, a more relaxed, informal atmosphere and the fact that it is a 'friendly method of investigation', which 'treats the interviewee in a respectful way' (Bruck and Stocker 1996, p. 48).

There are, however, also a number of shortcomings. In the group situation, 'group pressure or dominant participants may distort or inhibit statements of other participants (Bruck and Stocker 1996, p. 48), which the moderator may counteract only to a certain degree. A further disadvantage, according to Bruck and Stocker, is 'a limited possibility to probe and ask more penetrating questions' (Bruck and Stocker 1996, p. 48). Therefore, interpretation of the data must consider both manifest and latent hierarchical relations within the group as well as the way a discussion unfolds.

There are a number of crucial factors which require careful attention: above all, the composition of the group and the selection of the participants, which, of course, will be determined by the purpose of the study. Basically, groups can be either homogenous or heterogeneous, formed artificially ('stranger group') or naturally ('family group') (Lamnek 1989, p. 142, Bruck and Stocker 1996, p. 49). Family groups do not try to avoid conflicts as much as stranger groups, while the latter's 'warming-up' phase is considerably longer. Bruck and Stocker recommend a number of between five and twelve participants as the optimal group size. The moderator, of course, plays a crucial role. The tasks of the moderator include creating an informal but 'focused' atmosphere, ensuring balanced participation and dealing with both reticent and more loquacious people in a sensitive way. The specific procedures used to analyse the transcriptions of group discussions are primarily determined by the purpose and design of the study.

5.1.2 The Study: Data Collection and Data Evaluation

Our study examines semi-public discourse on Austrian identities. We wanted to investigate individuals' attitudes and statements about identities, generated under specific group conditions. Focus group discussions seemed well-suited to these purposes. In particular, we were able to follow closely patterns of recontextualisation and the transformation of élite concepts of national identity during group interactions. In other words, we were able to gain powerful insights into how meanings of important concepts such as 'nation' are jointly shaped and negotiated, or 'co-constructed', during the discussion.

We conducted seven group interviews altogether, each with eight to ten participants. Most discussions took place in different locations, thus ensuring a wide regional and occupational diversity in the sample. Ordered chronologically by date of their meeting, these groups have been assigned the following names:

Pilot Group (P)[1]
Group of Non-Austrians (NA)
Group Simmering (S)
Group Vorarlberg (V)
Group Carinthia (C)

Group Burgenland (B)
Group Styria (ST)

The research team was assisted by a consultant professional moderator, who also conducted the pilot group interview. With the exception of Group ST and P, all group interviews were conducted by the same moderator. Groups P and NA were organised by the research team based at the Department of Linguistics of Vienna University, Group S by the employee representatives of a particular firm. The recruiting of the other four groups was undertaken in consultation with personal or professional contacts in the respective provinces. With regard to participants' occupation, Groups P, S and ST form homogenous groups, while the other groups reflect the social networks of the groups' organisers and thus cannot be considered representative of the Austrian population as a whole. After the discussions, the participants were asked to fill out a short questionnaire to gather personal information about citizenship, age, training and occupation, place of birth and residence, leisure time and media consumption behaviour, native language, and political party preferences. The data revealed that members of Group S were predominantly SPÖ voters, whereas Group ST consisted mainly of participants who voted Conservative. In all other groups there was a higher percentage of sympathisers of the Greens and the Liberal Forum than is the Austrian average. There were no women in Groups P and ST; in the other groups males slightly outnumbered females on average.

Each discussion lasted about two hours, was recorded on video and audio tapes, and subsequently transcribed. During each focus group discussion, the moderator introduced the following core set of questions:[2]

1. 'Please introduce yourself briefly. What in your opinion makes you an Austrian?'
2. 'Which events do you consider most crucial for Austria in this century?' (The participants were asked to make notes before discussing this question in the group.)
3. 'On June 12th, 1994, Austria voted with a two-thirds majority in favour of joining the European Union. A year has passed and the situation has developed differently than expected. What considerations would be important for you if the referendum were held today?' Following this question, a short extract from the text of an address by current Austrian President Thomas Klestil on the occasion of Austria's national holiday in 1994 was shown on an overhead projector. The excerpt dealt with the question of Austrian neutrality (see 5.2.1.4 for the text). Afterwards the participants were asked: 'Do you agree with the President's statement or do you think what he says is wrong?'
4. 'Today Austrians are living in their country with people of different ethnic origin. Which of these people do you think are entirely different from Austrians?'
5. 'Does Austria have an obligation to compensate the victims of the Nazi regime fifty years after the end of the Second World War?'
6. Do you think that Austrians and Germans speak the same language?' To

stimulate discussion, participants were informed or reminded of the slogan '*Erdäpfelsalat bleibt Erdäpfelsalat*' from a newspaper advertisement used during the campaign leading up to the EU referendum. This slogan addressed the issue of Austrian lexical variants and correspondend roughly to 'chips will remain chips' (i.e. not 'French fries'), which was intended to assure the Austrian population that their regional particularities would also be preserved inside a larger Europe.

Although this sequence of prompting questions was the same for each group, there was considerable variation in the significance of the individual groups of questions, because each group had its own dynamic of discussion intensity.

We processed and analysed the data in a number of steps. The primary data sources were transcripts, together with field-notes and brief summaries taken during or immediately after the discussions. We interpreted the data as discursive utterances of individuals in a semi-public context, and focused our attention on the thematic contents which are constituent parts of a constructed national identity, and on how individuals articulated ('realised') these contents linguistically in group situations. Group processes and group dynamics were not our focus of interest *per se*, but we recognise that individual contributions may not be taken as isolated utterances but must be seen within the context of the group discussion as a whole. Undoubtedly, the group situation affects the statements made in the discussion as it encourages participants to share in co-constructing and negotiating the meaning of key concepts relating to national identity, a point illustrated below.

At the same time, it is important to note that real or perceived power relations in the group seem to have influenced participants towards expressing opinions they believe to be socially desirable and towards avoiding taboo subjects. Utterances felt to be undesirable or those opposed to the (perceived) prevailing group opinion were frequently more cautiously formulated, especially at the beginning of a speaker's turn (cf. Section 5.2.1.3).

In addition, participants tended to avoid open conflicts in the group and to work towards achieving group consensus, even in heterogeneous groups. This meant that extreme positions were only rarely expressed, while the dynamics of the group discussion sometimes resulted in the group attempting to convince individuals taking opposing positions that their views were wrong (cf. section 5.2.1.4). Potential conflicts were sometimes defused by individual participants' resorting to general or vague statements (cf. 5.2.1.2). Another possible strategy of conflict avoidance was to ignore extreme positions that had been expressed.

Finally, frequently a particular topic or argument, after having been introduced by one participant, was taken up by others in the group. It appears that participants voiced opinions they might not have expressed in other contexts. Despite, or perhaps, because of this relatively strong political and social group control (which normally does not obtain in discussions, say, at a pub or on the street) these focus groups were able to yield valuable insights into semi-public discourse which would otherwise be difficult to obtain.

5.1.3 The Group Discussions

5.1.3.1 Pilot Group (P)

Date of discussion: 7 July 1995
Venue of discussion: Department of Linguistics, Vienna University

Five male and five female students at Vienna University took part in the discussion of Pilot Group (P). This group differed from all the others in that it did not take place during the immediate pre-election period.[3] Furthermore, it was conducted by a moderator who intervened by throwing in questions and interrupting more frequently than the other two moderators. Participant contribution was evenly balanced, and the group seems not to have felt any particular need to reach consensus. Conflicts within the group were acknowledged, for example in the discussion of 'restitution', yet never came to a head. The discussion of question 1 (approximately 35 minutes) and of the Nazi past and 'compensation'[4] was particularly detailed. Question 5 triggered a lengthy, controversial discussion on the issue of 'collective guilt'. The participants almost unanimously rejected the statement made by President Klestil as 'politician's babble' and some also refused to answer question 4 (on differences between Austrians and non-Austrians), which is also striking. The experience of returning home from abroad came up repeatedly and was linked to the Austrian national consciousness and the feeling of belonging.

5.1.3.2 Group of Non-Austrians (NA)

Date: 10 October 1995
Venue: Department of Linguistics, Vienna University

Group NA (Non-Austrians) comprised eight foreigners between the ages of 24 and 43 (four women and four men, coming from Germany, Italy, the former Yugoslavia, Denmark, Iran and the United States) who were then living or had lived in Vienna for a substantial period. Participants described their occupations as student (three), translator, adult educator, university lecturer, university employee and freelance artist. The participants of this group also refused to discuss the question of 'national' differences. On the whole, participants in this group avoided generalisations, statements were repeatedly mitigated, relativised and withdrawn. Nevertheless, the group did not attempt to achieve consensus at all costs; the participants managed to express different points of view without coming into conflict. One notable feature of this group was its more critical attitude towards Austrian history and Austrian neutrality compared to the groups of Austrians. In addition, participants emphasised the significance of differences between the capital Vienna and Austrian provinces.

5.1.3.3 Group Simmering (S)

Date: 13 November 1995
Venue: Premises of a plant run by the municipality of Vienna

Participants of Group S were recruited from a typical Viennese working-class district (Simmering) and represented a relatively homogeneous group, since all eight participants (all of them men) were employed by the same company, a plant run by the Municipality of Vienna. The participants gave the following occupations: automobile technician, foreman, head of department, civil servant (*Beamter*), engine fitter, crew supervisor and power fitter. Their ages ranged from 33 to 54 years. The presence of elected employee representatives among the group, and the fact that all worked in the same company, as well the imminent general elections, resulted in some participants exerting a strong influence on the discussion. For example, SM3, an employee representative as well as a district councillor, exercised a dominant position, as did SM2, though to a lesser extent. SM1's role in the discussion was also quite remarkable: he expressed with a high degree of self-confidence views that did not conform with the group. SM1 also highlighted the general conflict in the group. He was the youngest and stressed this fact repeatedly. He even had something favourable to say about FPÖ politician Jörg Haider ('he says exactly what we think'). The dominance of SM3 was evident, for example, in that he interrupted the concluding remarks of the moderator and himself provided a 'final word', prompting SM1 to do the same. In contrast, there was a 'quiet person' in the group (SM5), who registered only four interventions, and who did not even speak when asked to do so by the moderator. The number of contributions made by the other participants was fairly balanced.

Group pressure was particularly marked during the discussion of the 'foreigner problem' (question 4). This issue had already been referred to in the introductory round, and participants tried very hard to formulate what might be called politically correct positions. Nevertheless, SM8, SM6 and SM1 expressed their prejudices towards foreigners quite openly. In the discussion of the EU, participants gave voice to a certain sceptical approval of the EU, which in other speech situations might have easily been expressed as rejection. The frequency with which certain subjects were reintroduced into the discussion and references to statements by previous speakers (for example, 'I am also proud to be Austrian') indicated relatively strong group pressure. In terms of content, the Simmering group discussion strongly emphasised the social and political achievements of the Second Republic. The participants repeatedly stressed that everything that had been achieved must be preserved. Accordingly, the responses to question 2 (important events) concentrated almost exclusively on the period after 1945. Interestingly, this question seems to have been construed as asking about the achievements of the Second Republic. Question 4, which this group immediately interpreted as the 'foreigner problem' (in contrast, for example to Group NA or Group P), was discussed at great length, and the group offered an implicit endorsement of current Austrian immigration policy. Many also demanded that immigrants be more willing to integrate themselves. Worth noting is the unanimous rejection of Klestil's statement on the role of neutrality.

5.1.3.4 Group Vorarlberg (V)

Date: 20 November 1995
Venue: Catholic community centre in Vorarlberg

Five men and three women aged between 32 and 54 years formed Group Vorarlberg. Vorarlberg, which borders on Switzerland and Germany, is Austria's westernmost province. The group was certainly not typical of this area, as one participant rightly observed (sympathisers of the Greens and the Liberal Forum were in the majority). The occupations given by the participants were: housewife (two), technical employee, consultant, adult education teacher, farmer, businessman, teacher. The province's differentiation from Switzerland and Germany and the relation of Vorarlberg to the rest of Austria were important thematic focal points. Particularly detailed and discerning discussion in the group centred on the issues of the European Union and Austria's 'coming to terms with its past' (question 5). The frequent reference to historical events which emphasised grass-roots political initiatives, for example Zwentendorf and Hainburg, or which had assumed public importance in the wake of the Waldheim Affair, was striking.[5] Prompted by question 2 (important events) and particularly by question 5 (restitution), participants criticised the official attitude towards the past and the perceived political lapses of the Second Republic. 'Experience abroad' was a motif which was repeatedly reintroduced into this group discussion. Creation of group consensus was an important feature of this group. Only VM5 sometimes attempted to upset it, for example by denying the alleged extinction of farmers caused by Austria's membership in the EU. The other participants did not, however, take up VM5's challenge. On 'coming to terms with the past' and the 'national' differences question, the participants were in agreement. This group differed from all others because the participants spoke partly in informal Alemannic dialect. VM1 and VM2 used their native dialect from the beginning, while the other participants switched between a modified standard German and Alemannic.

5.1.3.5 Group Carinthia (C)

Date: 1 December 1995
Venue: Chamber of Labour, Villach/Beljak

The next group to meet was in Carinthia, Austria's southernmost province, which borders on Italy and Slovenia and contains an autochthonous Slovenian-speaking minority. Four men and five women between 27 and 51 years participated this group discussion, including three native Slovenian-speaking Carinthians. The occupations given were teacher (three), university lecturer (two), old-age pensioner, housewife, technician and freelance artist. Pronounced regional pride was an important topic in this discussion. The issue of bilingualism did not play a significant role despite the bilingual composition of the group. Proximity to and differentiation from their neighbouring Slavic countries and from Italy were important to the Carinthian group members, unlike all the others. Neutrality and the role of Austrian German also figured prominently in the Carinthian group's discussion, but with a noticeable ambivalence. With the exception of CF1, who spoke very little, discussion time was distributed relatively equally. This group, too, showed a strong desire for consensus and there were hardly any points of conflict. A potentially contentious situation created by CM1 was defused by shifting the discussion to a more general, abstract level (cf. section 5.2.1.2).

5.1.3.6 Group Burgenland (B)

Date: 25 November 1995
Venue: Cultural centre in the bilingual area of Burgenland

Group discussion B took place in Burgenland, Austria's easternmost province, which borders on Hungary. In Burgenland, Croats, Hungarians, Roma and Sinti live as autochthonous minorities (cf. de Cillia et al. 1998). The discussion was carried out in a bilingual cultural centre in a community with a Croatian-speaking majority. Three women and six men took part, four of whom were native speakers of Croatian. Three participants were teachers, and in addition there were one farmer, one brick-layer, one student, one adult education teacher, one housewife and one kindergarten teacher. One participant's mother tongue was English – she had been living in Austria for 30 years. Their ages ranged from 21 to 56 years. The multilingual situation in this province and the peaceful coexistence of the different ethnic groups were important topics througout the discussion. One participant (BM5) had consciously moved into this area in order to enable his children to grow up in a multilingual environment. Multilingualism was discussed under both question 1 (introduction) and the issue of 'national' differences (question 4). Unlike other groups, group B quickly moved from the 'foreigner question' into a discussion of the exclusion of linguistic minorities inside Austria. On the whole there was a great deal of interest in linguistic issues, as is evidenced by the detailed discussion of Austrian German. BM1, a 'quiet person' in this group, spoke only twice throughout the entire discussion, while BF2 and BM4 also spoke relatively little. Among the others, dis-cussion time was distributed more or less equally. The participants in this group shared a particularly strong desire to achieve group consensus. A number of potential conflicts which centred on BM6's clearly dissenting and socially undesirable positions on 'national' differences (question 4) and on 'restitution' were defused by others in the group.

5.1.3.7 Group Styria (ST)

Date: 15 December 1995
Venue: An agricultural college in Styria

In a certain sense Group ST, which came together in a small locality in Styria, may be regarded as a counterpart to the previous group. In many respects ST was rela-

tively uniform compared to other groups, for example with respect to their occupations (four farmers, three teachers at an agricultural college and a consultant in
fruit cultivation), their political preference (for the ÖVP) and in their being a rural
group. There were only men in this group, aged between 20 and 56 years. One
participant did not have Austrian citizenship, but had studied in Austria and had
been a resident for nine years. The discussion was held two days before the general
election, a fact which obviously influenced the course of the discussion. This group
discussed the EU issue at great length (approximately 45 minutes), which was
undoubtedly due to the fact that agriculture is particularly affected by Austria's
joining the EU. The problems of small farmers in the EU, the threat to landscape
conservation as a result of the decreasing number of farmers, the lack of ecological
orientation of EU agricultural policies, and the absence of cost transparency in the
area of transit of goods were the dominant themes. In contrast to Group S, this group
fully agreed with President Klestil's statement, and unanimously rejected neutrality.
Question 4 was immediately interpreted as the 'foreigner question' by this group as
well. Participants considered any notions of multicultural co-existence to be utopian.
Also striking was the strong emphasis on the role of landscape and the regions in
constituting identity. Once introduced, these topics recurred frequently, which may
indicate a high degree of group homogeneity, at least superficially. STM2, an agricultural consultant with high local social status, and STM7 both influenced the
group dynamics of the group discussion. STM2 offered lengthy opinions deriving
from his expertise. The other six participants contributed to the discussion relatively
evenly. Participants exhibited a certain tendency to avoid conflict; consequently,
certain controversial questions such as restitution (cf. section 5.2.1.3), were not
developed. During the discussion of neutrality, which was rather consensus-oriented,
a potential conflict between proponents and opponents of joining a defence alliance
remained below the surface.

5.2 ANALYSIS

First, a preliminary note. Any discourse on nation and national identity always
implies a linguistic construction of international differences. The following analysis
focuses first on identity in a narrower sense and is organised under the rubrics *Homo
Austriacus*, 'concept of nation', 'facing the past', and 'neutrality'. Our discussion of
these themes is followed by two shorter sections on international differences
(between Austrians and non-Austrians). Our analysis emphasises the specific content
of the participants' utterances; their argumentation strategies and the linguistic
forms of realisation they employ will be only briefly examined, in the final section of
this chapter.

5.2.1 The Discursive Construction of National Identity in a Narrower Sense

5.2.1.1 *What Does 'Being Austrian' Mean? – Concepts of the* homo Austriacus

Question 1 of the group discussions – 'What makes you an Austrian?' – has been primarily designed to elicit spontaneous associations about what it means to be an Austrian and thus to obtain statements about the conceptions of 'typically Austrian' features, qualities and the like. Some participants find it difficult to answer this question, at least they initially claimed to have difficulty, for example STM1: 'why I am Austrian – for me that is very hard to answer – but I am Austrian – I know that – and that is – / there are many factors which actually make me an Austrian'.[6] In the end, everybody had an answer to this question, ranging from mere 'coincidence' to typically Austrian 'mentality'. Virtually no one mentioned only one characteristic. Even where 'coincidence' was the first answer, other aspects are added in the course of the discussion.

An initial spontaneous answer to this question was frequently a comment on the random quality of national membership in one form or other, for example, that it is more or less 'coincidence' or 'fate' (VM1), it 'has simply happened this way' (STM4), or is simply 'natural' (BM3, CM2, CF5). 'First, I am Austrian from habit – just naturally, in a completely banal, formal sense. I have Austrian citizenship – don't I? the necessary passport and therefore by law I am defined as an Austrian', argues CM2.

Other important elements were place of birth and place of residence – the fact that Austria is the country where one was born, where one lives or has spent the major part of one's life, where one's family and friends are, where one works: 'I think what makes me / an Austrian is the fact that I was born here and actually – have spent my whole life in this country – and therefore I naturally feel Austrian' (PM4). Indeed, participants often took a certain pride in describing themselves as Austrians: 'one can actually say – – that one can be glad that one was born here – and – one / that we can live here' (BM1).

A similar, though less frequently expressed argument, was socialisation. Thus, CF5 claimed:

> [...] really and as to my being Austrian – umm – I'd say I am / well I like being Austrian – I have been fed on it since I was a small child, one is taught that in primary school 'Austria this is my country dadada' well that's because – really I am Austrian that's what I like to be it is completely natural for me.
>
> (CF5)

This passage highlights a very important element in the discursive construction of Austrian identities in focus group discussions, namely, the extremely strong emotional attachment most participants felt towards Austria. Speakers stressed again and again that one is glad or proud to be Austrian. This impersonal construction was used especially frequently. For example, the first speaker in Group S began with: 'right my name is [name] – and I am actually quite proud to be Austrian', whereupon all the other participants took this up, for example, SM3: 'my name is [name] – naturally I am like the others – proud and happy – that I can be Austrian'.

Although participants critical of current Austrian politics were over-represented in the groups, national pride pervades all the discussions, repeatedly complemented by explanations of what made participants proud, for example, political peace, social achievements or the fact that nuclear power stations have been prevented in Austria by a referendum. Particularly conspicuous was the statement of BM6, whose ambivalent formulation was most probably unintentional:

> [...] what makes me into an Austrian is that / is interesting because I lived through the rebuilding – of Austria – first as a young boy – and then – when I was working, right? – and I think that you shouldn't, you can't, you even have to be proud to be an Austrian, I can't imagine anything else.
>
> (BM6)

The close emotional relationship of participants to Austria was usually based on their perception of Austria as 'home' (*Heimat*) (again and again the formulation 'Austria is my home' was used), and was often coupled with the recurring motif of returning from abroad, as for example by PF4:

> And umm ... it's love for this country maybe I'm exaggerating a bit now – because I came back from France three days ago, I was there for ten months – and – / you know it's when you leave the country you realize how proud you are of your country.
>
> (PF4)

Such episodes of 'returning home from abroad' were evident in all the groups. They were linked to the strategy of singularisation, or to the emphasis of national uniqueness, the telling examples of which were Austria's political and social achievements, everyday culture, mentality, or the Austrian landscape. Reports or stories of how Austrians became aware of their national origin and uniqueness only when abroad also occurred, most frequently when speakers distinguished themselves from 'the Germans'.

Finally, participants' continual reference to such things as a supposed Austrian mentality or a presumably typically Austrian behaviour suggests that they were content to ascribe certain traits to *Homo austriacus*, even while they expressed doubts as to whether there could be a typical Austrian mentality. Thus, CF5 believed it would be typically Austrian not to interfere, to doubt and to procrastinate. VM2, discussing neutrality, believed it was simply 'a typically Austrian solution (XXX) just to sit it out and wait'. And STM7 thought that he had acquired the Austrian mentality, which, however, he thought might not be unique. The cliché of the famed Austrian *Gemütlichkeit*[7] occured more than once, as did views that 'the Austrian' is 'a bit slow, a bit lethargic' (PM4).

Such statements about supposedly typical Austrian qualities and behaviour promote an assimilative presupposition of sameness or similarity within an ingroup. At the same time, such statements also encourage a singularising emphasis on national uniqueness, which, for its part, may be linked to the dissimilative presupposition, in other words to an emphasis on differences between one's own and other groups, which in turn are themselves assumed to be also internally homogeneous groups. Thus, interpersonal relations in Austria were described as less superficial and artificial than in other places; the Austrian was characterised as 'basically as / a friendly – an industrious – a very persistent person' (STM1). In Austria, one knows how to celebrate; this contrasts to Switzerland, for example 'where the significance of work is already too exaggerated that is where the ethnic achievement is too extreme where there is no *Gemütlichkeit* any longer' (STM8). According to participants, politicians, too, exhibit a presumably Austrian easy-going way of communicating with one another (STM1). BM4, coming close to the *locus amoenus* in his description of presumed Austrian traits explained:

> [...] here simply everything so – umm uncomplicated is umm much – simpler let's say easier to understand – it is / there is not as much – hypocrisy but everything is so somehow – obvious and simple you understand it right away and it's not as rational – less complicated and so absolutely classified and categorised, umm – in politics / in politics – or so in – everyday life that you / – that you – can have a certain distance – umm you feel emotionally closer and you can – understand it more with your heart / so to say mm umm / more than with your mind.
>
> (BM4)

Only very seldom did participants refer to physiognomic stereotypes, typical appearance or, for example, origin in the sense of a hereditary Austrianness.

5.2.1.2 On the Concept of Nation: an Exemplary Analysis of Two Text Extracts

As suggested in the previous section, the national self-conception – the national identity – of the participants was based on both state-oriented pride of Austria's political and economic achievements and on culture-based national identification with cultural characteristics Austrians are believed to share, such as language, presumed mentality or typical modes of behaviour. The emphasis put on these elements varied from individual to individual, and a conception based purely on the 'nation-state' was rare. Even those participants who initially viewed citizenship as the crucial element of their Austrianness referred to other elements of national identity in the course of the discussions. One criterion frequently mentioned in this context was whether somebody had been born in Austria or had spent her or his whole life there. Such a criterion would actually reflect a concept of *ius solis* and would in fact contradict the current citizenship law. The analysis of the following two text extracts is intended to demonstrate the intricate process of negotiation, the co-construction of national self-perception in the group situation as well as the blending of linguistic and cultural national elements with purely political elements of nationhood.

5.2.1.2.1 '... actually I have felt it more that I am Austrian' – an Extract from the Vorarlberg Group Discussion

VM4:   my name is – [name] – I am umm I work as a consultant a management consultant – and I also have teaching assignments here in (name of place) at the polytechnic well at the technical school (name). – – so far I haven't actually thought about Austrian identity but actually I have felt it more that I am – Austrian – mainly actually because of my contact to other countries – I have realised where where I somewhere belong more than through this / it actually felt almost like a mirror effect – my place is actually here and I would like to add to what has been said before about Germany somehow I'd also like to mention Switzerland umm – for me Switzerland has never been an alternative to to Austria even umm though my mother is Swiss and we have many relatives in Switzerland and as a child I used to spend my holidays there but Switzerland hasn't been the country which has somehow attracted me but – I prefer to live here as an Austrian. Where for me Austria plays a role is on the one hand the culture which we have in our country or which we built or which our ancestors built for us – important for me is – the – what I have also felt – the geography – as it plays a part here in Vorarlberg but also in large areas of Austria – another important element for me is the language – that is the – the dialect we use here in Vorarlberg – because the language we here – well we – – were also – more than ten years in Graz – and and there actually we also this language – now I don't mean just the Vorarlberg dialect but the kind of language we have in Austria – umm – just attracts me.

MO: well what is meant is not not – just Allemanic but – somehow an Austrian variety of German.

M4:   yes right yes yes in this / in this form it is actually meant. – then there is something else the history – which we have behind us Austrian history if I think of – in particular of – contact to the East – how these people still often also feel as well let's say as belonging to a 'Greater Austria' – in particular older people still have strong ties to Austria and for them Austria is actually a lot – much bigger – than this small bit left we now see on the map – and so when I talk to them they open up a much much broader horizon – for – for these people and also I myself have profited a lot. Something which I very much appreciate in Austria is a – a kind of Gemütlichkeit which we – have here in Austria – and which I think is umm a – an important element of the quality of life – actually and on the whole also a little the the mentality as we live here and how how we live our lives well in this we are different I think umm in a lot of ways from Switzerland and also from Germany if one looks at these neighbouring countries.

(VM4, Moderator, Group Vorarlberg)

In this sequence, which was VM4's first contribution to the discussion, he formulated what in his view made him an Austrian; he immediately referred to the emotional dimension ('to feel Austrian') and introduced the topic of suddenly realizing where one belongs when in a foreign environment. 'My place is actually here' pointed to the underlying concept of one's native country, whereas differences between Austria and the neighbouring countries Germany and particularly Switzerland were stressed for the first time.

The speaker went on to define his concept of national identity by introducing a number of dimensions: the common culture (in particular the collective cultural past), the common territory (as a landscape – 'the geography'), the country's small size, and a kind of historically expanded 'Greater Austria'. In addition, he mentioned the common language, both the dialect and a not precisely definable 'kind of language we have in Austria'. History as an identity-constitutive element was also mentioned, in this case the more remote Austro-Hungarian monarchy. Finally, he pointed to common features of mentality and behaviour in everyday culture, a certain kind of '*Gemütlichkeit*', indicating once again how he believes Austria differs from Germany and Switzerland.

At the same time, VM4 mentioned neither the collective present and future, nor the political and economic achievements of the Second Republic, nor political state-centred nationality as elements of his identity, articulating instead a more culturally based concept of national identity.

The strategies employed by this participant to express, or 'realise' these contents, included emphasising national similarity and common features (language, mentality, everyday culture), a notion which in turn resists on a presupposition of national singularity (in terms of culture, history, territory); and specifying the differences, both between Austria and its neighbouring countries Germany and Switzerland (this despite having relatives in Switzerland), and employing a mirror metaphor, between Austria and other countries in general.

The speaker's frequent use of the deictic personal pronoun 'we' was the main linguistic device by means of which he constituted the group of 'Austrians'. At the beginning of his turn, VM4 used 'I' ('that I feel Austrian', 'I prefer to live here as an Austrian'), but soon shifted to 'we' where he began to define his national identity in terms of the common group 'culture which we have in our country'. In this particular excerpt 'we' referred to three different groups: to Austrians, to residents of Vorarlberg and, to the speaker's family ('we were [...] in Graz'). In the majority of cases, however, his 'we' referred to the first group, although boundaries between a historically-expanded 'we' and a 'we' which refers to the Austrians of today may become blurred ('the culture which ... we built', or 'the history – which we have behind us'). The speaker's emphasis on the historical dimension suggests its particular significance for him.

Interestingly, with one exception (contact to Austria), the participant did not employ tropes for the designation of the 'we-group' ('Austria is ...'), although he used them for the definition of the 'group of others', Germans and Swiss: 'We' are different 'in a lot of ways from Switzerland and also from Germany'. The personification of the landscape was also very apparent ('the geography – as it plays a part here in Vorarlberg').

Finally, VM4's frequent use of the mitigating particles 'actually' (nine times) and 'somehow' suggests his wish to moderate somewhat his otherwise fairly straight-forward culturalistic discourse of national identity.

5.2.1.2.2   Of Slovenian-speaking Residents, Carinthians and Germans – a text extract from the group interview in Carinthia

CF4:   [...] well for the first time when I somehow realized that Austria is some-how different when I was in France for the first time when I was eighteen – and when I was working in a French family and which then – / the first question was 'are you German?' and I 'no no I am Austrian' and the others 'thank God' you know? and then it somehow happened – 'aha thank God' yes just like that – see? – so that / I / I can only describe my experiences in this way umm – so 'well there must be something' don't you think? – And umm I now think / I mean it is / I live in this country and what now maybe makes me so consciously an Austrian is simply that – that I / it's not only politics and the culture which influence me in this country where I live but that I also try to take part in the politics and culture of this country and to get involved you know?

MO: mhm

CF4:   I don't know that is – this is now just a first somehow / I don't know / theoretical definition for myself and I also have a lot of that emotional stuff as well

MO: mhm – – okay

CF 5: my my name is [name] – now comes the first now I think / yes some say what a kind of Carinthian one is yes and what kind of Carinthian am I? Right? Am I A Slovenian-speaking Carinthian? Well I would say – Slovenian / I am a Carinthian Slovene aren't I? – and then / really a Slovenian-speaking Carinthian – but I also speak German don't I? only you're already defining yourself this way.

MO: why?

CF5:   right? – because – if someone says just Carinthian: one thinks that they can only speak German, only in inverted commas now

MO: mhm

       [...]

CF5   really and as to my being Austrian – umm – I'd say I am / well I like being Austrian – I have been fed on it since I was a small child one is taught that in primary school 'Austria this is my country dadada' well that's because –

really I am Austrian that's what I like to be it's completely natural for me really

MO: right – / okay – if – / right

CM2: the more difficult this is the simpler the solution ((laughs)) as everything that

CF5: well

CM2: you take in from the beginning comes into my mind and which actually is so complicated ((laughs))

CF5: yes maybe / umm yes I could add – umm – this idea of being different from Germany which has been mentioned – I've never really thought about this problem in this way – well I'd say – the differentiation from Germans not Germany that for me is further away – well Austria right – it's interesting

CM1: the separation is only / – it's / is only arbitrary or that is

CF5: well well

CM1: only an arbitrary separation from Germany I'd say

MO: right – mhm

CF5. well what I mean now is rationally well – mhm

CM1: because I myself as: – / well because I see / I see Austria rather – so as a whole it is a political construction – nothing more – because I can't / for instance if I take the separation from Germany I can also easily include Bavaria in Austria can't I? I could also add South Tyrol to Austria – but only: bec / well because of the: present border this is not the case – but this doesn't intrinsically make any sense for me why a border is in a certain place or if there is no border

MO: could one also say that Slovenia for example could also be a part of Austria?

CM1: yes o / of course umm I don't know

MO: – well in the same sense – / well because /

CM1: well in this sense you can even include Kranska Gora to Austria or Ljubljana – I think

MO: mhm

CF1: I had at the time too

CM1: because the / the thing surely not – the / it's the regions that are so precious – for example Carinthia – I think – or / or Salzburg / or Upper Austria –

I know or / or – umm – the area around Königsee is / belongs to Germany it's so much like Austria / umm – maybe it is also the other way round

CM3:   umm but there you have – you'll have / umm I think a very big problem that's the problem of borders basically the question is also – how did a border come about and how did it come into existence – I mean if you look at the history of Austria – it happens like this doesn't it? well in one place it separates in another it converges and meanders here and there and at the moment it is where we have it now

MO: mhm

CM2:   well this is I think a very difficult question – umm if one wants to say what also belongs to Austria – umm count as – I think one / one used to include the whole of Northern Italy to Austria down to Triest – and right now one doesn't you see well for me / that's a very – delicate issue somehow that's how I see it

                     (CF4, CF5, CM1, CM2, CM3, Moderator, Group Carinthia)

This passage is an extract from Group C, recorded towards the end of the initial round, where the last two participants explicitly expressed their understanding of the Austrian identity. CF4 had previously discussed the difficulties she had about feeling primarily 'Carinthian', although 'rationally, of course … [she is] primarily an Austrian'. In this passage she defined her Austrian identity in terms of differentiation from Germany (experience abroad, a topic which was discussed earlier in this group) and in terms of political and cultural socialisation. She also introduced the idea of participation in Austrian politics and culture as a constitutive component of her Austrian identity. Further, she vaguely alluded to the importance of 'that emotional stuff'. Modifying particles such as 'somehow' and 'maybe' occurred frequently, as did relativising formulations as, for example, 'at least that's how I see it', 'I mean', 'I don't know', which generally emphasises a speaker's subjectivity and/or uncertainty.

CF5 began by clarifying her regional (Carinthian) identity. This topic had also previously been discussed by others in the group. The recurrence of this theme may simply be the result of the dynamics of this particular group discussion, or may be traceable to a pronounced Carinthian regional consciousness. However, she was not at all sure whether she considered herself primarily 'Carinthian' or 'Slovene' and finally settled on the order 'Carinthian Slovene […] and then […] Slovenian-speaking Carinthian'. In any case, she argued, bilingualism is an essential factor, as 'just Carinthian means that one can only speak German'. The lexical differentiation made between differing Carinthian identities such as 'Carinthian Slovenes', 'Slovenian-speaking Carinthians' and 'just Carinthians' is an interesting one. CF5 defined her Austrian identity on the basis of emotional attachment and socialisation at school, but at the same time denied that separateness from Germany might be a problem 'in [her] head'.

Taking this up and interpreting it literally, CM1 commented on the ostensible arbitrariness of the Austrian-German border and claimed that both Bavaria and

South Tyrol could be regarded as Austrian regions. Asked by the moderator whether this also applied to Slovenia, he agreed, but expanded his argument by remarking that 'it's the regions that are so precious'. He offered another example which in his view demonstrated the similarities between Austria and Germany ('the area around Königsee' could belong to Austria). Finally, he insinuated a position based on a cultural and linguistic nationalism, but formulated it rather cautiously, making use of qualifying parts of speech such as particles, the subjunctive, verbs of opinion and conjectures such as 'I think' and 'I know'.

A potential conflict, which might have erupted because of the presence of Slovenian-speaking participants, was prevented by interventions of other group members. CM3 defined the issue as a completely abstract 'problem of borders', and in this way digressed from the question of the concrete German-Austrian border; his whole utterance is characterised by great vagueness. CM2 found it 'very difficult' to decide what 'one' may allocate to Austria and what not. By using the impersonal 'one' CM2 attempted to lift the discussion to a more general level, thus defusing the 'somehow very delicate issue'. Finally, CF1 offered an even more abstract statement concerning 'borders and identity' thereby steering completely clear of the conflict.

In this passage, the argumentation strategies employed emphasised the differences between Austria and Germany (CF4), and at the same time were used to obscure these very differences and emphasise similarities, in particular between southern Germany and Austria. This extract clearly shows how various constructions of identity can emerge from a group discussion in which individual participants pick up on and respond to thematic issues introduced by others. It also shows that controversial positions may be mitigated and relativised through group intervention. In this particular instance, the tensions implicit between the concept of state-based nationalism and a cultural-linguistic nationalism (which is propagated in the shape of regionalism) never led to a conflict in the group, as individuals intervened to hinder it. This latter objective was made easier by the most prominent linguistic feature of this passage, namely the frequent occurance of modifying, relativising devices which stressed the individual subjectivity of the respective views. This relates to the fact that no 'we-discourse' emerged in this extract (only CM3 used 'we', which sometimes referred to the discussion group, sometimes to the Austrians as a whole).

5.2.1.3 The Construction of a Common Political Past: Nazi Era – Victim Hypothesis – Restitution Policy

The second question used to prompt discussion, regarding crucial twentieth-century Austrian events, aimed to examine the role of history in the construction of identity and to distil those historical periods and events from the repertoire of the participants' collective memory which they perceived as the most crucial. In this subsection we will offer a brief overview and will then look at one fundamental aspect of Austrian postwar identity in more detail, that is, how Austria has or has not 'come to terms' with its Nazi past.

An indication of the important role of history in the construction of identity was given by the early and repeated references in all discussions to a perceived 'common past', and the frequency with which the topos of 'history teaching lessons' occurred. The dates and events most often mentioned and assigned the greatest importance were, first and foremost, the year 1955 and the collapse of the Habsburg Monarchy. The First Republic, the Corporatist State, the *Anschluss* and the Second World War, the fall of the Iron Curtain in 1989 and joining the EU all featured less prominently, as did the years 1945, 1968, and 1986 (the Waldheim Affair), and two other events 'Zwentendorf' and 'Hainburg'.

For the majority of the participants, the signing of the State Treaty in 1955 was the most favourably evaluated historical event. In this context, moreover, Austrian neutrality is interpreted, at least historically, as having been highly successful. In contrast, 1945 was seldom mentioned at all, and even less so in a positive context. This seems all the more surprising, as our group interviews were carried out in 1995, the fiftieth anniversary of Austria's liberation from National Socialism. Among group discussions, the year 1945 was widely viewed (as only) a first step towards independence; on occasion, the end of the Second World War was even interpreted as a defeat.

The most frequently mentioned historical event with a negative connotation was the collapse of the Austro-Hungarian monarchy, followed by the First Republic, which most participants viewed as a period of crisis. In contrast, only a minority of participants characterised the subsequent period as a fascist period ('Austro-fascism'); they usually described it as the period of the 'Corporatist State' [*Ständestaat*].

The Nazi period and the Second World War were, of course, regarded as times of crisis. The terms used to designate the occupation of Austria in 1938 reflected the way this event was perceived: *Anschluss*, current in public usage, prevailed in the discussions although it suggests a certain voluntary nature (the image of 'joining'). Other expressions used as more or less synonymous for '*Anschluss*', included 'entry into the German Reich', 'joining to the German Reich' and 'Austria relinquishing its existence in 1938'. Formulations such as 'invasion by German troops', 'occupation' or 'annexation', which would actually correspond to the official postwar conception of Austria as the first victim of National Socialism, occurred only sporadically.

It seems that National Socialist rule itself did not occupy a particularly prominent place in the collective memory of the participants. It was described as the 'Second World War' and thematically touched upon only briefly. However, several participants pointed out that Austria needed to work out this Nazi past. A few participants regarded the Second World War as an Austrian war and Austria as one of the defeated nations. STM6 even claimed that the Austrians 'in the Second World War prob / were probably the only losers'.

When asked follow-up questions, in particular those related to 'restitution policies', participants did refer to culpability repeatedly. CM4 thought that Austria had no reason to be proud of this past, and suggested that it had still not found a way of dealing with Nazi crimes: what had happened was 'abominable', and one had to accept 'that Austria has, sadly, contributed – to this' (SM4). In groups V, C and P,

Austria's way of dealing with the Nazi past, and in particular the 'victim thesis', was also criticised: 'It is a shame' one group member argued, that apologies towards the victims had been made so late (CM4); every year on All Souls Day, claimed another, the 'fighters' (*Krieger*) are remembered, but not the victims (VM1); 'the lid is still kept on the Nazi period' (VM1), yet another believed it was not remembered, but forgotten (VM3); Austria, a participant noted, had been successful in presenting its 'victim role' abroad, 'and the Austrians probably thought that they might get away with it – and now history has caught up with them' (CM1). It is worth noting that in this statement the speaker excluded himself from the 'we' group by using the third person plural. The criticisms that Nazi victims had not been sufficiently compensated and that the past had not been dealt with appropriately occurred in all the groups.

The so called 'victim thesis', according to which Austria was primarily Hitler's victim and therefore had no share in responsibility for the events of the Nazi period, is explicitly endorsed by only a few participants. Thus, STM6 acknowledged a certain co-responsibility on the part of Austria, but continued:

> Right. Well how shall I put it we were certainly roped into it we are also guilty – you can't deny that there were simply too many Austrians involved in the war – but – you – then it / all turned out as if it only concerned Austria, didn't it? many nations have / Germany has let's put it like that has got away with it and in this country now / they all stood there and said 'well. what shall we do with those people now' – didn't they?'

> (STM6)

In a similiar vein, BM6 finally contended that 'it is not as if we – for – / for the crimes which perhaps – to ninety-nine point nine percent were committed by the Germans we had to suffer on top of everything else. [...] there must finally be [an end to it]'. The strategies BM6 employed were primarily those of denial and shifting responsibility for Nazi crimes onto others. At the same time, he distinguished himself from the Germans. The overall impression given in the (admittedly non-representative) group interviews was that the 'victim thesis' no longer occupies the central place it did from 1945 to the mid 1980s.

If we look at the issue of 'compensation' or 'restitution' (*Wiedergutmachung*) more closely, however, a slightly more discriminating picture emerges. Around one third of the participants unconditionally accepted Austria's present obligation towards the victims of National Socialism. For those who held this view, these victims' claims were considered legitimate; Austria had a moral and material responsibility towards these survivors which did not decrease over time. Other participants emphasised that although there was an 'obligation to compensate', it was important that history did not repeat itself: 'that simply must not happen again'. Finally, some group discussants argued that material compensation was really beneath human dignity.

An alternative way in which speakers attempted to shift responsibility was by using a 'yes, but' form of argument, in the sense of 'morally, yes, but financially?' – Thus, SM7 remarked:

Yes. Well I think morally yes, financially no – umm it's not my fault, is it? – that my grandfather or / father was grandfather – if he was somewhere in the – somehow was involved – it wasn't of his own free will surely – but I see no reason why our generation – or the generation after us – still has to pay compensation.

(SM7)

Particularly conspicuous was this speaker's emphasis on the difference between the grandparents' and the present generations, as well as the relativising emphasis on heteronomy. SM3 accepted a limited 'obligation to compensate' by arguing that Austria was renowned for helping those in need:

[…] well as has been said good contacts to that country and if help is needed there – to help – where it is needed but where perhaps money has been piled up in the meantime and there is somebody who feels morally still somehow because of what happened – / and now wants to make money out of it well there I would say – there we need not do it.

(SM3)

This passage, like the discussions of the Nazi period as a whole, clearly suggests that the topic was taboo to such an extent that the words 'Jew' or 'Israel' hardly occurred, while those most afflicted by the Nazi crimes were vaguely termed 'those people' or 'that country'. The excerpt from SM3's statement did, however, implicitly allude to the prejudice of 'unscrupulous Jewish business practices'.

Several participants felt that they were continually under pressure to justify themselves for Austria's Nazi past, particularly abroad, and explicitly rejected the notion of collective guilt. Nevertheless, one-fifth of the participants clearly denied any responsibility for compensating the victims. For example BM6, who remarked: 'we have really paid enough since the State Treaty. We had to hand over crude oil for every I don't know what (occupying XXX) we had to give loads. I don't know how long (they) should go on.' He went on to equate different groups of victims and to play off the claims of one group against those of another, in the process excluding Jewish victims from the group of Austrians altogether: 'therefore I – would well somehow say / well one must go about this (really in a different way) / do it the same. if one counts there were enough Austrians in the concentration camps and / and / and / (returnees) and they get nothing for it and their children (get nothing). that really I don't think is right.' Another participant assumed that 'compensation payments' were illegally cashed in by the descendants of victims and were used to finance a life of luxury. He disguised this accusation by relating a (second-hand) anecdote:

What shocks me really is – / what shocked me I was stationed at Oberwart and there I also – with the – umm Gypsies – / had / well not those who live there but those who travel from country to country I mean that did shock me – if you listen to them – they really just drive around and cash their compensation payments and if you look at them the expensive cars they drive the jewellery they wear and everything and they even admit it that this is the money – then I feel – / this has been over a long time so what's the point? Don't you think?

(STM6)

Here, the denial of responsibility for the Nazi crimes culminated in the defamation of victims and their descendants.

In two instances, participants, although they accepted Austria's obligation to compensate, pointed to the fact that the Sudeten Germans, who had been expelled from their homes, had still not been compensated; they also recommended that other countries should also confront their pasts. Taken together, these views ultimately suggest a kind of modified *tu quoque* strategy. In short, the discussions of restitution presented a very varied picture of coming to terms with Austria's past. It might be condensed to the formula: 'as long as it does not cost anything, we are all in favour of it, but …'

5.2.1.3.1 ... 'I think – compensation yes, but' – an Extract from the Pilot Group Discussion

MO: now my question would be ((clears his throat)) – well the Second World War ended – umm fifty years ago – – umm is there – for us today and do we today as Austrians – still have an – obligation to compensate – vis-à-vis the victims of the Nazi regime – –

PF2:   of course.

        ((5 seconds))

PM5:   I would say yes – absolutely –

MO: F2 [name] says – 'of course' – M5 [name] 'yes – absolutely'

PM4:   I would say it depends – – because – if I pay compensations now to / to – former victims this is clear but what annoys me a little is this – collective guilt which perhaps comes with it somehow – I think – compensation yes but not now in such a way that the present young generation must still feel guilty that I find a little bit wrong ...

PF2:   ((clears her throat)) I /

PM4:   it is also enforced somehow

PF2:   I think that this is no / no umm guilt / no guilt / I don't know – well not as compensation – well it / of course that one just – I / don't know / compensation payments and such things – they have to be – but I believe the most important well – a very important thing is that one is still aware of these awa / of what happened

PM4:   right

PF2:   and that one doesn't suddenly forget it for such things

PM4:   but it should be free of values

PF4:   well one can still be aware of it but I need not feel guilty in the third generation. – – Must. – But I must feel guilty because I must justify myself

MO: is there, would you say, an obligation to compensate? For yourself? Umm
        – and if yes in what way – –

PF4:   yes financially – that / that – I would accept but I see no reason why I
        should – justify myself when I say I come from Austria that would then
        be the negative side of all those good things – yes. first one must say 'oh
        bad. Hitler. But really so stupid'. as soon as you say that you come from
        Austria the first word that they put into your mouth – 'Hitler'. – I don't
        see why I have to justify myself in this case if I was born in seventy-
        six – –

PF3:   you don't have to justify yourself

PM1:   I also think besides that compensation is only possible financially there –
        is no other way to make up for it I feel

MO: say it again speak up I couldn't /

PM1:   Sorry umm th / th / well compensation I think is only possible financially
        because – well there is no other way to make up for it

PF4:   yes right it's over

PM1:   besides – I think also – only / not only that it is over but generally one
        cannot make up for everything that happened. only in the sense that one
        remembers it and that one – / that one passes it on I think – that is quite
        important

MO: M3 (name) what do you think?

PM3:   well well – obligation or / or compensation in the sense of a financial
        settlement this obligation I cannot see if I look at it now purely from my
        personal point of view. – Umm I also think what you have just said I think
        that actually also very stupid if for example abroad you are addressed and
        that has also happened to me 'aha Austria Hitler' and so on and so forth
        – that – I for myself do not accept because – / well never mind but – an
        obligat / an obligation towards other – people I do see that is – simply to
        make sure that such things will not repeat themselves. and that one is
        simply aware of the fact that such things happened and that of course
        potentially they may happen again – and that we / – that that simply
        mustn't happen again well this obligation I can accept.

        [...]

PM2:   perhaps – it also depends on now this is put very – wickedly but – umm
        – – it is partly based on facts how well – this group of victims is organ /
        organised and vis-à-vis the – the Austrian state or the state of Germany
        can assert their claims. and I think now umm coming back to the general

– the Austrian state certainly has a responsibility here and the – individuals take their share anyway partly if they identify with the state. and – that is a moral responsibility not a – financial one in the sense that umm now I as an individual person – should pay any compensations but that I umm as part of the Austrian state should contribute that similar tendencies – umm cannot come to the surface again.

MO: F4 [name] do you accept this moral responsibility? – does it mean anything to you? – –

PF4: to a certain degree

MO: where do you draw the line? – –

PF4: yes if / if I really / that is – as soon as I quite logically / that one talks about it that well that now one umm – because of well these – celebrations of the various anniversaries and so one begins to talk about this again and as she has already mentioned it was certainly prompted a bit by Waldheim – but – it is absolutely illegitimate that I must in – second third – generation justify myself really for that – – not even my parents had anything to do with it

PF1: but also the second and third generations of those people still have to cope with this. therefore why shouldn't the so-to-speak the other side in second third generation deal with it? – – that's what I wanted to say

[…]

PF4: what would you do now fifty years afterwards in the year ninety-five what do you do? –

PF1: the problem is that I belong to those who ((laughs)) whose families get compensation

(PF1, PF2, PF3, PF4, PM1, PM2, PM3, PM4, PM5,
Moderator, Pilot Group)

The Pilot Group discusses the issue of 'compensation' at great length. The moderator raised the question whether the Austria of today still had the obligation to compensate, which PF2 and PM5 answered in the affirmative. While PM4 acknowledged compensation payments to 'former' victims, he rejected supposed accusations of 'collective guilt', 'which comes with it somehow' […] 'compensation yes but not well in such a way that the present young generation must still feel guilty that I find a little bit wrong …' The strategy of pre-emptively rejecting an accusation previously made (that is, of collective guilt) made it possible to render harmless Nazi crimes and shrug off responsibility. As PM4's position conflicted with that taken by the others in the group, he was obliged to formulate it carefully; this was achieved through the use of modifying particles, for example, 'a little bit wrong'.

PF2's attempts to counter this collective guilt thesis failed (this is indicated by the frequent occurrence of fragmented sentences). Although she emphasised that it is important to remember, her formulations were rather vague; she stated merely 'that one doesn't suddenly forget it'. To this, PF4 reacted by reintroducing the collective guilt thesis, but conceded a responsibility for making financial compensation. However, she shifted the focus on the supposed compulsory justification vis-à-vis an ambiguously defined group of others ('they'). Following PF3's remark that there was really no need for PF4 to justify herself, PM1 offered his concept of compensation, which he thought should be limited to financial payments. He also stated that it was important not to forget. The moderator then called on PM3. The latter argued against financial compensation, a statement that was rather unpopular in the group. Because of the controversial nature of the issue he formulated his comments very cautiously and emphasised that it was purely from his personal point of view. He then shifted to the earlier topic of having to justify oneself abroad, a view he rejected. For him, the obligation consisted primarily in taking that 'that such things will not repeat themselves'. PM2 presumed that well organised groups of victims had a better chance of asserting their claims, and acknowledged that the state bears material and moral responsibility and that individuals bear a moral responsibility if they identify with the state. When asked by the moderator whether she accepted moral responsibility, so defined, PF4 answered 'to a certain degree', but then repeated her earlier rejection of the supposed obligation of the second and third generations to justify themselves, although it was 'logical' 'that one talks about it'. To this, PF1 replied that also the second and third generations of 'those people' still have to cope with what happened. At this point PF1 disclosed that she herself came from a family whose members had been victims of the Nazi regime.

The discussion continued to revolve thematically around the compulsion to justify oneself until, towards the end of this segment, PM4, whose family had been expelled from Czechoslovakia in 1945, attempted to draw comparisons with other countries. These, he stated, should also come to terms with their pasts:

> what I would perhaps also find important is that one / there is in many countries – in Europe – still no mastering of the past that one also – that looks / if I just look at Italy – where the Neo-fascists are again represented in parliament – and nobody really talks about this either – – or in Czechoslovakia where in the / in the / in the course of the liberation of Czechoslovakia from the Nazis – the Sudeten Germans were driven out and in this context compensations are not even mentioned.

> (PM4)

The discussion of this topic as well demonstrates the great variety of different positions that were put forward, but also negotiated, 'co-constructed' in the group. None of the participants openly rejected the obligation to compensate, none openly supported the victim thesis. The views expressed ranged from unconditional acceptance of Austria's moral and material obligation towards victims of Nazism to the acceptance of a moral, but not material, responsibility towards these victims, to a rejection of even a moral obligation towards the victims 'descendants'. This view was linked by some participants to social pressures. They claimed to feel obliged to justify themselves because of Austria's Nazi past. Consequently, they also categorically rejected the accusation of collective guilt, which in their view had been both directed against or forced upon the Austrians by groups they did not clearly define. Such statements, which in this group and in this setting were undesirable, were invariably expressed very cautiously (PM4, PM3).[8]

That this topic represented a taboo is suggested by the fact that virtually no one took up the 'national we' offered by the moderator. The participants used either the first person singular or impersonal 'one', which referred both to the 'I' and 'we'. Even within statements, a shift from 'I' to 'one' occurred (PF4). These formulations are the linguistic means which enabled the speakers to distance themselves emotionally from the topic. At the same time, personalisation was employed (for example by PM3) in order to limit the general applicability of statements. The effect of this taboo was also clearly suggested by the fact that the participants avoided naming the victims of National Socialism: in one case they were 'former victims' (PM4), or an obligation was expressed 'towards other people' (PM3), or 'this group of victims' (PM2); even PF1, who herself comes from a Jewish family used the formulation 'those people'. It is only much later in the discussion that PF3, when asked by the moderator, designated the victims as 'Jews, Gypsies'. Similarly, the Nazi crimes were described vaguely as 'such things' ('that such things happened', PM3).

5.2.1.4 Austria's Membership of the European Union and 'permanent neutrality'

At the time the focus groups were conducted, Austria's joining the EU was not perceived as threatening Austrian identity. Although most participants stated that they had not changed their minds since the referendum, a slight increase in sceptical or undecided positions was noticeable. Participants exhibited very little enthusiasm for EU membership; even the proponents used arguments such as 'choosing the lesser evil' or 'you can't have one without the other'.

Of the various reservations expressed by proponents of Austria's membership in the EU, perhaps the most important related to the maintenance of Austria's neutrality. In their view, Austria should not join a military pact such as the WEU (the Western European Union), let alone NATO (the North Atlantic Treaty Organisation). Some participants, especially those in group S, frequently made maintenance of neutrality a condition of their continued support of Austria's EU membership. Others, such as VM2 or VM5, were favourable to the EU, but felt 'that we shouldn't join NATO – – under no circumstances do I want to be part of this alliance' (VM5).

More details illustrating the ambivalent attitude of the participants towards Austrian neutrality will be presented below. Considering the nearly unanimous emphasis on the importance of neutrality as historical achievement, this ambivalence seems to suggest that a major shift is underway (Benke and Wodak, 1999). The different reactions to the following statement made by President Klestil, which all the groups discussed, only reinforces this view. We will illustrate this point by analysing the relevant sections of the groups from Styria and Simmering.

Today, on the evening of our national holiday, I would like to present to you my views on some basic questions concerning our republic – first on the national holiday itself – in particular during the last few days it has been suggested that the 26 October might perhaps be an obsolete date – because neutrality has lost its original meaning – I don't see it that way – because for me this day has always been associated with the recovery of our freedom – seventeen years under the dictatorship of war and occupation had to pass until the Austrians regained their freedom on 26 October 1955 – our neighbours in the East had to wait for another three and a half decades before they were able to experience the happiness of freedom – today Austria is surrounded only by democracies – for the first time Europe has a chance of growing together under the sign of freedom – and so an entirely new era has begun for us Austrians as well – with new rules of the game and new players in the team – the security concepts of yesterday are obsolete – to be on your own is no longer an advantage but a weakness.

(From President Klestil's television address on the occasion
of the national holiday on 26 October 1994)

Each of the two groups proved to be homogeneous on the issue of neutrality. Whereas all members of Group ST approved of the President's statement, with one exception, those in Group S clearly rejected it. In other groups, particularly in the Pilot Group, some participants were neither for nor against Klestil's statement but dismissed it as typical 'politicians' babble' because of its ambivalence and vagueness. Thus, PM5 observed: 'I think he doesn't say anything real, does he? he says nothing [...] nothing – the whole – / well I don't know the / the / there is no meaning behind this' and PF2, resignedly: 'the whole thing is politicians' babble – one can / what is now (there in / a / a /) what is it now in keywords / what is it what he says? – I can't say'.

5.2.1.4.1 'For me neutrality is a hollow thing: which is empty inside' – an extract from the group discussion in Styria

STM1: well umm this is actually taken / out of a / of a – umm out of context where he in actual fact – about this natio / I happened to hear this speech umm – where he in actual fact does – neutrality as such – as an important element in the / and / that is a stage in the development towards the country as it is today you know? / the moment the / when the Soviet Union collapsed neutrality collapsed as well because then you didn't have a counterpart any more which actually / guarantees neutrality in the sense guarantees who guarantees it to us from the East? – if / if one is completely honest I mean whether one / whether I like it or not is another question – who guarantees it from the Czech Republic from / from Hungary from / from all those countries? well for me neutrality itself is a / yes. If I say: the twenty-sixth is an obsolete date anyway just like my birthday

[...]

MO: well as neutrality as it existed umm

STM1: which / which doesn't exist any more

MO: until before the accession to the EU that is be / before the fall of the Iron Curtain

STM1: the one before the Iron Curtain? yes then neutrality made sense to me you know? but it lost its meaning the moment it lost its partner

MO: that means it's no / well for you in the sense of an Austrian attribute

STM1: for me? – No.

MO: the:

STM7: well that / there I have to say it's a hundred per cent clear that for me neutrality is a hollow thing which is empty inside.

STM1: right

STM7: that has no function any more – today – and partly this neutrality is now right. somehow which which is hypo / umm very hypocritical I think I just think about / about Switzerland the Swiss still have not joined the U / the / the UN – although one of its headquarters in Geneva so to speak the central / one of the main seats is in Geneva – why haven't they joined the UN? Umm

STM2: because they (XXX)

STM7: it's because then they simply don't / have to spoil

STM1: that's the only reason

STM7: and can do business with everybody – that's why one doesn't declare oneself and identify with one has so-to-speak no opinion – one withdraws to the / umm to the neutrality one can / if one is neutral one can't / shouldn't / say the truth so to speak or because it would spoil one's business wouldn't it?

MO: well neutral in your your opinion means – try to please everyone?

STM7: that's what it means pussyfooting to have no opinion because one doesn't get involved in conflicts always holds back: and as one says 'yes. They should do it themselves' and one / one tak / one doesn't take on any responsibility for a / for a third so to speak

MO: mhm

STM7: because one simply can't yes. Support anyone because one is neutral isn't one?

MO: yes – yes

STM7: and – I think that's the only problem which today I – if we're no longer neutral is whether we should join a military alliance instead / immediately join

STM1: that is the other question

STM7: that is the question

MO: but this isn't / what I hear is (XXX) yes say it

STM7: right. – Well there I have a problem: because if I think the Spanish have / now supply – umm the / the NATO secretary-general and are / they themselves are not even in the NATO – they are not a NATO member you see? And / and if I imagine that we also don't

STM2: nor are the French are they?

STM7: nor are the French so why do we have to join by all means a / a / a WEU umm / not a – milit / a military what's its / what is the name of this integrated /

MO   West European

STM2: Defence let's put it like that

STM7: Defence alliance

STM2: Union

STM7: and that we join that – then I would rather think that this is umm an exaggerated rejection for that no longer has anything to do with neutrality that is … a question whether it is wise to join a military alliance. Don't you think?

(STM1, STM2, STM7, Moderator, Group Styria)

STM1 opened the discussion by explaining that he had heard Klestil's speech and observed that in his view the present passage had been taken out of context. Klestil stated, he had in fact emphasised the historical importance of neutrality, but since the fall of the Iron Curtain and the collapse of the Soviet Union the issues of neutrality and October 26th had become obsolete. No one could guarantee 'us' neutrality 'from the east' – Hungary and the 'Czech Republic' were mentioned explicitly in this context. STM7 took up this point (for me 'neutrality is a hollow thing which is empty inside' and 'which has no function') and moved on to define neutrality in general as something negative. His initial remarks were formulated very cautiously ('partly this neutrality is now right. somehow which which is hypo / umm very hypocritical I think I just'). He continued by listing further negative attributions of neutrality, which in his view distinguished Austria from Switzerland. Switzerland was seen as a negative example, because it still had not joined the UN even though one of the main UN seats was in Geneva. At first STM7 only referred to the Swiss, 'who can do business with everybody [...]' but then shifted to an impersonal 'one' to characterise neutrality and neutral behaviour in general: in his view, one would not declare oneself, one would not identify with anything, one would have no opinion, one would not be allowed to say the truth, one would never get involved in conflicts, one would not take on any responsibility for a third party. But, he wondered, using 'we', 'whether we should join a military alliance [...] immediately'. That STM7 was rather uncertain about this point is evident from the interrogative form he employed on several occasions, and from his use of the subjunctive, implicitly modifying his views: 'then I would rather think that this is umm an exaggerated rejection [of NATO]'. These comments also provided an opening for the other participants to continue more systematically the disparagement of neutrality that STM7 had begun, and this is in fact what happened. STM5, who also stressed the historical relevance of neutrality, advocated joining a military alliance: 'I think there is so much hypocrisy in that – that's not good I mean if a European Union then also in terms of a defence union'. Interestingly, nobody, not even STM7, contradicted him, but nobody, on the other hand, reacted to this potential point of contention. Group consensus, which in this case consisted in the unanimous refusal of neutrality, seemed more important.

Thus, this politically homogeneous group exemplified a position which was favourably inclined towards the transformation of neutrality initiated primarily by President Klestil and his party the ÖVP, but also by the Liberal Forum and the FPÖ of Jörg Haider. This seems all the more remarkable as both STM1 and STM7, who have been quoted extensively, are members of an older generation. Austria's central postwar myth of neutrality had apparently already been shattered beyond repair for the participants of this group: how and by what it should be replaced, however, remained open.

5.2.1.4.2 'What I expect from him as Federal President – is that he actually
does preserve neutrality' – A Text Extract from the Group Discussion
in Simmering

SM3: right. May I say something – I think that a Federal President before he is
elected (XXX) and that – he must be aware of – at the time he was elected
to preserve neutrality – this I think is what he has to do and it's high time
that he does it. – That's what I expect from him as an Austrian. – But I
grant him that he is also an Austrian and a citizen – as it may occur to him
this is now a purely moral effect – whether he says this in his – New Year's
speech or whether he declares it just anywhere

MO: that was on the national holiday (XXX XXX) mhm /

SM3: national holiday – whether he declares it just anywhere – umm where he
says it in a private environment let's say – as a private person Mr Klestil
that's his business – whatever one thinks about it – (as I said) 'aha does he

believe in what he represents'. – But what I expect from him as Federal President – is that he actually does preserve neutrality. Because I think that this is a piece which belongs to us all – and that's why we have a President to take care of it.

MO: that what's in this text means for you – / what he wants really – / he talks in a very complicated way (XXX) well well

SM3:   well so sure – and by so many democratic umm countries and states – if I look at it closely – I don't know whether it's really so democratic every-where the borders have been been opened – but countries where things are OK I can't see – very many around us in the East looking to the West things have been stabilised really for – a long time but looking eastward I can't see it. That's why – I don't think that as President he is entitled to make this statement.

MO: yes – Mr. M6 [name] wanted to say something

SM6:   The way I see it is that he gives up neutrality. by saying this. that's how I understood it – but that's not why he was elected that I must really say.

MO: yes mhm – – and you are in favour of it.

SM6   I am for it – yes right

MO: one must preserve it right? Because that now really has been (in the XXX) discussed now – again and again for the last two years hasn't it?

SM6:   no now I have the feeling one should give up neutrality.

MO: yes mhm – – and (how is it) for the others?

SM1:   well I am actually not totally – of this opinion that one should at all costs maintain neutrality – I mean I don't want to fight in a war and – I'm certainly the last who wants this or I don't want it – – for my children somehow but – well I mean I can't join a union of states and then say 'okay now you protect me but I don't get involved' that – won't work. – That's how I see the security policy – especially in the EU – a very important – / because there is so much unrest – and I also say I can't say 'watch it! The five of us stick together if someone attacks us' – and then I say 'the four of you fight and I sit back and watch' that won't work like that – – and I think all of us: we have no protection at all. Because that we are now sitting here saying 'I am neutral' – that won't work either – because if someone comes along who thinks – that this is not so – then you are on your own then nobody is going to help you. don't you think? That's how I see it and – then I must the others also: sometime – all that (XXX) /

SM6:   I think / I think you are not quite right there because with the UN we have participated in peace-keeping operations anyway for a very long time

– well – whether – with or without neutrality. we have always done that well but – you're also

SM1: the defence policy of the EU doesn't have anything to do with the UN

SM6: it does actually in a foreign country with a war zone – –

SM1: yes – right

MO: M7 [name] /

SM1: but voluntary /

SM7: well. one mustn't forget – the umm European Union has – has approved of this that we can remain a neutral state. – – what they said that is actually – quite interesting yes so that's also

SM1: that's what they've told us (if) that is really so?

SM7: it hurts me even more – – if – the President /

SM1: if that had been the case such a discussion would never have been started. – – that's what they have told us /

SM7: well right – there are (then) other interests behind this. Are partly economic interests behind – and the line which has been actually pursued which is actually the yes – the line of the ÖVP which has never really cared about

SM?: well –

SM7: and I think the very moment the Europe / European Union says 'yes okay you can stay neutral' – then we ourselves shouldn't put that into question don't you think?

SM1: but in that case it wasn't about a security alliance. Was it? Because a neutrality wasn't even mentioned any more if we say anything. Because that doesn't work. how should that work (name). You say 'I am neutral I don't do anything and you – bash each others' heads for me' –

SM5: yes okay / but that was / you – but excuse me. – – Switzerland is not in the UN – – but- is neutral isn't it? (XXX)

SM1: look the Swiss haven't at all / you cannot compare Switzerland with Austria / in no way although the people do it all the time – because it's a small country but Switzerland is for example first economically – not dependent on anyone (XXX) /

SM6: when / when Switzerland is compared with Austria. it's only if one wants to show us something negative the positive things we have got there one doesn't compare us with Switzerland. If it's about the insurance companies and so on. One must always consider the point of view – when do I compare who with whom? is (there) – / for what reason? don't you think?

MO: M5 [name] said something before which I didn't quite / –

SM5:   well because of Switzerland I said. See? – With Switzerland that's okay with the neutrality. Isn't it? – and it's not that anybody attacks them because you said – ('well if we must be afraid' /)

SM1:   they aren't in the EU either

MO: they think that they have to keep neutrality

SM5:   we should keep it shouldn't we? Because clever people and efficient people have squabbled I don't know how long (and did it XXX) no?

SM7:   one shouldn't forget one thing. – If one day we have given up neutrality – how soon we will join a NATO alliance. Much sooner than with neutrality. because by that you open the doors wide for them. – – And whether the NATO alliance brings us the small Austria so much – I am not so sure about that. Except costs.

(SM1, SM3, SM5, SM6, SM7, Moderator, Group Simmering)

In contrast to Group ST, neutrality is not an issue for Group S, whose political preferences are closer to the SPÖ. Therefore the statement by the President, which is unanimously interpreted as putting neutrality into question, is met with brusque refusal from all participants, with one exception. The discussion is opened by SM3, which is probably not by chance, as he has a domineering role in the group: he thinks that Klestil, in his political function as president, does not have the right to question neutrality. He may do so as 'private person Mr Klestil', but as President, as guardian of the constitution, he has to 'take care' of neutrality because 'this is a piece which belongs to us all'. He continues by expressing his doubts whether in the East 'it's really so democratic everywhere', whether 'things really are OK'. He argues for retaining neutrality because of a 'threat from the East', which he also uses to criticise the President, who is not entitled to make such a statement. SM6, too, is for retaining neutrality and criticises the President. On this, SM1, the youngest participant in this group, points to the problematic nature of the neutral status using a cautious formulation ('well I am actually not totally – of this opinion that one should at all costs maintain neutrality') and referring to security policy arguments: one cannot be part of a union of states and at the same time not want to get involved: for him EU security policy is a very important issue. This he illustrates by a vivid fictitious scenario, which shifts the general, abstract neutrality and security debate to a concrete, 'tangible' level of a personalised potential face-to-face confrontation, that is by means of a fictitious dialogue from a fight among males taken from everyday life: 'I also say: I can't say 'watch it! the five of us stick together if someone attacks us' – and then I say 'the four of you fight and I sit back and watch' that won't work like that'. And he continues: 'I think all of us we have no protection at all. Because that we are now sitting here saying 'I am neutral' – that won't work either – because if someone comes who thinks – that this is not so – then you are on your own: then nobody is going to help you. don't you think?' SM6 interrupts him rather brusquely ('I think you are not quite right there') and points to Austria's participation in UN operations. However, SM1 insists on the 'security alliance of the EU'. Now SM7 intervenes and remarks that Austria was granted the right to remain neutral by the EU. He criticises the President and assumes economic interests are behind his willingness to give up neutrality, but also 'the line of the ÖVP which has never really cared about neutrality'. Still, SM1 is not convinced and now even the 'silent person', who has hardly said a word so far cuts in. He points to Switzerland as a positive example of a neutral state ('and it's not that anybody attacks them') and stresses inter-national sameness. In this he is assisted by SM6, who argues for maintaining neutrality and quotes anonymous authorities ('clever people and efficient people'). SM1 rejects this arguments and points to inter-national difference. Now SM7 warns that if Austria gave up its neutrality, it would not be long before it joined NATO. He expresses his doubts by referring to the relatively small Austrian 'national corpus' in terms of a 'we-body' using the metonymic deictic 'we': 'and whether the NATO alliance brings us the small Austria so much – I am not so sure about that except costs.'

The discussion continues along the same pattern. The group criticises the President (SM2 even thinks such a statement on the national holiday 'perverted'), using the 'we' form extensively, and attempts to persuade SM1, who, however, insists on his position. Thus at the content-level the strategy of perpetuation dominates. Discursive transformation in the sense that the vague European security policy plays a part in a reinterpretation of neutrality, as it was propagated in the *Neue Kronen Zeitung* before the EU referendum, is not discernible. On the level of group processes the attempt to correct non-conformist positions by means of group pressure failed. At the same time, the discursive strategies of transformation of neutrality, as they were expressed in the mass media, had clearly influenced SM1's views. Indeed, this extract reveals how elements of the discourse of the élites, of the media and of political discourse in general were recontextualised and reformulated in semipublic discursive environment (cf. Chapter 3).

On the whole, it seems that these group discussions fairly accurately mirrored domestic political debate on neutrality. In particular, participants close to the ÖVP favoured the renunciation of neutrality, while the majority of participants favoured maintaining it. However, all participants found it difficult to define what Austrian neutrality actually meant, and most of them had ambivalent feelings towards neutrality – an attitude which is neatly summarised by CM2 in a passage not excerpted above:

it is something which has well so to speak as [...] political compromise umm umm all things considered – / that is as a foreign policy compromise so to speak / now this sounds very mawkish – has entered our hearts – umm well that is really strange that this has so to speak become our flesh and blood.

(CM2)

Here, CM2 defined neutrality rather dispassionately, as a foreign policy compromise, while at the same time using a metaphor of somatisation ('become our flesh and blood') to suggest that neutrality had become 'incorporated', a 'natural' component of the Austrian national habitus in the sphere of habitualised emotions and attitudes: neutrality had become a matter of the heart.

Taken as a whole, the discussion of neutrality in the groups clearly demonstrates the highly varied reception and selection, as well as the recontextualisation, in a semi-public sphere of certain discursive set pieces dealing with a transformed neutrality, that have been floated in the media at least since the EU referendum. In addition, this discussion exemplified the very different perceptual and normative filters through which listeners understood a concrete statement of a politician; how such views were received depended partly on party identification, but also on a certain 'critical' attitude vis-à-vis politicians in general.

5.2.1.5 The 'Outside Perspective': The Group of Non-Austrians

In this section we will briefly address the specific differences between the 'outside' and 'inside' perspective. It is interesting to note that the participants in the non-Austrian group made hardly any references to a specific *homo Austriacus* in their attempts to define Austrianness. Instead, they draw on the categories 'citizenship', 'passport', 'coincidence' or ' place of birth' and 'place of residence'. Frequently, the similarities between countries were stressed and differences between countries minimised. At the same time, participants pointed to differences inside Austria (for example F3). Nonetheless, in this group, generalisations are made very cautiously, and several participants refused to answer the question of how Austrians differ from other collectives. Yet we did find accounts of negative experiences (by an Iranian participant while flat-hunting) as well as references to the high degree of resentment towards foreigners, in particular on the part of the older generation. Two participants, in contrast, mentioned experiences of positive discrimination, in this case towards South Tyroleans in Vienna.

One interesting feature of this group is its perception of historical issues, which differs from the other groups. The year 1955, the year of the State Treaty, was mentioned less frequently, while more importance was attributed to the National Socialist period, to fascism, to the belief that 1945 was not a liberation for Austria ('the liberation, which was not quite wanted' – F3), the Waldheim Affair, and, with positive connotations, the Kreisky era. The need for Austria to finally come to terms with its past was also mentioned. The issue of Austrian neutrality was discussed at length, though most participants did not take Austria's neutrality seriously. For one participant, Austria had actually never been neutral after 1945, it had always positioned itself among the Western capitalist states (M1). In reference to Austrian everyday culture, two participants claimed that there was a particular rhythm to Austrian life, while other participants doubted whether such a thing existed. When discussing the language issue, the NA group exhibited the same confusion about the range of dialect varieties as found in the other groups. One participant assumed that

Austrians possessed pragmatic differences ('to beat about the bush', 'not getting to the point'). Others attributed this feature to something specifically Viennese, contrasting this to Western Austria, thus shifting the issue to a subnational level.

5.2.2 Strategies and Linguistic Realisation: a Few Comments

In the present data, constructive discursive strategies clearly predominate. Most frequently, we find explicit emphasis or presupposition of intra-national similarity and sameness as well as emphasis of national singularity and autonomy. Inter-national differences, primarily, are employed in the differentiation from foreigners living in Austria and to a certain extent in differentiation from neighbouring states and nations. Rather less frequent is assimilative emphasis of inter-national sameness and similarity – if it occurs it is usually in the form of formulaic expressions. In the context of subnational group formations (provinces, minorities), intra-national group differences are pointed out. In the discussion of neutrality as well as of the topics of the EU, social benefits, the economic achievements of the Second Republic or the 'foreigner problem', the strategy of warning against the loss of Austrian uniqueness and/or autonomy is employed. In one group (ST), the strategies of transformation and demontage are conspicuously coupled with the topic of neutrality.

In the discussion of the past and the 'compensation' of Nazi victims, the strategies of relativisation and justification such as shifting guilt (to 'the Germans'), denial of and, in extreme cases, even defamation of victim groups are evident. In a few cases there is also balancing with other war victims (that is, equating of victims, even including soldiers), for example, with the victims of the crimes of other nations and countries such as the Czech Republic or Italy.

Linguistic devices and other strategies constituting groups, for example the deictic 'we' including all its dialectal forms and the corresponding possessive pronouns, played a predominant role in the focus group discussions. 'We' might have widely different referents according to the context. In most cases, of course, it referred to 'the Austrians', meaning contemporary Austrian citizens. An historical 'we' included many Austrians no longer alive. Indeed, one metonymic usage, if interpreted literally, would have restricted the category 'Austrians' to those already dead. For example, responses to question 1 – which was designed to elicit individual answers – frequently displayed a shift from the first person singular (sometimes via a neutral 'one') to 'we', as in: '[...] that one can be glad that one was born here – and – one / that we can live here' (BM1). The group of 'others' is frequently referred to very vaguely or impersonally by the pronoun 'they', without making clear, however, to which group of people 'they' actually referred, as in: 'as soon as you mention that you come from Austria the first word that they put into your mouth – "Hitler"' (PF4).

In other contexts, 'we' also constituted the wider group of 'Europeans' ('we have to form a front against the United States and Japan', from the EU discussion), or particular sub-groups such as the groups of Carinthians, Slovenes, Croats and so on, or the occupational groups of farmers or civil servants. The prevailing implication of 'we', however, remained the group of 'the Austrians'. The suggestive force of this 'we' was so strong that even those participants in the discussions who critically addressed nationally motivated generalisation could not avoid its usage: sooner or later every participant resorts to 'we' meaning 'the Austrians'.

Another means of constituting groups was by using anthroponymic generic terms such as 'Austrian/s', 'German/s', 'Swiss', 'Italian/s', 'Turk/s', 'Bavarian/s', 'Berliner/s' and so on (in the singular German these terms almost exclusively occur in the masculine, for example '*der Österreicher*' for the Austrian) and the corresponding adjectives (such as 'the Pakistani grocer'). In addition, participants used derogatory informal group labels (such as '*Ungar*' (Hungarian) or '*Krowodn*' – a derogatory term for an Austrian Croat) or vague designations of 'out' groups, such as 'the foreigners' or, sometimes, 'the aliens' (*Fremden*).

Various tropes were used more or less implicitly to construct sameness within groups. For example, 'Austria', the country, was often used metonymically to present persons, or the group of 'Austrians'. At the same time it was also anthromorphised, as in: 'well Austria is not born for fighting that / well we've lost every war so far – / we've lost every war, haven't we?' (STM5). Similar examples could refer to other nations, as in: '[the fact] that in the Second World War Italy turned away from the German Reich and changed sides' (CM1); and 'the mentality as we live here and how how we live our lives well in this we are different I think umm in a lot of ways from Switzerland and also from Germany' (VM4).

Synecdoche in a *pars pro toto* usage occured frequently with 'the Austrian', connoting the whole group, as in 'the Austrian is a bit slow'(PM4), or 'well I think: that an Austrian is somehow different from anyone else otherwise we wouldn't be our selves / we wouldn't be Austrians, would we? Sure we wouldn't all be one people, would we?' (STM6).

Analogous generalisations through synecdochal particularisation also refer to the group of 'others' as in: 'I mean this is because – umm – simply because probably the bloke from the South – because of the heat down there is used to during the day – umm taking a siesta and lying around and really only waking up in the evening. don't you think?' (SM2).

As we have seen above, in the focus groups synecdochal references to 'they'-groups were frequently linked with derogatory attributions and ascriptions of negative features to individual groups: 'The foreigners', it was claimed, 'do not subordinate themselves' or ' they don't get on with each other' (SM6) and 'the Turks' are said to '[...] appear practically only in groups of – ten fifteen twenty'.

There are also striking lexical peculiarities in the discussion of the past in the focus groups: the year 1938 is above all, referred to as *Anschluss*; the Austro-fascist period was referred to primarily as the 'Corporatist State'. In the discussion of 'restitution', the taboos clearly attaching to the words 'Jews' and 'Israel' meant that they were scarcely mentioned. Instead, speakers usually referred to Jews as 'those people' or to Israel as 'that country' ('well as has been said good contacts to that country and if help is needed there – to help', SM3).

As was mentioned above, members of Group Simmering exercised an interesting means of linguistic control when discussing the subject of foreigners. Keen to adhere to what they perceived as politically correct views, participants stated their expectation that foreign immigrants 'integrate', not 'assimilate', as in:

> Right – on the whole I have – not yet had negative experiences with foreigners but – what I find striking – / umm I don't want to say that this – is provoked by them – only they think they can – behave as they do at home and continue their: way of life as they are used to. And that causes friction. Because the Austrian well well – simply doesn't understand – that he doesn't at all subordinate himself / subordinate is nonsense – but not / not integrate and not / umm how shall I put it – somehow umm tries – to live with the Austrian but umm they say we just live the way – we are used to. And that – often causes much resentment. – – Apart from that I must say umm personally I have actually never had any problems there that is I – can't complain.
>
> (SM4)

SM4's statement could be a recontextualisation of a linguistic guideline, that a political party had its officials use when discussing this issue. At the same time, the statement featured an important device used to express views that the speaker felt might be controversal or socially undesirable, that is, the use of introductory and concluding formulae, which are desired to promote a certain image ('I have – not yet had negative experiences with foreigners'; 'apart from that I must say umm personally I have actually never had any problems there that is I – can't complain').

One means of expressing prejudices towards a group of foreigners frequently employed by speakers in the focus groups was to relate a personal (experienced or invented) narrative, or of more general fictitious scenarios. One such 'story' is told by STM6:

> What shocks me really is – / what shocked me I was stationed at Oberwart and there I also – with the – umm Gypsies – / had / well not those who live there but those who travel from country to country I mean that did shock me – if you listen to them – they really just drive around and cash their compensation payments and if you look at them the expensive cars they drive the jewellery they wear and everything and they even admit it that this is the money – then I feel – / this has been over a long time so what's the point? Don't you think?
>
> (STM6)

However, participants also told stories to 'prove' positive features of a group of others. Thus CM4 reports that an Arab once helped him to move, and concludes 'I don't think that any of the Austrians would have done that with / so / so decently – really'.

Similarly, SM1 produces a fictitious scenario in order to explain what he meant by 'integration' and 'non- integration':

> I say they don't integrate. Now I go to Hungary and – there I move around – so that I don't stick out in Hungary. I also move around in Yugoslavia so that I don't stick out there and I move around in England so that I don't stick out there. –

but I would surely not go and – and won't go to Yugoslavia and yell – 'Milosevic bullshit' or I don't know what and that is what they are doing in this country. – because who is interested whether they stage a hunger strike at the Karlsplatz. – and then they are given more time and then I give them something of this and then give them of that you just try that in Istanbul. – There you are arrested the next day and you are gone (in prison) bye-bye! That's how it works ...

(SM1)

In closing, we would like to mention one other means through which discursive strategies were espressed in language. Frequently statements were formulated very cautiously in order not to upset group consensus or to avoid potential conflicts that controversial beliefs might have been presumed to provoke. In such cases, speakers used modifying *verba sentiendi* such as 'I think' and 'I mean', as well as relativising particles, as the following example convincingly shows:

umm I mean I don't know / I can / I don't know either what shall I say to that? but / but that are those questions umm where I say to myself so. Now this conflict umm East-West is over that was actually the umm / was actually that was umm what constituted this neutrality now umm one keeps insisting see?

(CF4)

NOTES

1. Transcript extracts will be quoted under the name of the speaker which is made up of the group and the speaker number; PM1 therefore means Pilot Group, Male participant no. 1, VF3 means Group Vorarlberg, female speaker no. 2.
2. The moderator tried to encourage all the participants to reply to all the questions. The second part of question 1 was not asked of non-Austrians.
3. Due to the breakdown of the budget negotiations, an early general election took place in Austria in December 1995. The Pilot Group discussion was held before these negotiations failed.
4. The two words 'restitution' and 'compensation' are used interchangeably as translations of the nearly untranslatable German word '*Wiedergutmachung*'.
5. In 1978, a referendum was held which decided against putting a new nuclear power station at Zwentendorf into operation. The Kreisky government had staked its prestige on a 'yes' vote in the referendum, and a referendum vote not to utilise a nuclear power station that had already been built was unique in Austrian, and perhaps world history. Several years later, in 1985 and early 1986, a large grass-roots initiative successfully obstructed attempts to construct a hydro-electric power station on the Danube near Hainburg by physically preventing the builders from entering the site; this led to police intervention and an unprecedented degree of violence. The 'Waldheim Affair' is the term conventionally applied to the controversy surrounding the disclosure of the previously unknown past of Kurt Waldheim, former Secretary General of the United Nations, which arose during his campaign for the Austrian presidency in 1986. The affair not only focussed international attention on Waldheim personally, but also raised broader questions relating to the history of antisemitism in Austria and the role Austrians played in the Nazi dictatorship and the 'Final Solution' (see Mitten 1992). This footnote was written by Richard Mitten.
6. The transcription conventions used for the focus group and interview data are as follows: a slash / indicates the end of a tone group; pauses are indicated by a full stop; – means a break in intonation, – – a short pause; material which is impossible to make out is represented as (XXX); double round parentheses indicate non-verbal features. When used to denote the specific linguistic sense of verbal articulation of a strategy, realiSe and its derivatives will be used. When used in the more conventional sense of to become aware, realiZe and its derivations will be used.
7. The term *Gemütlichkeit* and its derivative *gemütlich* are words for which there are no real English

language equivalents. In both their historical and contemporary usage, they suggest a mood or ambience rather than one specific quality, and can connote positive stereotypical images which non-Austrians (within German-speaking Central Europe) have about Austrians and which Austrians also have about themselves. *Gemütlichkeit*, for example, normally evokes positive associations (the words such as friendliness, easy-goingness, conviviality, joie de vivre all come to mind), and a situation or an experience which is *gemütlich* could be described as one which is cosy, friendly, or relaxed. Culturally, the term is frequently understood to distinguish Austrians from Northern Germans, with whom such traits as excessive fastidiousness, efficiency and assertiveness are associated. Combined with other traits also conventionally associated with Austrians such as *Schlamperei* (laxity), however, *Gemütlichkeit* can acquire slightly negative connotations of moral laxity as well. We are grateful to Richard Mitten for providing this clarifying note.

8. On this strategy, which is widely employed in right-extremist publications, see Benz 1992, p. 117.

Chapter 6

Semi-Private Opinions:
The Qualitative Interviews

6.1 METHODOLOGY

As one of the aims of our study was to include 'subjective' aspects of the discursive construction of Austrian identity we carried out a number of topic-orientated qualitative interviews, to determine informants' views, attitudes and levels of awareness. The interviews took place in a relatively relaxed and flexible setting, which enabled the interviewer to react to unanticipated turns in the conversation and provided ample opportunity for feedback and clarification of ambiguous points.

Since the interviews were structured to resemble informal open-ended, private conversations there was little observable pressure to articulate statements conforming to group opinions or politically correct statements, as observable in focus group participants. Due to the dialogic nature of the interviews, moreover, respondents were able to produce sequences of thoughts and utterances without being interrupted or being pushed in a certain direction by other participants.

Of course, we make no claim to present a representative sample. The material collected in these interviews can, however, throw light on how patterns of national identification and identity find expression in individuals; and can illustrate the subjective dimension of the contents and figures of argumentation, and the construction of Austrian identity conceived on a more 'macro' level. It can also help trace the diffusion of specific information units about Austrian identity from public (media) or semi-public discourse down to the opinions expressed by individuals. As Hölzl explains:

> Basically, what is involved here are open, semi-guided interviews, designed to give the interviewees the greatest possible scope of speech. The interviews then centre upon one particular problem, to which the interviewee is led ... These are ... 'objectively' existing problem areas which may be of interest to the interviewees, who are required to participate in reconstructing them. ... The topic-oriented interview is therefore a very suitable tool in all those areas where the subjective views of interviewees on socially relevant areas are required.
>
> (Hölzl 1994, pp. 63f.)

Two pilot interviews were conducted between December 1995 and June 1996 to test and improve the quality of the interview protocol; these were followed by twenty-four intensive interviews lasting between one and one and a half hours each. In most cases, the interview took place in the interviewee's home or workplace in order to ensure a relaxed and 'normal' atmosphere. After the interviews, the respondents were asked to complete a short demographic questionnaire in order to provide information about their age, sex, education and training, their occupation, the size of their place of residence and whether they were born in Austria or, if not, for how long they had already been Austrian citizens. The questionnaire also contained questions relating to hobbies and leisure-time behaviour, holiday and travel habits, knowledge of languages other than German, and the newspapers and journals regularly read. In contrast to the participants in focus groups (see Chapter 5), individual interviewees were not asked to indicate their preference for a political party. After each interview, the interviewer noted down what she thought had been particularly interesting or striking about the interview situation and commented in detail about the overall interview context (the way the interviewee had been contacted, conversations before or after the interview, description of atmosphere, and so on) (cf. Hölzl 1994, p. 65). The interviews were taped and transcribed in their entirety. In our discussion of the interviews below, individual interviewees will be defined by combination of their interview number and either F or M, indicating their sex, for example 1F for interview 1, female interviewee; 2M for interview 2, male interviewee.

The age of the interviewees ranged from 22 to 84 years. Thirteen of them were men and eleven women. The following occupations were represented: secondary school teacher (two), architect, bank clerk (two), biologist, employee of the City of Vienna, geologist, housewife, journalist, cutter, salesperson, kindergarten teacher, old-age pensioner (three), psychotherapist, law trainee, locksmith, student (two), and technician (three). At the time of the interviews the individuals resided in the provinces of Vienna, Lower Austria, Carinthia and Vorarlberg.

Of the Viennese residents, two had been born in Burgenland and still had close contact to this province, identifying with it and visiting it frequently. There were also two individuals in Vienna who had originally come from Upper Austria; although somewhat less than the Burgenland natives, these also stressed their attachment to their province of birth. One interviewee had recently moved from Styria to Lower Austria, but in his self-definition still very much referred to his original province. Seven interviewees, or their families, were members of ethnic or religious minorities (some of autochthonous Austrian minorities). Four of the interviewees were immigrants, two of whom had come to Austria as children, whereas the other two were foreigners living in Vienna at the time of the interviews.[1]

The interviews followed a protocol in which the questions were grouped around several thematic areas (question sets). This largely open method of questioning allows the interviewee to elaborate lengthy narratives which capture his or her feelings and attitudes very clearly; indeed, the interviewees are encouraged to illustrate their statements with 'stories' and anecdotes. 'By emphasising the narrative component, it is left to the interviewees how they structure a topic' (Hölzl 1994, pp. 64). Frequently, questions are posed 'indirectly'. Although the answers to such questions do not yield immediate insight into knowledge and awareness, they nevertheless provide interesting clues to opinions or facts (cf. Scheuch 1973, pp. 87f.).

The questions of set 1 centred on the central issue of 'what does Austria mean?'. The interviewees were asked to describe spontaneous associations and self-images that formed in their minds, and to explain what they assumed others thought about Austria. They were also asked to provide personal, subjective definitions of Austria and to describe what, in their view, is characteristic or typical of Austria. Question set 2 focused on the topic: 'who is an Austrian?', that is who belongs to the Austrian (national) people, and the criteria used to define who is Austrian and who is not. Set 6 dealt with the rules of access to the national community of Austrians, that is the conditions necessary for acquiring Austrian citizenship. These three sets of questions were designed to gather subjective, individual concepts of nation defined either in political or in cultural terms, including various ideas of a *homo Austriacus* (see question 1 of the focus groups).

Set 3 dealt with the contextualisation of Austrianness and of the consciousness of the interviewees of being Austrian. Interviewees were prompted to relate anecdotes or report situations in which they have felt (particularly) Austrian and those in which they became aware of being Austrian. Set 4 concentrated on the differentiation between Austrians and those outside Austria, which we have already encountered as the discourse of international difference (analogous to question 4 in the focus groups). Here, interviewees were asked about subjectively felt or imagined differences between members of one's own nation and members of other nations. Set 5 was organised around the topics of internal homogenisation and internal heterogenisation and focused on perceived or imagined similarities and differences within the group of Austrians, both with respect to regional points of reference and to subgroups referred to as 'different'.

Question set 7 dealt with the construction of a common political past (cf. questions 2 and 5 in the focus groups) and to historical events existing in the collective memory of the Austrians which are evaluated as significant. The thematic focal points in this question set were the subjective attributions of meanings to those named periods of (contemporary) history and to the foundation myths of Austria. Another point of emphasis was the individual perspective on the debate over Austria's Nazi past, including the victim and perpetrator theses. Set 8 tried to elicit opinions on how geopolitical transformations influence Austria, Austrian neutrality and Austria's membership in the European Union. In other words, this question set dealt explicitly with essential aspects of change in Austrian identity, particularly in the concept of the constructive elements of a common political present and future (see question 3, and the additional question following the impulse text, in the focus groups).

Set 9 was designed to obtain material on the subjective attitude towards, and the subjectively perceived importance of, the Austrian variety of the German language and to gather information about the role of language in the individual's conception of nation and national identity (see question 6 in the focus groups). Finally, set 10, which dealt with current political challenges and problems in Austria, gave the interviewees the opportunity to address topics which had hitherto not been mentioned, which, however, they deemed subjectively to be important areas of Austrian identity and the Austrian concept of nation.

The entire sequence of question sets was introduced in all the interviews in identical order. Specific questions were omitted only if the interviewee had already talked about the topic at length. The temporal organisation of the individual question sets varied from interview to interview, as the interviewer reacted in a flexible manner to signals coming from the interviewees. Of course, interviewees frequently (due to the open organisation of the questions) tied together several topics in one answer, anticipated topics or resumed a topic at a later point in the interview. In the analysis, all responses relevant to a specific topic were combined in one analytical step. The interviews with the two non-Austrian respondents followed the interview guide less strictly, as some questions had to be adapted or reformulated due to the interviewees' not being Austrian citizens.

Using transcripts and summaries of the interviews, the interviewer interpreted the material in such a way as to allow both the influence of specific (lifeworld) contexts, and that of individual socialisation as an Austrian (gender-specific experiences, experiences as members of majorities or minorities, age-related experiences and recollections, the experience of immigration, and so on) as well as the influence of distortions caused by the interactional character and the specific atmosphere of the interview, to be taken into account. In a further step, the interviews were subjected to a content analysis on specific subject areas (where comparative-contrasting techniques were employed). For the purposes of this latter analysis, the interviews were considered utterances of individual speakers in non-public 'quasi-private' contexts. A selection of such 'typical' statements and patterns of argumentation will be given in original form below.

The analysis of the interviews – like that of the focus groups – concentrates on the discursive construction of national identity. The results are thus not organised according to the interview protocol but according to the main thematic categories of the present study. Finally, we would like to emphasise once more that the analysis concentrates on the content-level and on the identification of constitutive elements and recurring patterns of argumentation in the subjective construction of national identity, as well as on the way interviewees choose to combine these elements.

6.2 ANALYSIS

6.2.1 The Discursive Construction of National Sameness

Virtually all interviewees replied to the opening questions asking about spontaneous associations and images related to the concept of 'Austria' without hesitation, and in their answers referred to typical Austrian clichés described in the scholarly literature, such as the traditional cultural empire of Austria, the Austrian landscape or a supposed typically Austrian mentality (see, for example, Bruckmüller 1996 and 1994; Schweiger 1992):

I always associate Austria with music [...] it most likely has to do with the fact that all those composers have their roots in Austria – but I suppose it was always like that – / it was always like that for me actually before I came to Austria – / when I think of Austria I always think of music.

(1F)

The common national territory was perceived as a key component in an individual's subjective construction of national identity. This territory is described as *locus amoenus*, as a 'picture postcard landscape' (2M), and as a country which has 'green a lot of green, water [...] brooks' (14F), using the strategy of positive self-presentation. As one interviewee expressed it:

Austria is a nationality [...] an independent state [...] kind of a lot of music [...] as far as the landscape is concerned it's beautiful – I would definitely tell everyone about that [...] lots of green and mountains – woods – that's what fascinates me.

(1F)

3M described Austria as 'highly indus / industrialized – – with pockets of – unspoilt nature'. Some of the interviewees also mentioned local or regional points of reference and symbols of landscape in individual Austrian provinces. Places such as the lakes in Carinthia, Lake Neusiedl, the Tyrolean mountains, the Großglockner mountain or the Bregenzer Wald region were frequently described as idyllic (cf. 8F, 9M, 14M and 16M).

Apart from these clichés of touristic interest, interviewees also mentioned politically related topics such as Austria's relatively high standard of living, its political stability, its image as a free, democratic and independent country, and Austrian neutrality; in some instances respondents referred to political figures of legendary status such as Bruno Kreisky or Leopold Figl. Negative associations, such as the connection with National Socialism, were very rare. The congruence between Austrian auto- and heterostereotypification, known from social science literature on Austria and from studies on the image of Austria, was reflected in the spontaneous answers to the question designed to elicit respondents' views on how Austria is perceived abroad. Again, the interviewees mainly referred to areas of Austrian high culture, in particular to music, other typical tourist clichés or the high standard of living. It is worth noting that none of these spontaneous associations, even the most hackneyed, seem to have been influenced by factors such as occupation, age, gender or ethnic background of the interviewees.

6.2.1.1 *What Does Being Austrian Mean? – Images of* homo Austriacus

The interview and the focus group data indicate that intermingling politically based and culturally based lines of argumentation seems to be the 'norm' in everyday discourse of national identification. Even where interviewees emphasised citizenship as a criterion for national membership and identity (which, by the way, did not occur very often), most of them pointed to linguistically, culturally and ethnically defined elements of Austrian self-perception at a later point in the interview. As in the focus groups, one-factor answers such as those specifying citizenship as the sole defining characteristic in the construction of national identity ('well it's citizenship which simply makes you an Austrian', 6M), or those calling attention to the random nature of national membership, determined by the accident of birth ('because I I can't really tell you why – I was born in this country', 3M), were invariably complemented by other more emotionally laden, if not precisely specifiable criteria:

> First of all I would look at his or her citizenship to say if someone was an Austrian or not, and then of course there are borderline cases for people who have been living here a long time and don't have Austrian citizenship yet and in that case I would say that how they feel is an important criterion for me and secondly / if they would call themselves Austrians or not.
>
> (18F)

20M, who is not an Austrian citizen, referred – in a politically correct manner – to citizenship as the sole criterion:

> the fact that you were born in this area and that you have Austrian citizenship not much else really anything else would be racist by the way.
>
> (20M)

By contrast, several interviewees (for example, 10F) made it very clear that for them citizenship (alone) is too limited a criterion for national membership. Disregarding both the legal realities and the political practice of naturalisation, these respondents regarded citizenship as a mere formality which has little bearing on national identity: 'because [...] it really means that you can actually organise this acquisition of citizenship quite easily – and – then the commitment to Austria simply is not there' (2M). Several interviewees emphasised that citizenship is important in 'formal' or 'bureaucratic' terms, and pointed to a number of advantages connected with it, for example, a permit of residence, but did not attribute any identity-constituting function (which they located at the emotional level) to it:

> I think anywhere where your life is concentrated you should maybe have citizenship don't you [...] well I see citizenship as something that / that gives me the right to live somewhere and to stay there and well / [...] not some big wonderful thing I'd shed my heart's blood for but like just a technicality you know?
>
> (19M)

In spite of their relatively low regard for citizenship itself, interviewees tended to evaluate dual citizenship fairly negatively. Although several interviewees were in favour of this option – 'I wouldn't mind if someone had ninety-five citizenships' (19M), or 'I'd be much in favour of this [...] because you never know what happens in a country politically and then it's possible for you to emigrate' (18F) – only 3M made the point that there are certain privileges connected with dual citizenship, for example, the right to vote, and that people with dual nationality are, therefore, privileged. A female respondent, who had immigrated to Austria as an adult, regarded dual citizenship as problematic, because national membership defined only by citizenship would lack those emotional aspects she believed essential:

> If they have no − / no feeling inside somehow some − kind of affection for Austria I don't really think that they should become Austrian − but if they like living here and if they like all the stuff that goes on around them the people and all that [...] I would definitely say that these people with dual nationality that they can't be both Austrian and someone else at the same time − so it / for example an Austrian and a Pole this person would certainly have to feel either more Austrian or more Polish [...] so I don't think that everyone / anyone − emotionally − can belong to two different countries to two different nations at the same time − I just don't think so.
>
> (1F)

The issue of dual citizenship exemplifies the ambivalence which characterises the private discourse of national identity construction: elements associated with the idea of *Staatsnation*, superficially political-rational elements, cultural elements, mandatory national-patriotic commitment and emotional attachment were all mixed in patchwork fashion.

As in the focus group data, numerous statements in the individual interviews stressed the importance of emotional identification with Austria for the subjective discursive construction of national identity: 'I don't know if I am typical but I feel [...] Austrian [...] somehow I feel at home here', stated 10F, an immigrant from a neighbouring country. Interviewees emphasised again and again that what makes an Austrian an Austrian is the desire and determination to be Austrian and to remain Austrian ('somebody who wants to be Austrian is an Austrian for me definitely', said 19M), a love for his or her country and for its culture and its people, and a commitment to a more vaguely desired Austria. Thus, F17 felt that 'somebody who is not loyal to his or her country vis-à-vis others and doesn't stand up for it and prefers to live somewhere else is no Austrian for me'. Another respondent, an immigrant, claimed:

> I would say that you'd have − to feel − at home in Austria and love the people and (the) country only then: can you feel like an Austrian [...] but when people and their children although they were born in Austria isolate themselves − / umm well like [...] it all boils down to which language you speak / but it / if they don't care to learn anything about our tradition, about our culture, then I would be hard pressed to call them Austrian [...] it's really − not really an important issue if they (XXX) have citizenship or not as far as the law goes. For me it's their lifestyle − their attitude toward Austria.
>
> (1F)

Respondents frequently used the conditional when answering this set of questions, in defining the rights, rules and conditions of access to the 'we-group' of Austrians, which is what argumentation theory would predict (cf. Toulmin 1996).

Being born in Austria and socialised as an Austrian in childhood and adolescence are criteria several interviewees considered essential to national identity. People are Austrian 'because they grew up in this country. because they've absorbed its culture its music its people its neighbours', stated 16M, a member of an ethnic minority. Several interviewees reiterated the decisive role played by one's place of birth and socialisation in national identity. In many instances the respondents correctly concluded that this would render problematic the idea that one could change one's nationality:

> If I was born in this country and have lived here – twenty thirty years and I move to another county – I don't think it's possible – to change mentality the Austrian mentality because [...] that [...] that's a matter of education because this is where one grew up and acquired certain characteristics.
>
> (15M)

In turn, 12F, an older interviewee, claimed that an immigrant, for example, 'a Yugoslav' or 'a Czech' with Austrian citizenship is:

> still a Yugoslav or a Czech or a [...] well wherever he may come from / well that's the place where he was born [...] I think somebody who was not born in Austria – will surely find it difficult / will surely find it difficult to be an Austrian.
>
> (12F)

An interviewee who is a member of an officially recognised ethnic minority in Austria doubted that non-Europeans could actually feel Austrian:

> Now let's take an African / a black who has an Austrian passport is / this document says he's Austrian but I don't think that such a person will feel Austrian inside. I don't know what he feels I haven't spoken with any of them; or take an Asian who first must learn to be Austrian.
>
> (16M)

Occasionally, racist concepts which imply a kind of genetically-defined Austrian-ness surfaced in the interviews, for example, when interviewees wanted to require that a person who wants to be regarded as Austrian have ancestors who had lived in Austria: 'I think a typical Austrian must have grandparents who are Austrian but not from I don't know where but really from Austria – you won't find this very often anyway if you try to trace it back' (7F). 12F, too, refers to a kind of 'hereditary Austrianness':

> Yes, I was born Austrian born in the tenth district of Vienna just your typical Austrian. My parents they were too and my grandparents too yeah and my husband and my in-laws. He was a building contractor you know? My father-in-law was and they lived in the Starhemberggasse. Yeah and my husband's last name [name X] it's a German name right? / Not a Bohemian name and before my name was [name Y] so my name didn't change all that much [...] and on my mother's side her parents were called [name Z] right? / So you don't pronounce / the 'er' at

the end that's typically Austrian so we don't come from any Bohemians ((laughs)).

(12F)

Here, the interviewee uses a *locus a nominis interpretatione*, although her interpret-ations of the two surnames, which cannot be given here for reasons of anonymity, are mistaken. Surname X has a Slavic ending, and though surname Z is a German name it designates a proper name which derives from a toponym indicating origin from a Slavic town.[2]

Questioned about which criteria were essential for defining membership of the Austrian people, interviewees' answers frequently suggested cultural foundations underlying the construction of a *Staatsnation*. 1F, who had come to Austria as an adult and later acquired Austrian nationality, defined the Austrian people in terms of linguistic and cultural criteria: 'well actually like any other – [...] not different from a French nation a nation with its language – and with its culture – with its tradition'. Similarly, 19M, whose family also used to speak a minority language, referred to language as constitutive element of the Austrian majority population: 'the Austrian nation – – – ((coughs)) well this nation simply consists of a majority of German-speaking Austrians and then you've got the minorities'. A member of the Slovenian ethnic group expressed a similar view:

Austrian nation [...] umm German Austrians – and minorities and I think that's part – of a – German / umm Austrian nation that belongs – to this concept I think.

(8F)

In this passage, the use of the adjectives 'Austrian' and 'German' is noteworthy, as it points to the polysemy and 'ideological polysemy' (cf. Hermanns 1982, pp. 95f.) of the adjective 'German', which can be used as flagword (that is as a programmatic, positively connotated, declarative concept such as 'freedom', 'democracy', 'solidarity' and so on, transporting strong ideological commitment). Whereas the noun phrase 'German Austrians' does not leave much scope for interpretation, because 'German' in this context can only define the Austrians in the sense of 'the German-speaking Austrians', the formulation 'Austrian Germans', on the other hand, would have been very risky because of its clear 'Greater German' connotation. In any event, since the phrase 'German nation' itself could suggest such a Greater German interpretation, the speaker immediately corrected herself and replaced the ambiguous, ideologically polysemic formulation.

14F formulated ideas about a multiculturally shaped Austrian nation, which is also effectively used in advertising campaigns for tourism:

That's really great I think that really we're such a mixed people. from the past. that we – [...] sort of have been patched together from everywhere. [...] a mixed people – that's what we are.

(14F)

Here, the interviewee expressed the idea of the multiethnic origins of the

Austrians through historically expanded forms of a deictic 'we' – in particular through the second 'we', which 'rubs off' on the other two. 13M endorsed a similar concept and referred to an Austrian pop song with which he identified:

> There's a song [...] that's me a typical Austrian [...] it goes [...] from umm from Croat to – Gypsy so – that's what Austrian people are for me really [...] I think a typical Austrian there is no such thing. It's just a mixture it's a historical mixture [...] that's why there's no such thing as a 'pure-blooded' (laughs) Austrian in inverted commas so-to-speak right?
>
> (13M)

Some interviewees reject the term *Volk* (people/nation) as not being politically correct. Thus, 5M thought that: 'the term 'Austrian *Volk*' has been a little discredited by contemporary history a little discredited I'd say'. And 18F was reminded of extreme right ideological phraseology and preferred to use terms such as 'state' or 'nation':

> Well, talking about a *Volk*, that reminds me of the right-wing party platform. I don't think there's any such thing as an Austrian *Volk* [...] so I would probably describe it in a territorial way like belonging to a certain country's territory right? So more like looking at it like a country and not something to do with 'blood and soil'.
>
> (18F)

Both in the focus groups (see Chapter 5) and in the individual interviews, place of birth was linked with regional identity. Thus, 4F, who had spent her childhood in Burgenland and later moved to Vienna, regarded the place where she had spent her childhood as her 'home' (*Heimat*):

> Right; the place where I come from [...] I call my home because when I go out of the house there I can see the meadows and the woods where I was as a child – that / that small piece practically is what I call home – simply the place where I grew up and was born.
>
> (4F)

By contrast, 2M, who had not been born and bred in Vienna, but moved to the capital only as an adult, regarded Austria, and not the province where he comes from, as his home:

> I'm no [...] cosmopolitan [...] I would feel homesick probably [...] I need I think I – – like you know – – a fatherland and stuff like that like something that's really there [...] like a point of reference you know for my sense of identity.
>
> (2M)

The *mirandum* 'home' was given a variety of meanings by interviewees and focus group members, which ranged from the parental home to a regional frame of reference to the state as a whole.

Also similar to the focus group members, the majority of individual interviewees frequently became aware of a national feeling or national pride when they were in a foreign country (this was particularly strong with reference to the German nation or 'the Germans') or on returning 'home' to Austria from abroad:

> Some years ago – we went on a trip and we visited several countries like we were in Italy in Switzerland and then Germany – and then we were finally back in Austria / when we crossed the border we were there – / and somehow it surprised me too it was like – a feeling of being finally back home [...] I was really happy like now I'm really home and I think that having experienced it I would now probably say that I'm really Austrian.
>
> (1F)

The majority of interviewees had particularly strong feelings of belonging to the Austrian nation when watching sports such as football or ski races: 'very often this / this national thinking is stronger – that one says I support the – / I support our own' (2M). Here, the nominalised adjectives enabled the speaker to appropriate for himself as an Austrian the achievements of Austrian athletes who in his view do not participate in these competitions as individuals, but as *pars pro toto* for Austria. In such situations, many interviewees felt themselves to be part of this synecdochic generalised group and experienced strong feelings of national pride or national desperation, as the use of 'national we' illustrates:

> Well at an international soccer match as long as the game's going on I think to myself, now we're going to win or, it looks like we're losing but / as soon as the game's over then I really don't care anymore / I mean like in sports.
>
> (19M)

17F expressed her patriotic enthusiasm in the following way: 'Of course I always support / no matter which sport / the Austrians / because I'm simply glad if an Austrian wins somewhere / because it's a good reputation for the country' (17F).

At some point in their interviews, most interviewees – again as in the focus groups – referred to a typically Austrian mentality, to typically Austrian modes of behaviour and to something like a typically Austrian national character (*Volkscharakter*), which implied ideas of a *homo Austriacus*. This Austrian mentality was contrasted to and differentiated from the German mentality, which was described as harder, more serious and more industrious. The Austrian mentality was often linked to the concept referred to above, of the Habsburg Empire as a 'melting pot' of nations:

> I also think the – [Austrian] people is – different softer a:nd probably this is also because of this mixture because of the mixed roots coming from the old monarchy – and – this is what I – prefer – you know being softer and more tolerant – compared to other nations.
>
> (1F)

In this passage, the interviewee qualified the collective singular 'people' by the adjective 'soft', an adjective which is normally used to define material texture, and referred to origin by means of a naturalising metaphor.

In several passages, individuals repeated clichés of the easy-going, humorous, easy-living and slightly superficial Austrians: 'cheeky [...] kind of roundabout' (2M); 'easy going: taking things lightly and – umm yeah / even if things get serious full of humour' (4F); 'something like we'll always get by' (18F). Apart from the frequently mentioned cliché of *Gemütlichkeit*, some interviewees also attributed negative aspects to the 'Austrian mentality', for example, the Austrian way of 'complaining' (*raunzen*) and 'whining' (*jammern*) as well as an attitude of 'that's they way we are and we're not going to change':

> A kind of self-pitying attitude but also a certain creativity among the population and – what Austrians don't like to do is to look across the borders well looking beyond their own backyard is something they don't care for much I think [...] Hans Moser and so on / and even the music in Austria sounds so pathetic [...] the Schrammelmusik [...] and the Austrians still like to watch those films you know?.
> 19M

6.2.1.2 *The Construction of a Common Political Past*

Historical or mythicised recollections which are stored in the collective memory of social groups are of particular importance for the construction of national identity.

The responses to the question about events and periods noted by interviewees as personally significant, and their evaluations of these, showed surprisingly clearly how efficient the marketing campaigns and the efforts of the press related to the Ostarrichi Millennium in 1996 have been. In contrast to the 1995 anniversary, all the interviewees were able to attach some meaning to the date 1996 and could provide interpretations which were at least in part correct. Alongside the political mythology of the post-1945 period of Austrian history, which has already pervaded Austrian consciousness, political references to a thousand year-old Austria, which at first appear politically innocuous, also seem to have entered the mind of the Austrian population, and to serve as a repository for the discursive construction of national identity.

We find a diversity of interpretations of the significance of the year 1996, ranging from 10F's equation of the 1995 and 1996 anniversaries (both commemorate 'the origin'), to 1F's vague knowledge ('a thousand years of Austria [...] but please don't ask me any details'), to many others, accurate descriptions ('the name of Austria was coined at that time', said 17F; 'the first documented evidence in 996 – a thousand years ago', from 2M; and 'that's umm the Ostarrichi celebrations – that's near [*Neuhofen an der Ybbs*] where you find the Ostarrichi stone – which was first mentioned in a document in 996 – under the name of Ostarrichi – the *Ost* / the *Ostmark* and / and from this they deduce a thousand years of Austria', from 6M). The message of this year's significance which had been delivered by the media and by official Austrian (cultural) policy was apparently successful: '1996 means a thousand years' (18F). M3 explained why:

> Every state looks for a day in its history which it could take as its foundation and

then this is simply celebrated – in this case it's this thing with the – [...] document.

(M3)

The interview results differ significantly from the data obtained in the focus groups (see Chapter 5). One reason for this may be that mentioning the date 1996 provided the respondents in the individual interviews with a more suggestive reference point. Another factor may be that the individual interviews were conducted later than the focus groups, at a time when the 'millennium campaign' had already found a wider echo in the media.

Only a small number of respondents referred critically to the fact that the millennium celebrations outweighed the celebrations around the foundation of the Second Republic in 1995. Exemplifying this view was 19M, who stated:

> Well, 1995 fiftieth anniversary of the end of the Second World War and celebrated much too little. The end of the Second World War was celebrated much too little. In Austria they celebrated forty years of I don't know what – end of occupation of Austria and 1996 has this thousand years of the Ostarrichi document right? That's a thousand years of Austria as it says in the document you know? [...] I think it was a completely different Austria / a completely different concept you know? I think if you can at all / OK they probably mean this area between Enns and / and / and Traisen or whatever you've got in this area / that's what they mean by it but I think between 996 and 1996 there've been / so many different concepts of Austria you see.

(19M)

Several interviewees emphasised the importance of the time of the Habsburg monarchy, frequently glorifying it retrospectively:

> The monarchy is gone / the monarchy was so interesting to me because well – I don't think of the monarchy as it really was, but – sort of made nicer by all those films you see right? So it's probably so that I – am a bit nuts but there was a bit of splendour still left and – it's / it's / I mean if I had actually lived during that period I'd probably have said 'For Heaven's sake!' right? But that's just the era I think is interesting they had a kind of you know style back then that I – / they had a certain etiquette / I mean I / I can / I could be totally wrong but it's / in that world that I think of when I think of the monarchy the etiquette was completely different right? Back then everything was not as hectic or stressful.

(5M)

1F stressed the monarchy's function as a political model for the coexistence of different nationalities and contrasted it to current political developments:

> Maybe it's – important to show how in a / in a huge monarchy different – nations managed to cope – and that it wasn't bad at all – leaving aside of course that politically / each of them wanted to be independent – well today you can see what you get from this independence – in Russia for example they'll all become inde-

pendent and these tiny countries can't – exist any longer – because they're not able to – well if you forget the nationalism – then it's ideal.

(1F)

In several instances, respondents addressed the European dimension of the Habsburg Monarchy. A non-Austrian respondent stated, for example:

Certainly the Austro-Hungarian monarchy [...] enjoys even today a great image in Europe / you can't forget that / in all those countries you see remnants of the monarchy whether it's in Zagreb / which the Austrians still stubbornly call Agram / or Maribor which they still boldly call Marburg [...] I think though that Austria enjoys a still better image in the former Habsburg crown lands.

(20M)[3]

The end of the monarchy was perceived as a decisive caesura by all the interviewees, frequently with nostalgic regret and described by phrases such as 'collapse of the monarchy' (14F) or 'fall of the empire' (15M). As in scholarly literature on this topic, the small successor First Republic of Austria was mostly evaluated negatively ('when suddenly such a tiny piece remained from the huge monarchy' (1F; cf. also *Klestil 27* in Chapter 4). 18F was one of the few to refer to the different political ideologies prevailing in the 1920s and 1930s, to 'Red Vienna' and the ideas and social concepts associated with it and to 'Austro-fascism'.

The choice of words in interviewees' statements about the (generally negatively evaluated) Nazi era is very interesting. Synecdochal paraphrases (*pars pro toto*) such as 'the time when Hitler invaded [Austria]' (4F), or evasive verbal denials, such as 'for a short time we had a dictatorship and so on but that – let's not talk about that right now' (5M), are typical. 12F talked about the antisemitic riots and persecution after 1938 in the following way: 'she [her Jewish neighbour] then had to leave too and passed away and her husband he'd died before her and she also died.' Here, 12F obscures the perpetrators by the euphemistic use of intransitive verbs ('had to leave', 'passed away', 'died'), employing a strategy of trivialisation and denial. Another interviewee described the Austrian Nazi past in a similarly trivialising way as 'a bad time for the Jews' (10F).

A term frequently chosen to describe the events of 1938 was *Anschluss* (19M, 1F). 1F thinks that Austria lost 'its own identity' in 1938, that it was from that time onwards 'suddenly simply – a puppet of Germany', and added: ' there certainly were – sections of the population who were unhappy about this – but there were many – on the other hand who – in contrast – were very happy about it and supported it' (1F). Another respondent viewed 1938 as:

the beginning of a worse dictatorship and of political and racist persecutions worse than ever before in Austria / that is politically they also existed before / but not racist ones I think.

(19M)

Several interviewees showed understanding for the 'war generation', often employing topoi such as 'external force' and 'external circumstances'. This period, they argued, has to be regarded from a contemporary perspective; it was a time of 'confusion', where people had no other option but to 'participate' in National Socialism in one form or other:

> Absolute economic insanity for the common people [...] no future no hope – no chance at [...] any kind of progress – no hope of finding a job, having a personal life / not even a glimmer of personal happiness – – and because of that / and all the opportunities – – for the extreme / for the search for the extreme and even to get everything straight and for something powerful which gives you the strength to climb up out of your own powerlessness.
>
> (3M)

The same interviewee also regarded the Nazi period as 'insanity – which you can't control [...] and against which you're absolutely helpless' (3M). Using the strategy of heteronomisation, he stated in trivialising manner that many people were 'simply tools', 'puppets'. 2M also showed understanding, though with somewhat more insight as to the intricacies of the situation, as he also addressed the racist Nazi ideology and politics:

> In all honesty I personally find it difficult [...] in such an economically difficult situation umm someone had to find a way to boost the economy only we couldn't just leave things the way they were but some wanted [...] to start a war and stuff like that – and all those other awful things [...] umm fringe groups and – to kill them in cold-blood and – – like stuff like race / all that race craziness they used to have.
>
> (2M)

10F, too, emphasised heteronomisation, yet she inexplicably made the SA (the *Sturmabteilung*, known in English as the Stormtroopers or Brownshirts) solely responsible for all forms of coercion: 'the people then had to do what the SA ordered them to do maybe not all [...] but many – couldn't do anything else or act differently'. 5M, a very young respondent, referred to the topoi of ignorance and non-justification in order to support his statement that subsequent generations are not entitled to form judgements about this period and that they'd better keep quiet about it:

> I always say – you should learn from the past – but – you shouldn't talk about it so much [...] it was a bit of a black era in Austria but / such a dark era – – / you just have to try to make sure that you've learned as much as possible from it / I mean the mistakes you should learn from them and – there you should leave it I think because it doesn't make any sense I think that we now – / generations later those people because of that I wasn't even there: I can / I / I only see what we – / what I have seen from photos and films OK? – a:nd I can't really debate about that era so that I could say that I – I really can't say anything it's / I mean I can talk about it but it umm but I can't judge if the people / if they did the right thing that there were no shots fired or not – I wasn't there – and that's why I find that our

generation says this too and hurls accusations – for generations, they weren't there / we / we / we're pretty well off we have food to eat – and whether I accuse someone of having shouted 'Heil Hitler!' or not – I can't say that – because I don't know if they were there or (if they had been there right?) – because no one knew how it would turn out right? why should I accuse others? – and it just makes more sense to leave it all whether someone was a Nazi or not – it's just important what he's doing now now that it's all over rather than if he was there. But if he was involved in anything bigger, like, I don't know / but they have all been – punished – but I'm really not all that interested in whether anyone in particular shouted 'Heil Hitler!' or not.

(5M)

The beginning of this passage is interspersed with several trivialising modifications; on the whole, the passage contains many fragmented sentences, which not only indicate individual difficulties in articulating statements ('a bit of'), but also hint at the tabooed and delicate nature of the topic. The impersonal 'you' is used fully four times in the first few lines, which may be due to the fact that the interviewee tended to avoid the topic of the Nazi era and the issue of guilt. After the rather impersonal beginning, he employed the topos of ignorance, of 'not having known anything', which also serves to avoid the subject of responsibility and guilt in a threefold way. Firstly, it refers to the speaker's absence and thus his ignorance ('I wasn't even there') to justify his apparent abstention from judgement. Secondly, it is used to form the group of 'our generation', making the speaker a member of this group by using the inclusive 'our', and moves on to deny this group of people born after the war (a group defined by age) the right to make accusations and judgements, because 'our generation was not there' and therefore cannot know what it was like at the time. That the postwar generations are not entitled to criticise is reinforced once more by the argument of current prosperity. Thirdly, 5M extends the topos of 'not-having-known-anything' to the war generation proper ('because no one knew how it would turn out'), and then moves on to repeat the already mentioned conclusion that it would make more sense 'to leave it'. He then reinforces his argument once again by saying that it is more important how former Nazis behave today. SM appears to find his demand 'to leave it' slightly too strong, for he immediately adds a trivialising and flippantly formulated condition of exception. However, he immediately relativises this exception by arguing that all culprits have already been punished anyway.

The year 1945, which marked the end of the Second World War and Austria's liberation from National Socialism, was hardly mentioned spontaneously. When questioned about it, respondents sometimes assessed it ambivalently:

The end of a very very long horror [...] and of course the continuation of this horror – wh / after – the destruction there's always a phase following the destruction which certainly wasn't pleasant [...] for instance there wasn't anything to eat.

(3M)

That the historical caesura of 1945 has largely been suppressed from the collective memory is reflected by the fact that many interviewees cannot associate anything with the anniversary year of 1995. Apparently, the largely marginal public celebrations commemorating the end of the war have made no lasting impression on Austrian consciousness. Asked about what precisely the celebrations were about, the interviewees provided answers such as 'ninety-five now what are they celebrating?' (4F) or 'what happened in 1995? [...] now you have to help me!' (14F). In the course of the interview, however, 14F remembered that it was the anniversary of the end of the Second World War which was being celebrated. 3M ('1995 was umm the end of the Second World War at least that's what I think right? or wasn't it?') and 2M ('Fifty years after the World War – now is there anything to celebrate?') were both uncertain about the occasion of the celebrations of the Republic in 1995, which is reflected in their use of hesitation particles ('umm'), interrogative forms, tags and modifying reporting verbs. 2M, however, admitted that working out one's past was triggered by anniversaries.

There are a few exceptions ('well nineteen ninety-five they certainly celebrated the wrong day – [...] the eighth of May / – umm the eighth of May that has been more or less: umm mentioned not at all really or only very rarely', said 9M, a member of an ethnic minority), but in most cases interviewees associated the following events with 1995, if they mentioned anything at all: Austrian neutrality ('right neutrality – fifty-five ninety-five forty years ((laughs)) one could celebrate that – umm what else – sorry I can't think of anything else', said 1F), the Austrian State Treaty ('1995 – – 1995 was / wasn't it fifty years of State Treaty wasn't this last year?' – 7F) or joining the EU. It is interesting to note how 1945 and 1955 are confused, for example in the following statement: 'sure the period immediately after the war. Right? well – signing the State Treaty which is well still in May 1945 isn't it? well – – that was certainly – very important wasn't it?' (13M). A member of the Slovenian minority associated 1995 with the festivities around the 75th anniversary of the Carinthian referendum, which she described in the following way:

> This year was exactly like the years before right? You can't say that w / that there was anything earth-shattering: that you can say that you'd absolutely have to celebrate yeah this year here in Carinthia they / umm – really celebrated October tenth the Carinthian referendum – and we had a great big crowd in Klagenfurt at the Neuer Platz and [...] that was a parade – you could say they marched – / around the whole city.
>
> (8F)

Similar to their counterparts in the focus groups, the individual interviewees attributed great importance to the immediate postwar period, in particular to the year 1955. This year was associated with the reconstruction of Austria ('now the period after the war [...] well for me – that's when Austria began to exist', said 15M) and with the (ultimate) restoration of Austrian sovereignty ('the State Treaty which so to speak again laid Austria's foundation stone', said 18F), and symbolised the postwar period, which was perceived by all interviewees as a successful period where:

simply lots of terrific things were done by the people and construction work was done from which we still profit today without which we wouldn't be so well off.

(17F)

This was also expressed by the glorification of the reconstruction generation ('well they reconstructed everything [...] although life was difficult which nobody can imagine today', said 8F) and by the glorification of Austrian 'political culture' at the time as a model for politicians of today:

The parties actually co-operated much more which is what would be really needed today because now we are again so – that they simply (XXX) / they've realized that they have to co-operate that they can't only think of their own party and that one has to put other things really – / that they / concentrate on the most important the main things; and I think that's what they did first and then – / then – it was lost again.

(14F)

The speeches of President Klestil, discussed in Chapter 4, also display a strategy of unification when talking about this topic.

Interviewees' views about which historical events and periods are considered significant coincide with the results found in the scholarly literature (cf. Bruckmüller 1996; Breuss et al. 1995; Plasser and Ulram 1991; Reiterer 1988a) as well as with the focus group data: the success story of the Second Republic with the mythicised date of 1955, which symbolises the State Treaty and the declaration of neutrality, is firmly anchored in the consciousness of the interviewees and was frequently used for the positive self-representation of Austria's past.

A surprisingly large number of interviewees (but not exclusively members of ethnic or religious minorities or members of the younger generation) remarked that the Austria of today must confront the Nazi period ('because it probably still – haunts [...] people's minds', said M3; it could again – spring up again right? [...] this problem should be talked about – much more [...] this is not so harmless', 8F). In this context, interviewees frequently pointed to the threat presented by the extreme right, for example, by referring to the right-wing populist politics of the FPÖ. Both members of the minorities and members of the majority directly connected FPÖ politics with National Socialist ideology. However, the overall condemnation of the cynical and racist National Socialist politics did not affect the interviewees' attitude towards the integration of foreigners or the issue of 'restitution', nor their inter- pretation of the Waldheim Affair. Thus, more penetrating questions posed to the interviewees revealed a variety of ambivalent attitudes and opinions. A few typical statements about the era of President Waldheim, whom many of the interviewees did not find a particularly likeable person (for example, 12F), and the Presidential election campaign of 1986, which all respondents remembered in detail, illustrate this attitude:

Well yeah / Sinowatz [...] dragged Austria through the mud. In the whole history of Austria I mean – what / what's all that about? The best man in / I mean the people decide – and the one who wins is the winner. And I don't have to go looking here and there to find out if he – umm – has hidden something away somewhere something you could make public to taint his image right? I wouldn't find that / wouldn't find that unfair. I mean I think it's blacken [...] he was actually – umm – he really had it hard in his era and he really tried – to really – deal – with it as well as possible right? They really made it hard for him I mean he couldn't even carry out his duties as federal president right – because he just couldn't right? Because they / they / hmm his own / his own people saw to it that he couldn't, didn't they?

(15M)

The commonplace of 'foreign and media interference' as well as the interpretation of the affair as primarily an intrigue incited by Waldheim's political opponents, which severely tarnished Austria's reputation, seemed to be firmly anchored in the collective view of recent Austrian history:

Yeah yeah. He was more on the Nazis' side, wasn't he? they really branded him they couldn't talk about anything else without debating that without fighting about that [...] well that's wasn't fair, was it? – wasn't fair [...] yeah and they talked about that thing with Waldheim too much, didn't they?

(12F)

Several interviewees, however, took a clearly critical position on Kurt Waldheim's way of dealing with his Nazi past ('I voted for him [...] that's still a problem for me [...] I think I didn't think enough about the whole thing at the time', said 2M) and, above all, criticised Waldheim for not telling the truth and trying to cover up his wartime activities:

for me personally – / umm what I didn't like was that in all the interviews with Waldheim himself (XXX) things weren't mentioned something was covered up because I think if you talk about it openly if you say that's how it was / don't forget there was a war and that's understood in this country and you have: to adapt to a certain degree somehow I can understand all that – but because of his strange / – to hide something something: I can't remember this I can't remember that umm that's what I didn't like – because in such a situation you think this is certainly somebody who has something to hide.

(1F)

Other interviewees described the situation in a similar way:[4]

and as to Waldheim what I didn't like – about him at all – was that – that he didn't say the truth and that's what I didn't like at all [...] and that he wasn't honest because – a person in such a position – where you can prove that he lied – that's really bad isn't it? – that / I thought much worse than the fact that he was one of them at that time right? yes I think that was much worse his telling lies.

(14F)

It is interesting to compare these statements to the 'outside perspective' of a German citizen, who thought that 'the majority of the Austrians who voted for Waldheim / voted against the international protest or international interference', out of a 'that's the way we are and we're not going to change' attitude 'which expressed that we didn't want other people to interfere with what we thought was right' (20M). The same interviewee asserted by means of the topos of non-justification that he did not intend to condemn the war generation, because he himself 'belong[ed] to the generation which came next' who are not entitled 'to give the thumbs down to people who were wavering weak or not courageous enough or simply just unconcerned and indifferent at that time', as he does not know 'how [he] would have behaved under the conditions at that time; whether [he] would have managed to be quick-witted, courageous, or clever enough or whether [he] would have been deluded by the Pied Piper' (20M). However, he demanded that somebody 'who was part of it and so to speak was not a member of the absolute minority of the resistance movement must openly admit this to subsequent generations.' In his view, Waldheim's 'crime' was 'to act as if nothing had happened as if he had lived in a sort of historical vacuum'. By doing this, Waldheim 'touched the nerve of those who had the same way of dealing with their youth who repressed it in exactly the same way.' The beginning of Austrian postwar history, he remarked critically, was:

> that a country which declared itself to be among the first victims [...] thereby confused the population and the institution of the state, because the state of Austria was in fact Hitler's first victim but the Austrian population was not the first victim / but they were standing at the Heldenplatz and couldn't get their right arms down that's how it is and nobody wants to admit it today or there're only few who do.
>
> (20M)

A note of pessimism is observable in the statements of 20M and 15M ('I think that within one or two generations this will have completely faded away; there'll be some sort of awareness but the majority will show no interest in this matter'), who argued against the topos of history teaching lessons, which was so frequently addressed in political speeches:

> Of course we have a problem with Haider. / And / and / and not just him but in general that one needs this / this leadership quality again not only in politics but in other areas right? And – also it signals to me / umm a kind fuss [...] that someone stands up and says 'Be careful remember what happened fifty years ago'. We haven't learned anything from history – we can look we can look back on the entire history of man – they just repeat their mistakes – and it'll be / probably when it / has to happen – it's probably going to have to happen again that some-one comes along and / and proclaims himself dictator; and – then we / then we definitely won't be able to stop it.
>
> (15M)

Discussing whether Austria is responsible for compensating the victims of National

Socialism, interviewees referred to the 'unmastered' past and its consequences, as well as to the complicity of many Austrians in the National Socialist regime. 18F referred to the exhibition on the Nazi war of extermination and the crimes of the *Wehrmacht* organised by the Hamburg Institute for Social Research, which in Austria was shown in Vienna, Innsbruck, Klagenfurt and Linz in 1995 and 1996 as well as in Graz in 1997:

> Most of all I believe that there are some things that haven't been dealt with yet [...] that they somehow [...] seem to be going on underground and I believe that fascism is definitely still alive and well and I just realised this because of this debate [...] because of the exhibition on the Wehrmacht during the Second World War. Yeah well in my opinion it just came rushing to the surface again like the / like you can say whatever you want but don't try to pin anything on the army; yeah that was really interesting for me how strong feelings were stirred up and how people got so upset over things I just took for granted. Of course the Wehrmacht has skeletons in its closet and some people just didn't want to know about it.
>
> (18F)

A non-Austrian interviewee referred critically to a programme on Austrian television on the construction of a memorial to the Austrian victims of Stalingrad:

> Everyone always said that the German army fought and lost and somehow Austrians were killed in the war as well / but the connection / to make the connection that someone says 'Not'; some Austrians really hated wearing the German uniform but others fought fanatically for Hitler / no / one ever really brought up that subject.
>
> (20M)

That an aid fund had been established for the victims of the Nazis was positively evaluated by the majority of interviewees. These results differed from those of the focus groups. For example 3M thought the discussion of compensation 'hypocritical', because this initiative was simply a public relations device motivated solely by political opportunism and concern about Austria's international reputation. 18F emphatically claimed that Austria was obliged to compensate victims at all events 'right in any case I think it's an absolute disgrace [...] that this wasn't done much much earlier and then I think that this is an example of all these / well that these fascist tendencies are still effective today' (18F). A – German – interviewee welcomed the attempts to confront openly Austria's Nazi past, which, he thought, was prompted by the debate about the aid fund for the victims of National Socialism:

> The term 'compensation' [*Wiedergutmachung*] / especially the way it has become so popular in Germany I think is completely inappropriate. the reasons they had for establishing these national funds is a late / a very, very late but I think not too late socio-political realization and admission of complicity and even if it's only – to use the fashionable word for it – peanuts. This admission and that was a huge step by Chancellor Vranitzky as I see it that he admitted in the fiftieth anniversary year of the Second Republic of Austria that it happened in Austria and we were

involved and not because we were forced, but that some of us were pretty enthusiastic about it. this / this step had a lasting cleansing effect on Austria [...] it can't be appreciated enough [...] Thomas Klestil expressed as well but very carefully in his address before the National Assembly for the fiftieth anniversary celebrations of the Republic of Austria.

(20M)

Several interviewees contended that although there was a moral obligation to 'compensate' – frequently accompanied by the remark that primarily hardship cases should be considered – this could not be effected by paying sums of money; in any case, they feel that this insight had come somewhat late:

When you can prove that there are some people – who today – for example – / elderly people who are all alone – because they lost their family their children and everything / everything in the war / in Austria because of the Nazis – and today – umm live in horrible / in horrible conditions then I think that Austria – it really is Austria's duty to help these people [...] besides I think it's a bit late – because after fifty years – who / umm how many are still alive – who really – umm like – suffered – like; and if they did suffer it was right after – the war – when times were really hard when people had to start from scratch and at that time it would have been appropriate but these days it's [...] certainly too late and somehow / you can't really compensate these people with money the only thing I say sometimes when there really are people who are still – suffering as a result of all that today – yes these people should be helped [...] I probably would have tried to do it differently – to do something positive in general – something political somehow something like – in any case not with money but maybe to show that we did make a mistake and we say / umm we are also – guilty – and we're trying to make matters right but that / nothing like that will come again – / like something like that won't happen again that's much more important I think [...] and that would be enough if we / if we talked about it openly and openly admitted to it by saying 'yes it wasn't right and – ' / so I have kind of / if someone lost – children – and family and everything and got those seventy thousand schillings I think that's insulting – because no one can give me my family back – no one can with seventy thousand schillings / not even with seventy million.

(1F)

The opinion (in many cases simply evasive) that financial payments were no 'compensation' and that it would be much more important to tackle political dangers, was expressed by 10F:

If you can / make up for anything with money? [...] I'd rather do it another way and [...] I'd really like to strangle Haider more than anything. [...] and I would fight against him and his followers. [...] And by this the / – victims certainly would profit more – or the families of the victims [...] because many are living in fear again.

(10F)

In a few instances, interviewees' beliefs mirrored the officially represented victim thesis, indicating that although what happened was regrettable, the current Austrian state could not be held accountable for the crimes of National Socialism and therefore must be absolved from paying 'compensation':

> But there's no need for them to – do such a thing / yeah. [...] because / then it'll be even more [...] if they set up such a thing for those people / right [...] well then perhaps we wouldn't be so well off [...] then we wouldn't be so well off.
>
> (12F)

It is worth noting that in the interviews – just as in the focus groups in Chapter 5 – the groups of victims were hardly ever referred to as 'Jews' or 'Roma and Sinti', but rather primarily by vague formulations such as 'the victims' or 'those people'.

On the basis of the data we examined, we can say that none of the interviewees supported the 'strong' victim thesis, according to which Austria was a victim of Nazi aggression and that National Socialism was imposed on Austria. This may suggest that the discussions conducted over the last decade have affected the subjective feelings and attitudes of Austrians. Virtually all interviewees argued in favour of an open confrontation with the past and regarded it as important for the political culture of the country. However, the interviewees scarcely ever indicated that they saw any connection to current and everyday racism and exclusionary practices. The topos of 'history teaching lessons', frequent in political speeches, seems to be of no relevance in the individual-private discourse of national identity.

1F, who had immigrated to Austria, expressed the fear that there were Austrians who had not learned their lesson from the experience of National Socialism and pointed out that her opinion on this issue had changed over the last years, becoming progressively more negative:

> I think umm that especially World War II and the time before that are actually in my eyes / well it seems that it's repeating itself somehow like this shift to the right and nation umm / this nationalistic movement and I think it's really important [...] because you – [...] hear politicians talk – then – I get the feeling that some would – like to forget it – or that people would just rather look back on those times positively just that it was bad luck that it ended so bad and didn't turn out different – – like I think the danger is there – – and there's this older generation and these right-wing associations and the way people talk at their local – so it hasn't been forgotten entirely [...] I lived for years / back then I thought that the past was over – there's a new generation now and a new Austrian people and umm – democratic and I only saw that as being positive – but now that everything is coming out of the woodwork – then I think up to now I thought it was all rosy because those who tend to think like Nazis – because they just were – in / in the background they just didn't publicly – give their opinion but they / they always – umm were always thinking that way / believed in it – and unfortunately today I think it has become an issue [...] I would definitely tie it to Haider because

somehow he – umm – encouraged them – to express their opinion and that's – umm – to dig up the past like that.

(1F)

6.2.1.3 The Construction of a Common Political Present and Future: Austrian Neutrality and the European Union

Interviewees frequently addressed current and potentially problematic issues which have emerged in the wake of recent geopolitical changes. In particular, those text passages which refer to the issues of Austrian neutrality and Austria's EU membership offer evidence of subjective private perceptions that a change in Austrian identity is underway. 'A small – / politically completely insignificant central European state with nothing particularly striking about it in comparison to its neighbours' was 3M's idea of an idyllic Austria, which still exists today but which had, according to this interviewee, been affected by far-reaching transformations in connection with the dissolution of the Eastern Bloc:

> There're a lot a lot of consequences so many consequences that you can't list all of them this evening [...] there are consequences on economics on the employment market there are of course consequences because it affects any major area [...] it was so to speak the – – / Cold War was of course very cushy for Austria [...] this special status [...] and now of course that's gone.
>
> (3M)

Similarly, 19M referred to the privileged status Austria enjoyed for a long time, primarily in the years of the Cold War, due to its geographical position in Europe. Quite remarkably, not only did he evoke simultaneously both the traditional image of Austria as a bastion against the East and that of Austria as a bridge between East and West, but also the image of Austria as an 'island of the blessed', a small peaceful country in the heart of Europe. These stereotypical reminiscences from the collective memory are discernible in the following passage, which is representative of similar statements in other interviews:

> Well in my opinion, Austria as the most easterly of the western countries even though it was neutral it was always very spoilt economically – politically and so on; all around it were / well east of Austria was the Iron Curtain – that was like an outpost kind of to the East somehow you know? And for sure they put a lot of money into it and / and well for Austria there were some companies / there were / a lot of companies had their eastern representatives in Austria just because it was good to do business with the East from there. But that's all over now right? I mean this special role this being spoilt a bit well I think Austria was actually very spoilt by the West. Austrians were always supposed to be so nice cheerful umm hard-working communicative friendly people right? [...] That special status it's gone now and the Austrians have to redefine themselves 'so what are we now here in Europe?' Or there's no Iron Curtain any more.
>
> (19M)

Most interviewees thought that in the wake of the geopolitical changes since 1989 Austria had lost its special status as mediator between East and West. In this view, Austria was now unequivocally part of the West, and it had to commit itself to western Europe 'to show its colours [...] say where you belong' as 18F put it:

> Well I think that Austria is part of the West now and it wasn't before well of course it really was but not so close to the West. Well now with the EU / with EU membership with the Iron Curtain down it's just / well somehow before the Iron Curtain came down and with Yugoslavia open / Austria was kind of a mediator / for me it isn't anymore / umm now it's just / the border runs along the Czech Republic and Slovakia and Hungary and so on that's sort of like the European border and I'm very aware of that; so really we're a Western state and the others are the Balkans.
>
> (18F)

Most interviewees perceived the political, economic and social changes in Austria following its joining the EU as unavoidable. None of the interviewees was enthusiastic about Austria's EU membership. There were a few pronounced EU sceptics; most frequent, however, was an attitude of critical approval of EU membership. Interviewees did not worry about membership having any fundamental effects on Austrian identity, which may be explained by the fact that they defined it primarily through 'cultural' terms:

> Well if you're part of a community of nations then you can't be different you must be like the others I think [...] but that Austria is still Austria that's no question for me.
>
> (1F)

The equality which is referred to in the first part of the quotation refers to joint supranational political decision-making, which, however, does not affect the continuity – understood in the cultural sense – emphasised in the second part of the statement.

Asked about the possible outcome of a referendum on membership, if it were to be repeated, almost all of the interviewees tended to predict a negative result. One believed that 'there wouldn't be so many in favour of it now I think' (12F), while another was convinced that there would be 'not as many' votes in favour in a second referendum (8F); at most, a third argued, Austrians would be 'in favour by a small majority' (2M). Most respondents did, however, claim that they personally not would vote differently in a second referendum: 'what I hear is that people are rather against [...] not that I am against it that's what I hear' (10F). This general assessment of the outcome of a second referendum probably reflects Austrian media discourse on the EU issue. At the same time, interviewees argued that the Austrian government's exaggerated pro-EU propaganda preceding the 1994 referendum had given rise to the ostensible disappointment which Austrians felt because the government had not kept the promises it had made about the benefits to consumers of EU membership:

Most Austrians are watching to see if there's a direct change economically / an improvement you know? If we get more for our money in the shops / if cars get cheaper / that's what most Austrians are interested in and that hasn't happened, right? Well except for flour and cream and all that right? / But that's what would've been important to most people and because it didn't happen the majority are against it.

(19M)

Furthermore, the sceptical attitude of the Austrian population towards the EU was explained by the effects of the austerity budget due to the Maastricht Treaty, which respondents believed was a consequence of EU membership: 'I think its outcome would be no and I think that's because of the austerity budget' (18F).

Several interviewees welcomed the fact that membership in the EU forced the Austrians to 'look across their fence' (19M) and show self-confidence and initiative; that, in other words, the threat of outside forces determining their fate would motivate them to develop more autonomy and self-reliance:

That we go and stand up for what we want in Brussels or especially in front of the mighty Mr Kohl or the mighty Mr Chirac and push through our own / our own interests / try to push them through and altogether it couldn't hurt the Austrians to become a little more self-reliant and learn something new right?

(19M)

'Our self-understanding is becoming more European which is a good thing,' says 2M. Sometimes interviewees also argued that sooner or later Austria would have joined the EU anyway, therefore it was better that Austria was accepted before other (East European) candidates.

I thought to myself 'okay. Rather better than – / than no:t.' [...] and after there had been and / that is of the East / of the countries of the former eastern block there were also candidates I think more or less I [...] its definitely better now than / than – / than later; simply because of the conditions which you can negotiate.

(11M)

Finally, we would like to quote one of the few statements sceptical of the EU which ran counter to the general tendency of the interviews and which provided economic and ideological reasons to explain this scepticism. In this excerpt, 3M refers to the train metaphor, which had been frequently used by politicians and the media in this context, and to the topos of the 'train which has already left the station', both of which suggest that the essential decisions have already been taken and are irreversible:

I think the situation is absolutely clear – the way things are today, the train is travelling towards Europe / to some kind of dubious supranational – state that – has an army [...] well I consider it absolutely undesirable – [...] imperialist powers are always a dubious thing – I myself wouldn't aim to live in one / in a major power that has to fight other major powers for resources and access to oil and markets, but of course you can't stop it now [...] this whole currency business and the EU is, umm [...] an economic concept that only works at the expense of the have-nots – and [...] some free European markets are only geared to snatching money away from the have-nots and filling the pockets of the capitalists.

(3M)

On the whole, our analysis of the interviews suggests that individual interviewees exhibited an attitude which was more favourable towards the EU than that of focus group members analysed in Chapter 5 (neither the problems of transit nor the ecological problems were mentioned in the individual interviews), although at the time of the interviews public political discourse and discourse in the media had becoming increasingly critical, and not infrequently reported the generally more critical attitude of the Austrian population. The processes which were evaluated rather critically by the interviewees – for example, increasing migration – were apparently interpreted as a result of the general geopolitical transformations due to the dissolution of the power of the major blocs and the war in ex-Yugoslavia, rather than as a result of European integration, which was primarily perceived in terms of its economic and socio-political effects.

Since nearly all interviewees linked the 'European issue' and Austria's membership in the EU to Austrian neutrality, we have looked at the way in which interviewees dealt with security policy, in particular the arguments they offered for and against it.

The interviewees can be divided into two groups on the basis of their personal opinions on the significance of Austrian neutrality, and on their degree of identification with this pillar of Austrian self-perception. Some respondents emphasised the importance and meaningfulness of neutrality for contemporary Austria in the context of its transformed political environment: 'The whole development up to / up to fifty-five and then neutrality is for me – something which / which is very important [...] because [neutrality] has liberated Austria' (10F). These respondents personally identified with neutrality and regretted the discussion about whether or not to renounce neutrality, to which they assign a certain protective function for Austria:

Well I have to say: for me neutrality was always important well of course not so much when I was a child because as a child you don't understand so well what it all means but from the age when you really know what neutrality means it was always important to me [...] I'm talking about our country I mean that we as a country are neutral and as I said for instance don't have to get involved in any wars; / and that protects my own life too [...] I think neutrality is always important [...] I think that staying neutral will [...] I would keep it [...] and I think that if war really broke out Austria couldn't defend itself with the army that we have maybe hold out for a couple of days but for sure not defend itself in a real emergency because we just don't have the wherewithal / all the weapons and tanks and aircraft and so on / I mean we're just way behind / that's why I believe neutrality is important / because I believe a small country just can't defend itself in the long run.

(17F)

19M argued along similar lines:

Well I think that a military neutrality and umm / we should have a small army because I just don't think defending the country should be left up to the police it should be kept separate right? But the army should stay more or less a / a small body because we couldn't win anyway and we can't defend ourselves anyway if anybody attacks right? It's practically just something to prove that we're prepared to defend our / our / our political system I think that'd be good but not more. Not armaments in a big way, no buying rockets, that's all / all just a big show.

(19M)

The line of argument employed by these two respondents clearly contains absurd arguments if looked at from the perspective of *Realpolitik*: for example, 17F's contention that neutrality was important because 'we' would not manage to defend ourselves for long.

The second group of interviewees claimed that Austrian neutrality may have been meaningful in the period after the war, but that now this was no longer the case:

Because I think that was signed by the Americans and the Russians at one time and therefore Austria had this very special position / I really think that this was important.

(18F)

Today neutrality seemed to be a 'remnant [...] of being somehow out of touch' which in the past meant that Austria did not 'not have to get involved in any of the / these dubious colonial wars like – in Iraq or so' (M3). M2 spoke of what had been taught at school about the importance of neutrality:

Yes it did have a huge importance [...] – because it came up everywhere and [...] they always talked about it in such an important manner as if this were some something really vital for the Austrian existence.

(M2)

However, he relativised the current importance of neutrality: 'It's really an important instrument I'd say – or was at one time [...] and I think it's getting weaker all the time'. 18F contended that in actual fact Austrian neutrality had been renounced a long time ago because 'those planes which fly over Austria to unknown destinations well this has happened already anyway.' She did, moreover, think there were currently more important issues in Austria because:

at the moment that's certainly more important this EU thing / which is only about that the richer countries forming a front against the poorer ones / and in this neutrality is not at all important.

(18F)

Previously she had viewed neutrality as 'one of those symbols of the mediating position [...] between East and West', but:

When the Iron Curtain came down – when we joined the EU then it [...] just lost meaning well then I let myself start thinking it over and not just keep carrying it around like some kind of icon and being proud of it.

(18F)

Another interviewee also addressed the emotional attachment one has to Austrian neutrality as an issue separate from the actual substantive content of neutrality itself. In doing so she also pointed to the ambivalence of political discourse on Austrian neutrality:

Politically I don't think it'll be possible [...] I think the Austrians [...] because they aren't so sure of themselves [...] will let the other countries get the better of them you know? [...] But in my opinion it's important and I think it ought to be possible [...] to just say 'politically and economically we belong to this Union to this European Union but not militarily' [...] I mean military neutrality that would be important not to get mixed up in any military conflicts and not to have any / any Austrian soldiers getting sent anywhere [...] I mean not a single Austrian soldier should have to march around anywhere in any foreign country you know? You can't be politically neutral anyway right? You can't keep out of what's happening in the world right? [...] And neutrality it's a kind of a sacred cow for the Austrians too right? Even though most of them don't even know what it is? Just like / 'Austrian State Treaty' and 'neutrality' they're just words, right?

(19M)

It can be assumed (and is also observable in the focus group data analysed in Chapter 5) that the issue of neutrality is undergoing a significant change in Austrian consciousness, and that the status of neutrality as the icon of Austrian identity will in future hardly be maintained in its current form. Although there are views such as that expressed by 8F, a very young woman, namely that 'actually I don't think about it much [...] but I think – – it will definitely stay neutral for a time', most respondents, even proponents of neutrality, predicted that it would have to be renounced sooner or later. 20M, who is not an Austrian citizen, summed it up in the following way: 'Now it's time for [Austria] to step out of this self-defined neutrality [...]'.

Finally, we can say that a number of strategies employed by politicians in respect to neutrality seem to have shown considerable effect in this semi-private setting. In particular, the discursive strategy of transformation, primarily emphasising the difference in political significance between the past and the present, and, to a lesser degree, the deconstructing strategy of heteronomisation, which tried to expose neutrality as the price Austria was forced to pay in the past, were the most prominent.

6.2.2 The Discursive Construction of Difference

6.2.2.1 Subnational Differences

The discourse of difference primarily emphasises differences between western and eastern Austrian provinces (as in 11M's statement, 'I'm quite sure that there's such a thing as this famous east-west divide or whatever [...] you call it / I think it exists'). Regional differences, 'distinctive regional features' (16M) between eastern and western Austria were taken for granted by almost all the interviewees and were interpreted as differences either in mentality ('a Tyrolean – now is different [..] I feel [...] that there's a connection to the area where you grow up', said 2M), in socio-political arenas (18F), in modes of behaviour, in everyday life, or in traditions:

> The peo:ple in the East / eastern provinces definitely have another mentality than those in the West because they are sort of more oriented towards Germany and Switzerland – and / and the eastern ones sort of more towards Hungary and Slovenia and / and a Czech and so right? Well I really think that there's – a difference between east and west.
>
> (4F)

Some interviewees from the eastern part of Austria believed that residents of western provinces 'tend rather to feel closer to Switzerland and Germany' (18F). Western Austrians rejected this idea, however (14F, 15M). 12F, who is Viennese, remarked that she found it easier to talk to people from Burgenland, the Waldviertel or Carinthia, since they are much friendlier than the Viennese. 'In the Tyrol now well people are really – very friendly you can say right?', said 8F, a Carinthian. Some interviewees, primarily those who are residents of Vienna, assumed that the residents of the more conservative western provinces 'look with suspicion' at 'Red Vienna' (18F), or, at least, are ambivalent about it:

> On the one hand it's a kind of admiration for the big city [...] on the other it's something like / well the Viennese always think they're something better.
>
> (18F)

16M claimed that:

> People from the western provinces see Vienna as being puffed up with its own importance and there's a certain amount of resentment. You hear 'oh, those Viennese' all the time, you know?
>
> (16F)

Several interviewees (4F, 9M, 13M and 16M) spoke explicitly or implicitly of their love for their home province. The synecdochal identification of Austria with Vienna (*pars pro toto*), well known from the Austrian scholarly literature as well as from tourist advertising campaigns, was emphatically endorsed by 19M, who equated Austria primarily with its eastern part, which he defined as culturally 'central European':

> Well for me Austria is actually eastern Austria around Vienna you know? Well for me that's Austria [...] Vienna and its surroundings and its history [...] for me what's typically Austrian is what you find in eastern Austria the culture the old culture centred in Vienna is Austria for me. That's what makes Austria different from other countries, right? I mean western Austria is well Tyrol and the moun-

tains and all the rest of it in my opinion it could just as easily be in Switzerland or in Bavaria or in / in / in any other Alpine area. I haven't had much to do with it up to now / I mean I've been there a few times but it's just / my Austria is well in and around Vienna / the west doesn't really interest me. And so I'd much rather / I feel more attracted to Budapest and Prague somehow than to Munich or Innsbruck or Zurich or places like that; that's what I meant when I said Austria for me is more / more eastern Austria.

(19M)

Although this passage contains a number of personalised and therefore slightly qualified ('for me', 'I mean') phrases, it nevertheless conveys an extremely rigid, unidimensional, antipluralistic and non-heterogeneous conception of Austria, which transforms eastern Austria or Vienna into a synecdochal *differentia specifica* in order to justify Austria's uniqueness. In this view, Austria can be distinguished from other countries only because of the existence of eastern Austria and Vienna. Discussing western Austria and its neighbouring regions, this respondent employed a dissimilation, which specifically disparages the idea of a politically unified Austria or *unio Austriaca*. In so doing 19M contradicts the view, widely promoted by Austrian politicians, of Austria being 'unity in diversity'. The emphasis on similarities between the west of Austria and Bavaria or Switzerland, which 19M set against the closeness of eastern Austria and Vienna to Budapest and Prague, should be understood as component of a discursive construction of subnational difference, including the specific individual possessive appropriation of Austria ('my Austria is well in and around Vienna') and the (explicitly dissociating) declaration of indifference vis-à-vis western Austria.

Members of ethnic groups and members of ethnic, linguistic or religious minorities were very much aware of their distinctive situation, of which, however, members of the majority group apparently take little or no notice:

I don't think I'm really all that different from my friends my Austrian friends – like I don't see any difference between us – aside from the language of course how well I can speak German – but on the other hand somehow – umm where I come from we have a different tradition and / but maybe it doesn't have anything to do with the idea of nation, so to speak, but with reli / with religion – with the Jewish faith because I have my holidays and my tradition and I always will.

(1F)

One interviewee played ironically with the stereotypical construct of the 'typical Austrian' promoted by the tourism industry (which, by the way, contradicts the clichéd image of a multicultural Austrian origin) and stated that because of her family roots she would not qualify for membership in this category:

No, I wouldn't say that I was a typical Austrian [...] because actually my extraction is / the fact is a lot of my family connections aren't very well-tolerated or appreciated here. Neither the Jewish side nor the Slavic and because of that I would say I'm not what anybody would call typically Austrian / what an Austrian would consider a typical Austrian woman [...] or what somehow is stereotyped as typical and then you picture some woman in a dirndl or something ((laughs)) now that was very / really very spiteful / but anyway more rural.

(18F)

Some members of ethnic groups told of specific discriminatory acts which had been directed against them, in particular because of their physical appearance ('because of my dark skin colour' – 16M). Another interviewee summed up his experiences laconically: 'as: a member of the Slovenian – community – you do experience: disadvantages now and then' (9M). 8F, also a member of an ethnic group, remarked that her identity was not anchored in her home province:

I'm – a bit – sad about how the Slovenians in Carinthia are treated how they – sometimes get ridiculed and then I feel I'm not a real Carinthian I'm Austrian and say so too – and even if somebody says 'well but you're really / you're Slovenian / you didn't belong to Austria / and you belonged to Carinthia and if so-and-so had happened then you would belong to Slovenia' I always say I'm Austrian, aren't I? [...] because I was – / I was born here – umm – even though I / I speak two languages but that doesn't make me a foreigner [...] I mean I can't find anything – untypical about me that would make me – not an Austrian.

(8F)

Commenting on the Carinthian referendum of 1920 she stated 'that [...] the majority – voted in favour of it – [...] therefore the Carinthians / the German Carinthians must be glad right?'
Basically, however, she thought that:

much too little – has been done – umm about integration with the Austrians / integrating the German Austrians and the minorities I mean – umm and I think that – minorities like us Carinthian Slovenians for example – umm speak up much too m / much too little – so that people will notice us like when I think of the / Roma – they're much more self-confident.

(8F)

What is most noticeable about these statements is the way the speaker linguistically constructed the groups of 'Austrians', 'German Austrians', 'Austrian minorities', 'immigrant Austrians', 'genuine Carinthians' and 'Carinthian Slovenes'. Although at one point she emphatically defined herself as Austrian, but simultaneously as a 'non-genuine Carinthian', in other passages she exhibited the same linguistic exclusion frequently constructed by German-speaking (Carinthian) Austrians. Although she corrected herself and turned 'the Austrians' into 'German Austrians', she went on to distinguish once again between those Austrians, 'Austrians – who have umm always been here' and the minorities of 'immigrant Austrians'. It did not seem to occur to her that this labelling of autochthonous Austrian minorities as immigrant Austrians is incorrect.

6.2.2.2 Inter-national Differences

6.2.2.2.1 Differences Among Nations Within a Single State

Most interviewees rejected any (culturally) racist distinctions explicitly: 'As to the individual person – it doesn't matter whether he is black yellow red or white. Therefore I think anybody can become Austrian' (19M). However, in this discourse of difference between Austrians and foreign nationals resident in Austria we found statements ranging from implicit to openly expressed racist prejudices against foreigners, to the view that Austrians were not able to walk in the street anymore, as they felt 'surrounded' by foreigners there:

> Now I don't like going shopping there [to the *Naschmarkt*, an outdoor market in Vienna] 'cause now there's only foreigners there anyway and it's all so disgusting [...] now it's / now there's hardly any Austrians anymore. Now when you walk down the street all you hear are foreigners /only foreigners [...] now I don't like / I used to like Mariahilferstrasse [a popular shopping street in Vienna] – I'm glad if I don't have to go there. [...] I mean even / even / no matter where you are, in one store or the other, everywhere you've got all these foreigners and you hardly hear an Austrian word spoken anymore.
>
> (12F)

In most cases, these stereotypes referred to (everyday) cultural modes of behaviour attributed to an alleged 'foreign' mentality which was contrasted negatively to that of the 'Austrians'; for example when 12F referred to an unspecified general 'they-group' of foreigners whose 'whole behaviour and / this fuss they're making / when they're speaking or eating or / somehow it's obvious that they are not Austrians' (12F). Linguistic and phenotypical features were also mentioned, as in 8F's comment:

> Well only because of the language / because of the skin colour – and otherwise I think / I think even if somebody from another nation – was born in Austria, that he was born here and that he – speaks the language and that he also speaks the dialect well then you can't notice anything – anything else – except if he really has another skin / skin colour or – I don't know the way he acts you can't tell either only by the skin colour – that he's not really / exactly an Austrian but I think if you just / if you just look well then you think to yourself 'aha, he's from somewhere else' but when you hear him talk / then you can tell – he's an Austrian – so then there's no difference.
>
> (8F)

In discourses of difference on Islamic culture, the status of women who are perceived as having no rights and being inferior ('women have nothing to say', 4F) was used as an argument several times – only, however, by women interviewees:

> even though I can't accept it for instance, or that the Turkish women wear headscarves here, either, that's / it's maybe prejudiced but I can't accept it – because I

think – I don't know I mean maybe it's wrong ... Because they / they have to because of their mentality.

(7F)

Although the speaker modified her statement by inserting the phrase 'I don't know I mean maybe it's wrong', she constructed a culturally racist causal relation by means of deontic modal modification. 8F took up pat phrases from media discourse about the book and film *Not Without My Daughter* in order to corroborate her view of problems raised by culturally or religiously mixed partnerships:

Well I think – umm – I think some – problems are / are very much to the point for instance when I think of women that – that are married to Turks or someone and then it's not until later that they – umm – start to realise the problems – I think it's in one way it depends on the woman she should – get to know the man much longer before she well commits herself – umm – the culture too – get to know much better what's different in the culture – different from the Austrian culture and so on – and I think then / then she should think carefully about how things will be you know? Because if she just ties herself down after one year – and then – when it really comes down to it so to speak for instance if all of a sudden the man takes off with the children – kidnaps them – and then the woman finds out – how things are – well then for sure it's too late – and you can't do much then – I think the / the whole problem is for sure every country has different cultures – different customs – and – people need to think about that much more – getting along with each other too / like for instance – if I'm a Catholic and he's a – a Muslim or – whatever – well that's bound to cause – big problems.

(8F)

Fears that national conflicts or even wars (as, for example, in ex-Yugoslavia) could be imported to Austria were also expressed:

I don't think it's right – although I don't have anything against Turks – that some people keep their / their whole mentality and their whole thing here with us – in their own / well I have to say I don't think it's right now / here there's these groups already / that I think / in my opinion – there's – these Turks and they think everyone has to have his rights – and I mean someday – I think – that this can lead to / to some kind of / can lead to something whether it's – like now down in Yugoslavia I really think it's because / sooner or later they'll demand their rights which of course / I feel sorry for the foreigners but somewhere there has to be a limit.

(7F)

This passage not only contains numerous fragmented sentences due to the sensitive nature of the transported content, but is in itself contradictory. Although initially the speaker used a disguised 'yes, but' figure, whose adversative part is emphasised by the assertive 'well I have to say', the normative postulate that 'everyone has to have his rights' raised by the speaker herself was rendered absurd by presenting the fulfilment of these rights in a negative way, that is by conjuring up a war scenario as its consequence.

The underlying tenor in all the interviews is that foreigners living in Austria must adapt to the cultural codes and behaviour common in Austria. According to 10F, who immigrated to Austria as an adult, immigrants were not perceived as Austrians:

> If they ((draws breath)) keep their own culture – and / and don't adapt / then rather not [...] although you should preserve your own culture – but – rather more like [...] adapt.
>
> (10F)

3M pointed out the importance of language as an identity-constituting criterion and emphasises the advantage of a *lingua franca* as a language 'which the majority understands'. 'I don't think everybody should only speak this one language of course not', 1F stated, 'but I think there must be a common language in a country'. The majority of interviewees, particularly those who had immigrated to Austria, thought that foreigners living in Austria should at least be reasonably competent in the German language. 'Well I do think if you live in a country – umm – you have to be able to speak the language I think that's important' (1F). 8F saw an advantage for 'the foreigner' because 'then he can integrate into the society – by being able to communicate with others'. Of course, 1F argued, how important it was for an individual immigrant to speak fluent German depended on 'the foreigner's way of life, his level of education', and continued:

> Because if you're only sitting at home – umm – and going shopping to the grocery shop too / you won't improve your language abilities, but if you lead – your life on a higher level, then you will need – to improve your language skills. But someone like that would be unhappy at being left out of – / theatre and the media, newspapers, magazines, someone like that would be very unhappy [...] I wouldn't require someone who per / to speak perfect German but at least to be able to make himself understood [...] he would have to be able to speak German at a minimal level.
>
> (1F)

In the view of 8F:

> At least you – should be able to talk to others [...] in German so that you can say – I am Austrian', because if you go somewhere and say umm 'I'm Austrian' and you speak English or / or Italian [...] then they stare at you open-mouthed – because you associate with – with the concept Austrian yeah the German language you know? – – among other things.
>
> (8F)

10F formulated this argument even more emphatically: 'I can't see why [...] you shouldn't learn German [...] if you decide to live here [...] I think in all areas of life it's absolutely necessary'. 18F, who first claimed that speaking the German language was not a precondition for being Austrian, at a later point in her interview stated:

Well I believe that in any case it helps if you speak the language of the country you live in and I also believe that it's necessary [...] and I think they should give everyone the opportunity to take a language course, I mean everybody who comes to Austria, they should be able to take a language course and it shouldn't cost anything. It should be offered as a service, so to speak [...] and in my opinion it's crazy to live in a country and not be able to / well to live in a country for 20 years and not speak the language, that seems somehow so absurd to me, you know? And I think it's necessary to know the language. I'm not saying it has to be perfect or anything but you have to be able to make yourself understood and also to under-stand what's / what's going on in the country.

(8F)

The suggestion that persons who want to live and work in Austria or want to acquire Austrian citizenship should attend a compulsory language course was welcomed by several interviewees, also by members of ethnic groups and by immigrant Austrians who had grown up speaking a different language. One interviewee, a Slovenian Carinthian, thought:

It would really – make sense because otherwise anybody can come and [...] yeah, it wouldn't be so bad at all – if at least you had to take a course and then a test – and then show a certificate – I think that wouldn't be so bad – although I don't – although I'm not – you know – racist or anything that I wouldn't give anybody else / give them citizenship but – it wouldn't be so bad.

(8F)

The following view was rather the exception:

Apart from the fact that most Austrians can't speak German properly why should somebody who speaks even less German suddenly if he wants to become Austrian suddenly has to speak perfect German.

(19M)

Several interviewees regarded immigration to Austria as problematical and were sceptical of or even hostile to immigration, for example, when they demanded that Austrian citizenship not be handed out irresponsibly:

Well when somebody comes from somewhere else and gets Austrian citizenship right away then / well I don't think so much of that you know? – I mean – I don't have anything against the athletes that get it right off although – it kind of makes you think doesn't it? Some guy just has to shove a ball around a little and / and be a good athlete and he gets citizenship right away – and I think that's unfair – something should be done – they should take other criteria into consideration: where he comes from and – because there's always so much talk about 'that person is a threat to Austria' when for instance a decent Turk or somebody comes into the country. Yeah and – – / and 'the other culture comes in and you'll see in a few years – the country'll be crawling with Turks and they – / they'll try to take over' and all the rest of it – well I don't know. – When really he's just decent and so on

– he's sometimes – less dangerous – than an athlete who comes from who knows where.

(8F)

12F thought that 'all those who are now / foreigners in this country they want to become Austrians. Right? [...] because at home things aren't going well for them'. 18F demonstrated understanding for prospective immigrants and asylum seekers, particularly for those coming from 'countries where the situation is totally chaotic [...] now if I were from Nigeria I'd certainly rather be Austrian' (18F).

A small group of interviewees worried that Austria might increase immigration control and restrict its asylum laws in the future:

> I think, too, the worse the economic situation is, the worse such things get as far as trying to force people of other nationalities out of the country and then I think it also makes a difference which country they come from. I'm sure somebody who comes from Germany has much fewer problems here than somebody from Uganda [...] for people who come from southern countries or from Asia or Africa I think it's almost impossible [...] for them to get a work permit here [...] because somebody would have to have really good professional training for any / for a company to decide it needs that man or woman and that sort of eliminates certain countries [...] well I / this restrictive immigration policy really gets on my nerves I must say and I would think / well in any case I would open it up and let more people come in ... it really puts me off how few refugees they took in from the people who came from Bosnia, I thought it was just awful, and a neighbouring country too.

(18F)

The fears about the restrictive nature of Austrian immigration policy referred to in the above statement were corroborated by a passage from an official notification of rejection issued by the immigration authorities in Vienna, which contained culturally racist arguments such as the following:

> Due to the fact that, even after years of residence in this country, the daily life of persons coming as adults from the same cultural area as the applicant [the reference here is to Turkey] evince scarcely any signs of integration with regard to language, communication with the established inhabitants, or adaptation to central European mores, customs, and lifestyle, a preferential treatment of the candidate's application, from which no circumstances which might facilitate integration could be inferred, would only further impede the exhaustive efforts being made to integrate foreign citizens living in Austria. Therefore no grounds for preferential treatment could be found.
>
> (Administrative decision by the Resident Permits Department
> of the Vienna Provincial Government, March 1996)

6.2.2.2.2 Differences between Nations (Defined by the State Borders)

Most of the interviewees assumed the existence of differences between nationalities or national cultures. In their view, these differences may manifest themselves in language, mentality, the culture of everyday life, or even (though this was the exception) in phenotypical features:

> Well first of course language [...] then – – well probably the / the skin colour that is primarily white or black or whatever. – – Then of course mental differences [...] that is the men / mentality.
>
> (11M)

3M assumed that:

> People in Bangladesh – [...] probably have a completely different umm – behaviour [...] that is a cultural umm social behaviour not (XXX) biological behaviour the biological behaviour of course is – umm is inherent in the way people are and pervades everything.
>
> (3M)

18F claimed 'that a certain social organisation continues to have an effect over the years', as does a particular school system or 'the special ways you become something and do things'.

In these interviews, and the focus groups analysed in Chapter 5, the discourse of difference between Austria and other countries or between Austrians and residents of other countries centred on the relationship between Austria and Germany. Alongside this discourse, the interviewees employed discourses of difference which distinguished Austria from southeastern European nations, using a criterion of the level of social and economic development. In contrast to the relatively inferior situation of southeastern European countries' Austria's own relative affluence could be portrayed all the more favourably. In a typical example of this discourse, 18F stated slightly ironically:

> Well for example if you take Yugoslavia / this war is somehow such a / such a / that makes me aware of the differentiation I think how / that the Slavs bash each others' heads and they're crazy right. Well this civil war doesn't bother us really because we are Europeans.
>
> (18F)

When discussing Islamic culture, it was primarily female interviewees who demarcated themselves with regard to gender relations and to the discrimination of women. With very few exceptions, this was the only case where interviewees considered the gender aspects of social issues and where the selection of topics correlated with the sex of the interviewee. However, the (female) interviewees tended to ethnicise (cf. Jäger 1996) the particularities of Islamic cultures in a rather sweeping manner.

The presumed need of Austrians to differentiate themselves from Germany and 'the Germans', in terms of language was frequently connected to experiences they had had abroad. This generally related to the interviewees' having occasionally been mistaken for German citizens, who are believed to be less popular than Austrians in other countries either because of their mentality ('much too self-confident', according to 10F), or because of the association made between Germans and National Socialism:

> Well partly / partly the Germans have a bad reputation abroad [...] that they've a lot of money and are really so arrogant and on top of it the Nazi past.
>
> (18F)

17F mentioned experiences of this sort she had had as a tourist, and referred specifically to the different reputations Austria and Germany enjoy respectively in connection with their Nazi past:

> Yes I'm usually aware of it for example when we're on holiday. Because if you're Austrian they like you everywhere. And I've never known that there's somebody who doesn't like Austrians [...] I think that's because of the past that / I mean you mustn't forget that Germany for example / the Germans really did many things against other countries which were not OK of course it's not the fault of the the German citizens of today but it's inside them in certain peoples and that I think / is not the case in Austria.
>
> (17F)

1F talked about experiences which suggest that many non-Austrians see no difference between Austrians and Germans and stated:

> Many don't make a difference – although others (regard) Austria as an independent country – well different – but that's happened more than once – where I 'well Austrians – Germans it's the same anyway'.
>
> (1F)

Almost all respondents stated that being mistaken for a German citizen would elicit protest on their part and the desire to put the mistake right (for example 10F, 19M).

The difference between Austria and other European nations was portrayed by 20M from an 'outside perspective', using a number of clichés about Austria:

> A region of Europe in which many things are still much more intact than in other areas of Europe that I have seen: from the magnificent landscape to the European architectural tradition and even the crucifixes by the roadsides, which for me are indications that here there is still a different attitude to life than just a motorway that you speed through on [...] I have the impression that in Austria life is quieter. That's not meant in a derogatory way. More friendly. That doesn't apply to Vienna primarily but it does to the rural regions, the small towns and villages, there may be [...] something small-time (about it) but I'm more than willing to overlook that because on the other hand the small-time aspect has preserved a world that the others, the big-time wasn't able to.
>
> (20M)

In this excerpt 'the crucifixes by the roadsides' became an Austrian *locus amoenus* – symbols of peacefulness and of a conservative value system – and were contrasted with cars and motorways which symbolised a more hectic lifestyle, speed and pollution. In addition, 20M introduced the topic of religion, which is unusual as it generally did not play a large role either in the interviews or in the focus groups, or in political speeches, at least not at the level of explicit references. The lack of emphasis on this theme contrasts with popular clichés about Austria as a country pervaded by Catholicism. Whether closer semantic analysis would have revealed the hidden influence of religious membership or non-membership on the subjective models of Austrian identity is an open question.

NOTES

1. Four interviewees had also taken part in the previously conducted focus groups. However, this fact hardly seems to have had a bearing either on their behaviour during the interviews or on their responses. All but two of the interviews were conducted after the general elections of 12 December 1995. Therefore it can be assumed that the Austrian electoral campaign influenced all the interviewees evenly. However, this does not hold true for the ensuing coalition negotiations, or for the political debate on the issue of neutrality, or for the media reports on the growing negative attitude on the part of the majority of Austrians towards the European Union. Thus, certain distortions in the argumentation patterns and narratives of the interviewees must be assumed and cannot be considered in the analysis in every case.
2. Onomastic analysis was also attempted in two of the focus groups. In the Pilot Group, one participant assumed his surname to be typically Austrian, and in Group Burgenland one participant whose mother tongue was Croatian remarked that his Austrian-sounding surname had spared him trouble in a number of situations.
3. President Klestil demanded that Austrians recall their European roots in his speech of 27 April, as a counter-model to the myth of smallness.
4. See also 19M, who remarked on the presidential elections of 1986 'that there was a Federal President with a past as an officer and Nazi officer / as an officer of the German *Wehrmacht* and I think also as a Nazi officer who always denied this / that was really the main problem' (19M). The distinction made here between an 'officer of the German *Wehrmacht*' and a 'Nazi officer' may be an indication of the myth of a 'clean *Wehrmacht*'.

Chapter 7

Conclusion: Imagined and Real Identities – the Multiple Faces of the *homo nationalis*

In this section we will tie together the key issues which have arisen from the analysis of our data in the light of the theoretical assumptions and hypotheses we outlined in the first chapter. We will first look at the content of the discursive constructs of national identities in general and of Austrian identity in particular, and then summarise the main strategies and forms of linguistic realisation.

7.1 THE INITIAL HYPOTHESES REVISITED

Over the past decade, the concept of nation as an imagined community has gained increasing importance in the relevant scholarly literature. The main objective of our study has been to identify this mental construct and to specify its emotional appeal and social binding force through an examination of different types of discursive practices related to the Austrian nation. Although our results cannot be generalised in every specific point, they nevertheless demonstrate tendencies in national processes of identification which are observable across contemporary Europe. Consequently, the methodological and theoretical framework of our discourse-historical approach (cf. Wodak et al. 1990, Matouschek, Wodak and Januschek 1995) is also applicable to investigations of the discursive construction of national identities other than the Austrian alone.

One of our principal operating assumptions has been that national identities are generated and reproduced through discourse. We have assumed further not only that institutional and material social structures determine the construction of national identities in important ways, but that institutional practices can conflict with discursive models of identity. The discursive constructs of national identities emphasise foremost national uniqueness and intra-national uniformity, and largely tend to ignore intra-national difference (the discourses of sameness). Above all, however, the greatest possible differences from other nations are frequently simultaneously constructed through discourses of difference, and especially difference from those foreign nations that seem to exhibit the most striking similarities.

We have also assumed that there is no such thing as *one* national identity in an essentialist sense, but rather that different identities are discursively constructed according to context, that is according to the degree of public exposure of a given utterance, the setting, the topic addressed, the audience to which it is addressed, and so on. In other words, discursive national identities should not be perceived as static, but rather as dynamic, vulnerable and rather ambivalent entities.

This applies to all 'official' and 'oppositional' models of identity provided by the political élites and the various institutions of socialisation. Discourses in different political and media publics stand in reciprocal relation to one another in much the same way as do discourses of powerful élites and 'everyday discourses'. We have described the details of such discursive 'exchanges' using the concepts of inter-textuality and recontextualisation.

The thematic content of discourses of national identity encompasses the con-struction of a common past, present and future; a common culture; a common territory; and the concept of a *homo nationalis*. In view of this, we have assumed that a strict dichotomy between *Staatsnation* and *Kulturnation* cannot adequately account for processes of national identification. Indeed, the discourses of national identity always contain elements referring to both *Kulturnation* and *Staatsnation*. While all these assumptions can be applied to nations and national identities in general, they also constitute the analytical framework for the study of particular identities, in our case Austrian identity and nation.

Writing on the Austrian nation, political scientist Anton Pelinka has argued that:

> The concept of Austria as an entity spanning centuries and encompassing a variety of religions, classes, sexes, regions and ethnic groups of course only exists in our imagination; the product of human invention projected from the present into the past and oriented towards the future. This refers to our case of Austria, but equally to France, Portugal, The Netherlands or Switzerland. All nations are political inventions.
>
> (Pelinka 1995, pp. 8f.)

In contrast to previous research done in this field, which has largely concentrated on the study of historical sources, and which has employed quantitative social science methodology to quantify predetermined response alternatives by means of standard-ised analytical procedures, our study was designed to illustrate the 'imagined' charac-ter of nations to which Pelinka refers, and which is expressed in concrete, authentic, more or less spontaneous discursive 'events'. In order to survey the broadest possible range of identity constructs and their dialectical interrelations, as well as identify in detail the recontextualisation of important concepts and arguments, the present study has investigated four different discursive contexts ranging from fully public to quasi-private. Specifically these were:

1. The discourse of political élites, as exemplified by the commemoration of the fiftieth anniversary of the founding of the Second Republic
2. Excerpts from discourse in the media (for example newspapers and pro-EU campaigns) on the topics of 'neutrality' and 'entering the EU'
3. Semi-public discourse as expressed by participants in seven 'focus group' dis-cussions

4. Quasi-private discourse based on a sample of twenty-four topic-oriented qualitative interviews.

With the exception of the media discourse, which can only be discussed here in
brief, all the above-mentioned sets of data were investigated along three analytical
dimensions: 1) content, 2) strategies applied in the discursive construction of
national identities, and 3) the forms of linguistic realisation. These three dimensions
were explored by testing a set of hypotheses which goes beyond general assumptions
on nation and national identity, and is addressed to the Austrian nation and the
Austrian identity specifically.

Among the assumptions we have had in connection with our case study is that
there is not *one* Austrian identity, but that constructs of identity are formed depending on context, and are influenced by factors such as social status, party political
affiliation, regional and/or ethnic origin, and so on. In addition, we assumed that
the concept of an Austrian nation encompasses elements of both *Kulturnation* and
Staatsnation and that a number of other dimensions might prove influential in the
construction of Austrian identities, for example differentiation from non-Austrians
resident in Austria or from other nations, in particular from 'the Germans'. The
attitude towards Germany, it was assumed, would be highly ambivalent in regard
to issues such as the common Nazi past, Austria's membership of the EU, or the
German language. We assumed further that the German language would be important to those informants who spoke German as a mother tongue, but also to
people from linguistic minorities whose languages do not enjoy the same status as the
majority language. The primary linguistic level of identification, however, would be
the dialect or 'everyday' colloquial language, since, we assumed, only a very small
number of the respondents could be expected to be aware of an independent
Austrian variety of German. The respondents' perceptions of history, moreover,
would be influenced primarily by the Second Republic and the Habsburg Monarchy,
while periods of conflict such as the Nazi era and 'Austro-fascism' would be less
present in the collective memory. After the Waldheim Affair in 1986 and the celebrations in 1988 commemorating the fiftieth anniversary of the Nazi occupation,
we assumed that the 'perpetrator thesis' would have gained prominence over the
'victim thesis'. Finally, we assumed that Austria's joining the EU would require a new
definition of Austrian identity and that in this connection Austrian neutrality would
have to be redefined.

7.2 GENERAL THEORETICAL RESULTS

The first point to note is that the analysis of our data has confirmed our initial
approach: highly diverse, ambivalent, context-determined discursive identity constructs could in fact be identified. Those we discovered varied from setting to setting,
and were additionally influenced by factors such as an individual's political affiliation
or regional origin. In the linguistic identity constructs, attempts were made to create
intra-national sameness and/or differences with other nations. In commemorative

addresses, constructive strategies of assimilation and unification predominated, whereas in semi-public and private discourse there was also considerable emphasis on intra-national difference. In the discourses of national identity, it was not only the construction of a common past, present and future and a common territory, but also the construction of a common culture and a *homo Austriacus* or a 'national character' which were perceived as essential. In other words, irrespective of the degree of formality of a particular situation, respondents drew on culture-based national elements in all the contexts analysed. However, this was particularly obvious in semi-public and quasi-private discourse, where culture-based self-perception was determined not only by 'high culture' but also by an imagined homogeneous everyday culture, an assumed national mentality and a concept of naturalised descent. This latter concept sometimes appeared cloaked as multicultural theory of origin, but was nonetheless rooted in nativism and had little in common with any political-based conception of a multicultural society. Consequently, any attempt to apply strictly the two idealised models of *Staatsnation* and *Kulturnation* to individual nation-states under the condition of mutual exclusion will fail; at best, a delimitation between these two concepts may serve to define differences in the national self-perception within one and the same state, for example between various political or ideological orientations.

The detailed discourse-analytical investigation of the five sets of data (including our study of poster campaigns, outlined briefly in this chapter) allows us to make a number of statements about the context-determined interrelation of contents, strategies and forms of realisation. Firstly, certain contents, strategies and linguistic forms of realisation in certain publics (which obviously determine the degree of formality of the speech situation in question), at particular places, on particular occasions, and before a particular group of addressees, are selected depending on the speaker's political function and party affiliation, age, occupation and level of education, and gender, and on his or her social position, regional ethnic, national, sexual and religious membership, as defined by the speakers themselves or by others. It is primarily these contextual factors which we have considered in our analysis. In addition, our case studies highlight certain intertextual connections, which include almost literal repetitions of passages from commemorative addresses and text extracts from books and articles by historians, political scientists and essayists, and hackneyed formulations transferred from the areas of politics and the media into semi-public and quasi-private areas (recontextualisation). A further intertextual dimension may be observed in allusions and evocations, which occur primarily in commemorative speeches. The detailed linguistic analysis of local (interaction-specific) co- and contextual factors in our data reveals a third important general result, that is that discourses about nations and national identities cannot be perceived as clearly distinctive and unified but rather that, depending on the social macro-function involved, at least four distinct macro-strategies are used invariably in combination. These are: constructive strategies, strategies of perpetuation or justification, strategies of transformation and destructive strategies or strategies of disparagement (cf. Chapter 2).

7.3 EMPIRICAL FINDINGS

7.3.1 Identity, Nation and Differentiation

Although the term 'Austrian nation' hardly ever occurs explicitly in our data, there can be no doubt that the Austrians who made up our sample perceived its existence in their speeches. Politicians strongly emphasised Austria's autonomy. The perception of an Austrian identity in everyday contexts in fact contained both state-based and culture-based elements. As we have seen, the majority of our respondents, both in the focus groups and in interviews, drew not only on the concept of citizenship and the positive presentation of political achievements and institutional practices for positive contents of identity, but also on 'high-cultural' achievements, on presumed shared properties in the areas of everyday culture, on language, and on the concept of a *homo Austriacus*. Even those participants and interviewees who for reasons of political correctness initially defined their national membership exclusively in terms of 'coincidence', 'passport', 'birth' or 'citizenship', usually mentioned cultural and essentialist features of Austrianness in the course of the discussions or interviews. By contrast, cultural elements were seldom mentioned in politicians' addresses.

The core elements of state-based national identity in our data were: citizenship; the economic and social achievements of the Second Republic, in particular the welfare state, social and political peace (in contrast to ex-Yugoslavia and eastern Europe and other states); the Austrian State Treaty of 1955 (to some extent); and neutrality. Members of the focus groups also positively evaluated Austria's environmental policy. Culture-based national features mentioned by the respondents in our sample comprised achievements in the areas of culture and sport, a frequently invoked 'Austrian mentality', and 'typical Austrian ways of behaviour' (such as *Gemütlichkeit*, for example). Further, language was perceived as being very important. Thus a unified national German language was regarded (even by members of the minorities) as absolutely necessary even if there were few who believed that competence in the German language should be a criterion for the granting of citizenship.

In semi-public and quasi-private discursive practices an essentialist conception of an 'Austrian people' predominated which was based on cultural elements such as the mentality, character, and behavioural disposition of the *homo Austriacus*. In a few instances the notion of an 'Austrian people' actually entailed the idea of a common origin and concepts of 'innate nationality'. Some of the participants and interviewees described the 'Austrian people' as a multicultural collective which had emerged out of the melting pot of the Habsburg monarchy, but did not believe that present-day Austria might also be multicultural in a similar sense. Both in individual interviews and in two of the focus group discussions, members of ethnic groups stressed their linguistic identity and the contribution their respective group had made to Austrian culture. Members of religious and linguistic minorities addressed the ambivalence, contradictions and fragmentation of identities more frequently than did members of majorities. At the same time those from minorities emphasised their pronounced

Austrianness and Austrian consciousness. In this connection they frequently related personal or second-hand experiences of discrimination and expressed the fear that they might not be perceived as 'real' Austrians by other Austrians.

Of particular importance was the affirmation of a 'commitment to Austria', which is a set piece of public discourse and of the political socialisation carried out in school. This was said to manifest itself in strong national pride and Austrian patriotism that were triggered by particular situations of everyday life (staying abroad, returning home from abroad, sport events or being under the ritual spell of state symbols). The most frequently mentioned objects of national pride were: the Austrian landscape; political, social and ecological achievements; political security; Austrian culture and everyday culture; academic and scientific achievements; success in sport; and national symbols such as the national anthem and the Austrian flag. It was, therefore, no coincidence that the government's pro-EU campaign preceding the referendum in June 1994 made frequent use of the Austrian and the European flag. Many respondents in interviews linked this 'commitment to Austria' to their rejection of dual citizenship. Similarly, many speakers demanded that immigrants to Austria must be culturally integrated or assimilated.

As we have seen, the conceptualisation of nation and of national self-perception is context-specific. Accordingly, political speeches were characterised by an understanding of nation which is based on the concept of *Staatsnation*. However, beneath the patina of an officially constructed national consciousness a self-perception shaped by a national culture is often discernible. In other words, as the degree of informality increased, cultural and essentialist definitions occurred more frequently. In quasi private discourse we encountered formulations or rhetorical set pieces that had probably been taken over from official political discourse on Austria (or which had been learned at school). Regional identities which were referred to in all the settings were frequently formulated as differences in mentality that were anchored in a vague concept of home (*Heimat*) related to place of birth or childhood. However, on the whole they seem to have been important to 'pan-Austrian' national identity. In none of the settings did ethnic minorities figure in the Austrian self-perception of the German-speaking majority population, indeed, apart from the minorities themselves hardly anyone took any notice of them. In the individual interviews, members of ethnic groups or religious minorities sometimes provided spontaneous narratives of their personal experience of discrimination. Multiculturalism was only important within the framework of a glorified past ('the multicultural monarchy', 'melting pot'). Minority languages were 'tolerated' in everyday life, but did not have the same status as the official language, German.

Differentiation along party political lines was found primarily in the political speeches and was often made indirectly through allusions, the only exception being speeches delivered to members and officials of one's own party.

The higher the speaker's office, and the more 'national' the occasion of the speech, the less frequent were instances of intra-national differentiation. There was, however, one exception: all speakers of all parties distanced themselves from the extreme right and political terrorism, although to varying degrees. There appears to have been a clear distinction in the party political characterisation of certain pillars of the Austrian identity, above all Austrian neutrality, which was evident in the political speeches, in the media and in the focus groups.

Strategies which presupposed or merely touched on inter-national sameness or similarity, or which implied a sense of affinity with other national collectives, played a subordinate role in the data we examined. Where spatial proximity and/or certain similarities were particularly striking, respondents felt compelled to emphasise inter-national differences between Austrians and either non-Austrian residents or nationals from neighbouring countries, specifically those in the former Eastern Bloc, ex-Yugoslavia, Switzerland, and above all Germany. In connection with Austria's membership of the EU, the strategy of discriminatory differentiation was extensively employed. Respondents constructed a hierarchy of 'foreignness' which ranged from Europeans in 'western' EU-member states to the EU as a whole (including the less wealthy countries), the remaining European countries and non-European countries (implicitly Third World countries).

At the same time, the explicit discursive exclusion and ostracism of non-Austrians living in Austria seems to be a taboo in public settings. However, in semi-public and quasi-private discourses this exclusionary usage was a constitutive element of identity construction. Thus the further east or south their country of origin, the greater the perceived differences in their appearance. The more they were perceived to have come from countries with Islamic culture (emphasised only by women interviewees), the more alien these non-Austrian residents were perceived by Austrian respondents to be. In addition, language was perceived as a crucial factor in differentiation (not being able to speak a language supposedly leads to alienation, fear and rejection), as was the foreigners' 'insistence on their traditions'. Integration, subordination and assimilation were demanded of foreigners living in Austria. In several focus groups classic prejudices towards foreigners (their not being willing to work, being noisy, and so on) were expressed and these in turn correlated with the social class of the speaker: the better educated the participants, the more politically correctly they behaved. The awareness that explicit resentment of foreigners was politically inappropriate and a taboo was evident in all our data.

For the most varied reasons, emphasis on differences between Austria and Germany played an important part: in the commemorative speeches, politicians distinguished themselves from Germany especially in contexts relating to the common Nazi past (relativisation of Austria's responsibility, legal prohibition against Austria becoming part of Germany). Austria's strong contemporary economic and cultural independence vis-à-vis Germany was often stressed. In semi-public and quasi-private discourse, differentiation from Germany seemed to be an emotional need; it is not clear, however, why this was felt to be so important and what exactly the differences between Austrians and Germans were perceived to be. One relatively straightforward, frequently mentioned difference was that Austrians are allegedly more popular than Germans in other countries. Apart from this specific reference, the interviewees mostly perceived such differences within the realm of everyday culture and mentality. The standard language ('high German') and literature, in contrast, were regarded as similar. Austria's relationship with Germany as revealed by our data may on the whole be characterised as highly ambivalent, which also holds true for the Austrians' attitude to the German language.

As the national language, German represented an important element of the Austrian identity in semi-public and private discourses. In political speeches, however, this issue was not addressed. Having a native language other than German was felt to be alienating and unsettling, both by foreigners living in Austria and by the autochthonous minorities, though members of Austrian minorities considered their own bilingualism to be self-evident. Austrian German was stressed in particular contexts as an important criterion of difference between Austria and Germany, hence the emphasis on typically Austrian culinary terms in the pro-EU campaigns ('*Erdäpfelsalat bleibt Erdäpfelsalat*'). At the same time, differences between Austrian German and German German were primarily located at the vernacular or dialectal level. The attitude of German-speaking Austrians towards their language exhibited schizoid characteristics: on the one hand, the language was an essential component of Austrianness. This applied especially to language use in certain symbolic actions (for example, the terms used on menus, or in forms of greeting), as well as the linguistic influence of the media (cable TV and suchlike) on children. On the other hand, there was hardly any awareness of an independent Austrian standard variety of the pluri-national language German. Moreover, the majority of our respondents assumed a common German standard, codified in the Federal Republic of Germany, as the linguistic norm.

7.3.2 *Homo Austriacus*

As we have demonstrated, argumentation patterns based on the concepts of *Kulturnation* and *Staatsnation* are usually amalgamated in semi-public and quasi-private discourses on national identity. Consequently, one can reasonably assume that the stereotypical image of a *homo Austriacus* and the concepts of a 'typically Austrian national character' (*Volkscharakter*), 'typically Austrian behaviour' and a specific 'Austrian mentality' are of great importance (cf. Liebhart and Reisigl 1997). Even interviewees who initially suggested citizenship as an important criterion of national membership (which on the whole did not occur very often), added linguistically, culturally and ethnically defined elements of Austrian self-perception to their argumentation. Although in individual cases doubts were occasionally expressed as to whether such a thing as a typical Austrian mentality actually existed, nevertheless in a number of arguments respondents drew on this concept to deduce an Austrian nation defined in cultural-essentialist terms. For example, a continuity from the Habsburg monarchy was constructed and the above-mentioned theory of origin was put forward in an attempt to derive today's Austrian from the 'melting-pot' of the monarchy. With some interviewees and participants, behavioural modes of everyday culture were linked to 'national mentality' and served as a signal for a negative differentiation from foreigners. The importance attributed by respondents to their place of birth and socialisation for the geographical genesis of the 'Austrian' suggests elements of the theory of milieu. For some interviewees and participants, environment and education shaped mentality in childhood and adolescence so decisively that it could not be changed later in life. As to Austrian mentality, Austrian behaviour and Austrian national character, the participants and interviewees drew upon a repertoire of well-established clichés. Images of humorous, easy-going, joking Austrians who enjoy good living, but also of the complaining or slightly superficial Austrians, who 'cannot see beyond their own borders', appeared again and again.

Such a culture-oriented basis of the national *homo Austriacus*, which today primarily occurs in informal everyday discourse, manifested itself in even the most formal political ceremonial discourse in the immediate postwar period. In contemporary political discourse, as our analysis reveals, the image of an 'Austrian person' typically connotes state-based rather than culture-based images. In any event, images of an 'Austrian person' played only a subsidiary role in the everyday discourse we studied. Thus, for example, in a speech on the occasion of the celebration of the Austrian Millennium on 19 May 1996, President Klestil emphasised that 'According to the experts, Austria is a *Willensnation*, that is a 'nation by an act of will'.

7.3.3 The Austrians and their Past

Of all the periods of Austrian history deemed particularly crucial in the construction of a collective past, the Austro-Hungarian monarchy and, in particular, the year 1955 were accorded pre-eminent importance and positive connotations. The founding myth of the Second Republic, a period largely perceived as the country's 'heyday' due to its political and social achievements, was associated with 1955, the year of the signing of the State Treaty and the declaration of neutrality. In contrast, the year 1945 ('liberation', 'rebirth', 'new beginning') seems to have occupied a much less prominent place in the collective memory, in contrast to official historiography, which stresses the liberation of Austria in 1945. In political speeches, Austria's entry to the European Union in 1995 was portrayed as a significant turning-point, whereas the Millennium of 1996, with one exception, was not mentioned. Similarly, 1996 was not perceived as an important date in the focus groups, but the evidence from the individual interviews suggests that the idea of a 'thousand-year old Austria' had already entered everyday consciousness. On the whole, however, this 'recent' myth has not (yet) fulfilled any identity-constituting function.

Most interviewees and participants in the discussions perceived the First Republic (1918–34), the Austro-fascist Corporatist State (1934–38), the Nazi era, and the Second World War (1938/9–1945) as periods of crisis. Politicians publicly acknowledged that these periods had to be 'worked through' and increasingly directed their attention to the 'perpetrator' aspect. However, this topic was often addressed in a trivialising and relativising manner, most strongly so by Jörg Haider. The victim and perpetrator perspectives were intermingled in public ceremonial speeches, although the contradictory nature of these two positions was not acknowledged. According to most (male) politicians, 'coming to terms with the past' should be pursued with moderation, as concentrating on the challenges of the future is far more important.

Although our assumption that Chancellor Vranitzky's speeches between 1988 and 1991, which viewed the Austrian past relatively critically, would initiate a new phase in dealing with the past has not been confirmed, a number of interviewees and group members regarded the Nazi period as an important topic which had been ignored far too long. They also recognised certain continuities between the Nazi period and today. However, a considerable percentage of respondents claimed that in politics and the media the Nazi era was presented in an exaggerated way in order to discredit politicians (the 'Waldheim syndrome'). They also pointed to the supposed demand to justify themselves whenever the Nazi period is mentioned. On the whole, members of minorities adopted a more critical stance in their evaluation of the Austrian Nazi past.

The explicit rejection of National Socialism and antisemitism had a direct bearing on the assessment of current political problems for only a very small number of respondents. Threats by the current extreme right were almost exclusively seen in connection with the far-right party, the FPÖ, and with its leader Jörg Haider. Thus it seems that the rejection of the Nazi era does not automatically lead to heightened moral sensitivity towards everyday racisms or to greater tolerance towards 'others'.

If the 'restitution policy' of the Second Republic was mentioned in the political speeches, it was in part accompanied by positive self-presentation and justification of previous policies. Many participants in the interviews and focus groups were sceptical of the necessity of the Austrian state to make restitution payments in general, and were hostile to the National Aid Fund, established in 1995 to aid surviving victims of Nazi persecution in particular. Moreover, participants frequently made statements that were wholly or partly inaccurate about the extent and amount of payments already made by Austria to Nazi victims, or about the details of the laws governing restitution payments themselves, or both. A minority of respondents even believed that the descendants of victims, in particular those 'living abroad', would unduly profit from these measures. In the focus groups, respondents' attitudes towards the obligation to pay restitution in principle, as well as the accuracy of respondents' information about the restitution issue, correlated with age, social class and level of education. In general, the older the respondents were, the lower their level of formal education and the lower their social status, the more they tended to overestimate the past achievements of restitution measures and to advocate limiting further compensation or restitution measures. Furthermore, the boundaries between different victim groups (concentration camp survivors, 'civilian war victims', soldiers of the *Wehrmacht* who fell in battle, Sudeten Germans who were expelled from their homes, and so on) were blurred, and sometimes an exclusionary contrast between the victims of the Nazis and those of 'the Austrians' was constructed. Views on 'compensation' varied among the respondents. We found unconditional approval of Austria's responsibility but also a predominant attitude which may be summarised as 'co-responsibility and compensation yes, but not materially and financially, only morally.'

The victim thesis, according to which Austria was a victim both of the Nazis and of the Allies, is still a core element of the Austrian identity in the public political sphere. Since 1988 it has no longer been possible to deny the Nazi crimes committed by Austrians, and the perpetrator thesis has now also entered quasi-private discourse. Here again, the age of the respondents was an influential variable. Members of the older generation based their assessment of political issues on personal experience during the Nazi or postwar period, while younger respondents frequently claimed that they were not entitled to judge their parents' and grandparents' generations from a contemporary perspective.

7.3.4 Neutrality and the European Union

A central assumption of our study has been that the conceptions of Austrian national identity would have to be newly defined in view of Austria's membership of the EU. As the analysis of our data reveals, a complex process of transformation has been set in motion which affects a central pillar of Austrian identity, namely neutrality. Austria's joining the EU was presented as a decisive turning point by President Klestil, whereas for Chancellor Vranitzky it only marked a caesura. Campaigning for EU membership, Klestil demanded that Austrians recall their European roots, and claimed that Austrian identity was threatened neither by EU membership nor by European integration or a 'European' identity.

For reasons of space we are not able to consider in detail a case study carried out in the context of our research project, which investigated the 1994 pro-EU campaigns preceding the referendum (cf. Wodak et al. 1998, Kargl 1996). However, we would like to mention some of our findings. They suggest that these campaigns were designed primarily to present European and Austrian identities as being mutually compatible. These campaigns interrelated with the EU debates in other public and private spheres by influencing the way the issue was discussed: for example by formulating the topics which were subsequently taken up in spoken or written discourse. In turn, advertising experts, political parties and other groups designed their respective campaigns in reaction to previously existing tendencies in public and private discourse. All of this suggests that these campaigns were attempts to meet demands and allay fears which had existed before the work of the respective campaign began.

The government's 'information campaign' had considerable visibility and attracted substantial criticism in the media. The overall influence of this campaign on how the issue was presented in the Austrian public should not be underestimated.

Viewed in terms of content, these campaigns were organised around three themes:

1. The tension between Austrian and European identification
2. Reinforcing the idea of an Austrian nation
3. Establishing a European (or, rather European Union) supranationalism.

By shifting the country's orientation towards a supranational community, the existing national identification was called into question. The ensuing tension between these two identities, the European and the Austrian, affected the social as well as the psychological level and reverberated through the campaigns both for and against EU membership.

The pro-EU campaigns assured the population, sometimes quite vehemently, that neither their regional nor their national identity would be in danger through membership of the EU. The two identifications were simply presented as compatible with no attempt made to resolve the tension (which could have been effected, for example, by adopting the supranational and simultaneously renouncing the national identification). Frequently, it was suggested that these two kinds of identification could be fused, without, however, specifying how this could work in practice. By presenting the two identities as simultaneously existing side by side, they were both made possible in a purely tautological way.

What was particularly remarkable in this debate was that both EU proponents and EU-sceptics strongly emphasised Austria's autonomy, uniqueness and national identity, thus making 'Austria' the lynchpin of any discussion. Paradoxically, the symbols of national identity were, at least at this stage, utilised to promote membership in a supranational collectivity, a strategy which, judging by the outcome of the referendum on 12 June 1994, proved highly successful.

The main visual symbols used in the campaigns were the Austrian and the European flags. Resembling the presentation of identity on the linguistic level, the Austrian flag was moved to the foreground, and its red-white-red colours, or red alone – striking colours, advertising purpose and reckoned to be suitably positively connotated – were employed throughout. Visually, Europe, or rather the European Union, was almost exclusively represented by the European flag and its dark blue and yellow colours. Other visual symbols appeared only sporadically.

Emphasis on the Austrian nation, however, was also accomplished by distinguishing Austria from EU member-states in general (above all, this was done by EU opponents from the right political spectrum) and, in particular, from the less prosperous EU states (by both proponents and opponents). On the surface, there was an almost naive emphasis on Austria's autonomy vis-à-vis the EU member states and their populations. Fears associated with these poorer EU members tended to be implied rather than expressed explicitly. What seems a perfectly plausible, if rather trivial, observation, namely that – other things being equal – the prospects of living in a wealthier country might 'encourage' those living in a poorer one to immigrate to that country, was seldom if ever debated at this level of abstraction, but rather in the language of fear. Whenever such fears of unwanted economic immigration (those countries mentioned were primarily Portugal, Spain and Greece) were mooted, they were either explained away or exaggerated, depending (broadly speaking) upon whether the respondent was in favour of or against Austria's joining the EU. European states such as Ireland, which has a history of economic emigration, were on the contrary regarded much less frequently as potential 'threats' to Austrian prosperity. This selective differentiation may indicate that behind the economic arguments mentioned explicitly lay deeper-seated prejudices against the countries of the 'olive belt', i.e. that this particular differentiation was in fact determined by purely racist motives.

In the course of the 'campaigns' for and against EU membership, a new concept of European supranationalism emerged which, however, did not replace but served to complement nationalism. Group formation was accordingly increasingly realised through the construction of differences along an inside/outside EU divide. Explicitly mentioned in this connection were above all the United States and Japan, against whose economic power the European countries would have to unite to be able to assert themselves. However, there were frequent (implicit) instances of differentiation from countries with economic problems against which, it was claimed, Austria could in future only defend itself by seeking co-operation within the EU.

On the whole, the campaigns were characterised by a hierarchy of 'foreignness', well-known from racist prejudiced discourse, with 'us Austrians' against, firstly, Europeans from 'western' EU countries ('first class Europeans'), followed by the EU as a whole including the poorer members, and then by the remaining European countries, that is, countries of the former Eastern Bloc (which, however, had been enthusiastically welcomed shortly after the fall of the Iron Curtain), and, finally, by non-European states (implicitly Third World countries), against which rather open resentment was expressed. In other words, in these campaigns 'foreigners' in Austria were not 'equally foreign'. Whenever one perceives that entry into a supranational entity will bring one into increasing contact, and perhaps conflict, with foreigners, one response is to establish how foreign individual groups of foreigners are. In our data, such a process continued to draw upon well-established, long-cherished elements of prejudiced discourse.

Individual elements from the EU campaign were, as we suggested, recontextualised in the focus groups. This applied both to Austria's compatibility with Europe and to the 'Yes to Europe, no to the European Union!' approach. Intra-European differentiation from the countries of the 'olive belt' (represented by concepts such as the 'Portuguese construction worker') occurred side by side with demands for an economic alliance to remain competitive with Japan and the USA. The discourses of the élites seem to have been enormously influential and more effective, while the arguments put forward by EU opponents seem to have proved less convincing.

At the time we collected our data, European integration did not represent a real threat to the Austrian identity. Rather, what seems to have influenced a change in identity were the geopolitical changes since 1989 and their effects on the countries around Austria. The majority of the Austrians in our sample still favoured EU-membership for economic and security reasons, yet we found a number of reservations and qualifications, the most important one being the perceived danger to Austrian neutrality.

In the commemorative speeches, the politicians made a distinction between the past and the current meaning of neutrality. To call neutrality into question was politically still rather taboo, and this is why only the FPÖ and the Liberal Forum challenged the myth of neutrality quite openly. ÖVP politicians and President Klestil rather cautiously addressed this sensitive topic in connection with the EU and issues of security, historicising neutrality by means of transformation strategies. In contrast, SPÖ politicians largely circumvented the topic.

The coverage of the EU membership campaign in the media, our second case study, has also not been included in this book (cf. however, Wodak et al. 1998). Only the *Neue Kronenzeitung* discussed neutrality relatively extensively during this period, while other newspapers dealt with it only marginally, generally from a critical perspective. Above all, strategies of transformation as well as attempts at strategies of demontage and disparagement dominated the discourse in the Austrian daily papers. The overall lines of argument may be summarised roughly as follows: a new definition of neutrality seems unavoidable after the end of the East-West confrontation; as Austria's security is threatened by the unstable situation in the East, in particular in ex-Yugoslavia, there is a need for Austria to react by joining the EU; neutrality affords only relative protection against new threats, as was shown, for example, during the Cold War, when it was only effective in combination with the deterrence offered by NATO.

In the *Neue Kronenzeitung*, 'security' was the central argument in support of EU membership. This aspect was primarily reported using quotations taken from politicians' statements. Traces of this emerged in a more diffuse form in the focus groups. To a certain extent, the *Neue Kronenzeitung* clung to the myth of neutrality rather than to neutrality *per se*, as it hinted at a change in attitude and meaning which increasingly reduced neutrality to a meaningless formula. By claiming that security conditions for Austria had changed, and consequently calling the protective function of neutrality into question, the *Neue Kronenzeitung* paved the way to the renunciation of Austria's neutral status.

Reflecting the diffuse character of the public political debate on neutrality and security, the essence of Austrian neutrality remained extremely vague and difficult for the group participants and the interviewees to pin down. Nevertheless, neutrality was still strongly anchored and bore positive emotional connotations for many respondents. It had become lodged in their heads, or rather in their hearts (as one participant put it), a constituent part of identity dating from the time of the Cold War which, as 'flesh and blood', had become a significant internalised component of the national habitus. As the reception in the focus groups of the statement by President Klestil revealed (see Chapter 5), there are strong party political differences in respect to the future role of neutrality: Participants closer to the ÖVP regarded neutrality as obsolete, those sympathising with the SPÖ favoured its retention, while the attitudes of participants who had not specified their party preference were ambivalent and contradictory. A transformation was obviously taking place; however, it was not easy to abandon a central myth.

7.4. STRATEGIES AND FORMS OF LINGUISTIC REALISATION

As our analysis of commemorative speeches, of the coverage of neutrality and security in the media, of the pro-EU poster and folder campaigns prior to the referendum, and of the focus groups and individual interviews has revealed, there are at least five different important macro-strategies which play a significant part in the discourse of national identity. These are: constructive strategies, strategies of relativisation or justification, strategies of perpetuation, strategies of transformation, and disparagement and/or destructive strategies. The following section once more explores their uses, and forms in which they are realised, in our five different sets of data.

7.4.1 The Discourse of the Political and Media Élites

Most conspicuous in the poster campaign of the EU proponents was the attempt to combine constructive and perpetuating strategies with strategies of transformation in such a way that Austrian identity was presented as compatible with EU membership and with a supranational European identity. This was also attempted through an emphasis on inter-national sameness. On the linguistic level, assimilative identity-enhancing strategies anthropomorphised both Austria ('We love Austria') and Europe or the European 'we-body' ('we are Europe') through personification. The use of visual devices and strategies, which were obviously characteristic of this set of data and distinguished it from all the other data, contributed to enhancing suggestive vividness and immediacy. The two coalition parties, the SPÖ and the ÖVP, both proponents of EU membership, attempted to refute the arguments of the two opposition parties sceptical of EU membership, the FPÖ and the Greens – namely, that membership would lead to the loss of national uniqueness and autonomy – by adducing negative arguments and evidence. Thus, strategies of singularisation and autonomisation occurred again and again through procatalepsis, frequently accompanied by the strategy of perpetuation aimed at the reduction of fears. What distinguished the SPÖ from the ÖVP, however, was each party's respective accentuation of perpetuation and transformation as well as their choice of particular linguistic and visual means of realisation. The ÖVP portrayed itself as the more conservative and patriotic party by means of the unifying 'we', and emphasised static and factive presentation ('We are Europeans – but remain Austrians'). The SPÖ partly abandoned the explicit 'we' and introduced elements of transformation ('We remain Viennese – and become Europeans'). Only one year later, however, these tendencies were reversed in the speeches commemorating the fiftieth anniversary of the Second Republic.

In the media coverage of neutrality and security we found predominantly strategies of transformation, which sometimes turned into strategies of disparagement, depending on the particular newspaper. What was common to all the papers was that they placed 'permanent neutrality' under the hypertheme of Austria's security, and attempted to justify its compatibility with EU accession.

In each of our closely analysed sets of data – political commemorative speeches, focus groups and interviews – we found examples of the whole range of macro-strategies. How much significance was attributed to individual strategies in the speeches largely depended on the topic and, obviously, on the overall context, including the political office and the party affiliation of the speaker, the occasion and place of the speech, and the target audience. Generally, we can say that constructive strategies and realisations were used more in the political speeches than in all our other data. To create and enhance identity through discursive acts is, of course, the job of every politician, but especially of those who presume to speak for a large imagined community. This professional wont may explain the high proportion of presuppositional and explicit assimilative strategies and unification strategies, as well as strategies of autonomisation, in political speeches. In no other data were personifying, generalising-synecdochal and metonymic references, as well as subtle shifts of 'we'-reference, so dominant and suggestive. Constructive strategies were linked primarily to the thematic clusters of a shared political past and a collective political present and future. However, whenever the issue of guilt was addressed, the past was dealt with by means of strongly justifying and relativising strategies. In addition, when addressing the past President Klestil and the ÖVP politicians frequently employed the topos of 'history teaching lessons'. In other words, insertions of a transformatory nature were used to relativise events of the past. In contrast, the opposition parties aimed primarily at dismantling the myths circulated by the 'official Austria' revolving around the foundation of the Second Republic, the 'founding fathers' and 'neutrality'. In reference to the past, neutrality was mainly disparaged by the FPÖ and by the Liberal Forum, but not by the Greens. In general, moreover, inter-national differentiation played only a minor part in the commemorative speeches, although politicians pointed out (inter-national) differences by attempting to distinguish Austria from other nations, in particular from Germany. In contrast, implicit differentiation occurred quite frequently, effected, for example, through the strategy of singularisation, which emphasised unmistakable uniqueness in contrast to other nations. Where inter-national differentiation was linked to the common political present, it was either done in the form of threatening scenarios posed by the situation in ex-Yugoslavia, or – associated with a *locus amoenus* – in comparison to other, less prosperous nations.

7.4.2 Semi-public and Semi-private Discourse

In contrast, the focus groups and interviews yielded data from less formal settings. Thus, apart from the key questions of the moderators and interviewers, this data consisted of spontaneous dialogic products. This type of discourse is characterised by turn-shifts (question-answer exchanges), by phatic feedback and continuation, and by a number of dialogic features such as hesitation markers, sentence fragments and syntactical deviations, reformulations, corrections, modifications, follow-up questions and so on. To have integrated all these factors into our analysis in a systematic way would have exceeded the scope of this study. Consequently, we focused on several striking features of this data, for example, the modifying function of modal particles, hedges and the subjunctives and the use of hesitation particles and linguistic vagueness when taboos were addressed. When the issue of the Nazi period arose, participants in group discussions employed the strategies of avoidance extensively. These aimed either at avoiding the topic altogether or at resorting to referential vagueness. However, this might have been also due to the fact that the Nazi era occupies a small place in the collective memory of particular groups of the population (the younger, those with a lower level of education). Strong group pressure may also have contributed to tabooing this topic; indeed self-censorship was less marked in the individual interviews.

One striking difference between the focus groups and interviews was that interviewees did not have to 'fight' for the floor, but had more time to formulate their contribution, although some group discussants were unable to wait until another person in the group stopped talking before speaking themselves. However, the more relaxed and informal atmosphere of the interviews seems to have been considerably more favourable to the 'gradual construction of thought' while speaking than the group situation. In the focus groups, strategies of perpetuation and transformation prevailed and were closely linked to party political preference (party affiliation was not specified by the interviewees). The distribution patterns in the groups fairly clearly reflected the constellation of macro-strategies in the political speeches. This could be best observed in connection with the debate on neutrality: the position in favour of maintaining neutrality, which had (at least until recently) been propagated by the SPÖ, was taken up by SPÖ sympathisers, while the attempts at transformation and disparagement conducted by the ÖVP politicians were reflected in the discussions by the attitude of their potential voters. Interestingly, the topos of threat was used in the groups as an argument both against and in favour of neutrality, depending on the specific party-political preference. Thus the group discussions perfectly mirrored the public political debate, and recontextualisation and intertextuality could be clearly traced. Clear differences between public political discourse and the group discussions were discernible, however, in the use of dissimilative or exclusionary strategies. Emphasis on inter-national difference was, on the whole, not an important feature in the group discussions – nor in the interviews – but it occurred more frequently here than in the commemorative speeches. Primarily directed against internal outgroups and other national collectives, this emphasis on exclusionary difference was realised by means of arguments utilising illustrative examples, typical in dialogic contexts and frequently used to convey stereotypes and prejudices in the form of anecdotes, (second-hand) narratives and fictitious threatening scenarios. Not infrequently, narrators drew on the particularising-synecdochal reference characteristic of prejudiced discourse.

Taken together, the five data sets selected for this study indicate that there is an interrelationship between the discursive identity constructs propagated by the political and media élites and those observed in semi-public and quasi-private settings. The discursive national identification 'products' offered by these political and media élites to their targeted audiences was influenced partly by the demand of these target groups for images to reinforce their national confidence. At the same time, these élites endeavoured to satisfy such demands for national identity, at times by creating, emphasising, or – as illustrated by the myth of permanent neutrality – by playing down particular features of this identity. It remains to be seen whether politicians, together with the media, will succeed in reducing demand for the neutrality myth (which at present still constitutes a means of identity construction) sufficiently to relegate 'permanent neutrality' from the 'national *habitus*' of the majority of Austrians to the collection of historical curiosities.

Appendix:
Speeches Studied in Chapter 4

1. Address by Federal President Thomas Klestil at the ceremony celebrating 'Fifty Years of the ÖVP', delivered at the *Konzerthaus* in Vienna on 21 April 1995 (*Klestil 21*)

2. Address by Klestil during the ceremony celebrating the fiftieth anniversary of the re-establishment of the Austrian *Auswärtiger Dienst* (Foreign Office), delivered on 25 April 1995 (*Klestil 25*)

3. Address by Klestil at the ceremony celebrating 'Fifty Years of the *ÖGB*' (Austrian Trades Union Federation), delivered on 26 April 1995 (*Klestil 26*)

4. Address by Klestil to the joint session of the National Assembly (*Nationalrat*) and the Federal Council (*Bundesrat*) celebrating the fiftieth anniversary of the foundation of the Second Republic, delivered on 27 April 1995 (*Klestil 27*)

5. Address by Klestil at the ceremony celebrating 'Fifty Years of *Gewerkschaft Öffentlicher Dienst* (Civil Servants' Trade Union)', delivered on 23 May 1995 (*Klestil 23*)

6. Address by Klestil at the ceremony commemorating the fiftieth anniversary of the restoration of independence of the province of Vorarlberg, delivered in Feldkirch on 24 April 1995 (*Klestil 24*)

7. Declaration by Federal Chancellor Franz Vranitzky before the National Assembly, made on 8 July 1991 (*Vranitzky 1991*)

8. Vranitzky's address before members of the Hebrew University of Jerusalem at the ceremony at which he was awarded an honorary doctorate by the Hebrew University of Jerusalem, delivered on 9 June 1993 (*Vranitzky 1993*)

9. Vranitzky's address before the joint session of the National Assembly and the Federal Council celebrating the fiftieth anniversary of the foundation of the Second Republic, delivered on 27 April 1995 (*Vranitzky 27*)

10. Address by Vranitzky at the ceremony commemorating the fiftieth anniversary of the Second World War and of the liberation of the Nazi victims imprisoned in the Mauthausen concentration camp, made in Mauthausen, Upper Austria, on 7 May 1995 (*Vranitzky 7*)

11. Address by Minister of the Interior, Caspar Einem, at the same ceremony commemorating the liberation of the Nazi victims imprisoned in the Mauthausen concentration camp. (*Einem*)

12. Remarks by Heide Schmidt, leader of the Liberal Forum in parliament, made at

the opening of the exhibition commemorating the fiftieth anniversary of the liberation of Auschwitz on 26 January 1995 (*Schmidt*)

13. Address by Deputy Chancellor Wolfgang Schüssel at the ceremony commemorating the fortieth anniversary of the signing of the State Treaty, delivered at Belvedere Palace on 14 May 1995 (*Schüssel*)

14. Speech by Jörg Haider, national chairman of the FPÖ and at the time Governor of Carinthia, at the *Friedens- und Europafeier* ('Celebration of Peace and Europe'), delivered at Ulrichsberg, Carinthia, on 7 October 1990 (*Haider 1990*)

15. Haider's keynote address to the FPÖ ceremony celebrating 'Fifty Years of the Second Republic – Looking Back and Looking Forward', delivered on 26 April 1995 (press release) (*Haider 1995*)

16. Address by Defence Minister Werner Fasslabend at the *Friedens- und Europafeier* (Celebration of Peace and Europe), delivered at Ulrichsberg, Carinthia, on 1 October 1990 (*Fasslabend*)

17. Address by Green leader Madeleine Petrovic 'For a Moral Renewal of the Second Republic' on the Fiftieth anniversary of Germany's unconditional surrender, delivered on 8 May 1995 (*Petrovic*)

18. Remarks by the Green Spokeswoman for Minority Affairs, Terezija Stoisits (*Stoisits 15*), and the director of the Boltzmann Institut for Human Rights, Hannes Tretter (*Tretter*), made at a press conference devoted to 'Forty Years of the State Treaty' on 15 May 1995; press release by Terezija Stoisits on the occasion of the Austrian National Holiday on 26 October 1995 (*Stoisits 26*)

19. Remarks by Second President of the Austrian National Assembly, Heinrich Neisser, made at a ceremony commemorating the fiftieth anniversary of the mass murder of 200 Hungarian Jews by the Nazis, at Rechnitz, Burgenland on 26 March 1995 (*Neisser*)

20. Address by the First President of the Austrian National Assembly, Heinz Fischer, to the joint session of the National Assembly and the Federal Council celebrating the fiftieth anniversary of the foundation of the Second Republic, delivered on 27 April 1995 (*Fischer*)

21. Address by President of the Federal Council Jürgen Weiss to the same joint session celebrating the fiftieth anniversary of the foundation of the Second Republic (*Weiss*)

22. Address by then chairman of the ÖVP Erhard Busek, at the ceremony celebrating fifty years of the ÖVP, delivered at the *Schottenstift*, Vienna, on 21 April 1995 (*Busek*)

23. Lecture by Member of Parliament Friedhelm Frischenschlager (Liberal Forum) 'Austria in a Europe of solidarity' at the *SPÖ Zukunftswerkstätte* ('Workshop for the Future') Conference 'Advanced Democracy', delivered on 1 July 1995 (*Frischenschlager*)

Bibliography

Alter, Peter (1985). *Nationalismus*. Frankfurt a. M.

Ammon, Ulrich (1995). *Die deutsche Sprache in Deutschland, Österreich und der Schweiz: Das Problem der nationalen Varietäten.* Berlin.

Anderson, Benedict (1983). *Imagined Communities: Reflections on the Origins and Spread of Nationalism.* London.

Andics, Hellmut (1962). *Der Staat, den keiner wollte.* Vienna.

Ardelt, Rudolf G. (1994). '"Wie deutsch ist Österreich?" Eine Auseinandersetzung mit K. D. Erdmann und F. Fellner'. In Botz, Gerhard and Sprengnagel, Gerald (eds). *Kontroversen um Österreichs Zeitgeschichte.* Frankfurt a. M., pp. 266–86.

Bailer, Brigitte (1993). *Wiedergutmachung kein Thema: Österreich und die Opfer des National-sozialismus.* Vienna.

Bailer, Brigitte (1995). 'Die unwürdige Diskussion über den NS-Opfer-Fonds'. *Kurier,* 1 June 1995.

Bailer, Brigitte and Neugebauer, Wolfgang (1993). 'Die FPÖ: Vom Liberalismus zum Rechts-extremismus'. In Dokumentationsarchiv des österreichischen Widerstands (eds). *Handbuch des österreichischen Rechtsextremismus* (2nd edn). Vienna, pp. 327–428.

Bamberger, Richard, Bamberger, Maria, Bruckmüller, Ernst and Gutkas, Karl (eds) (1995). *Österreich Lexikon,* Vol. 2. Vienna.

Bauböck, Rainer (1991). 'Nationalismus versus Demokratie'. In *Österreichische Zeitschrift für Politikwissenschaft* (ÖZP) 1, pp. 73–90.

Benhabib, Seyla (1996). *Democracy and Difference.* Princeton, NY.

Benke, Gertraud and Wodak, Ruth (1999). '"We are no longer the sick child of Europe": An Investigation of the Usage (and Change) of the Term "Neutrality" in the Presidential Speeches on the National Holiday from 1974 to 1993'. In Wodak, Ruth and Christoph, Ludwig (eds). *Challenges in a Changing World: New Perspectives in Critical Discourse Analysis.* Vienna, pp. 101–26.

Benz, Wolfgang (ed.) (1992). *Legenden, Lügen, Vorurteile: Ein Wörterbuch zur Zeitgeschichte* (2nd edn). Munich.

Berger, Peter L. and Luckmann, Thomas (1980). *Die gesellschaftliche Konstruktion der Wirk-lichkeit: Eine Theorie der Wissenssoziologie.* Frankfurt a. M.

Bernstein, Basil (1996). *Pedagogy, Symbolic Control and Identity: Theory, Research, Critique.* London.

Bischof, Günter, Pelinka, Anton and Rathkolb, Oliver (eds) (1994). *Contemporary Austrian Studies 2: The Kreisky Era in Austria.* New Brunswick and London.

Blomert, Reinhard, Kuzmics, Helmut and Treibel, Annette (1993). *Transformationen des Wir-Gefühls: Studien zum nationalen Habitus.* Frankfurt a. M.

Botz, Gerhard and Sprengnagel, Gerald (eds) (1994). *Kontroversen um Österreichs Zeitgeschichte: Verdrängte Vergangenheit, Österreich-Identität, Waldheim und die Historiker.* Frankfurt a. M.

Bourdieu, Pierre (1990). *The Logic of Practice*. Cambridge.
Bourdieu, Pierre (1993a). *Outline of a Theory of Practice*. Cambridge.
Bourdieu, Pierre (1993b). *Sociology in Question*. London.
Bourdieu, Pierre (1994a). *In Other Words: Essays towards a Reflexive Sociology*. Cambridge.
Bourdieu, Pierre (1994b). *Zur Soziologie der symbolischen Formen* (5th edn). Frankfurt a. M.
Bourdieu, Pierre (1994c). 'Rethinking the State: Genesis and Structure of the Bureaucratic Field'. *Sociological Theory* 12:1, pp. 1–18.
Bradley, Harriet (1996). *Fractured Identities: Changing Patterns of Inequality*. Cambridge.
Bredin, Hugh (1984). 'Metonymy'. *Poetics Today* 5, pp. 45–58.
Breuss, Susanne, Liebhart, Karin and Pribersky, Andreas (1995). *Inszenierungen: Stichwörter zu Österreich*. Vienna.
Brubaker, Rogers (1992). *Citizenship and Nationhood in France and Germany*. Cambridge, Mass. and London.
Bruck, Peter A. and Stocker, Günther (1996). *Die ganz normale Vielfältigkeit des Lesens: Zur Rezeption von Boulevardzeitungen*. Münster.
Bruckmüller, Ernst (1991). 'Die Frage nach dem Nationalbewußtsein in der österreichischen Geschichte unter sozialhistorischem Aspekt'. In Wolfram, Herwig and Pohl, Walter (eds). *Probleme der Geschichte Österreichs und ihrer Darstellung*. Vienna, pp. 49–56.
Bruckmüller, Ernst (1994). *Österreichbewußtsein im Wandel: Identität und Selbstverständnis in den 90er Jahren*. Vienna.
Bruckmüller, Ernst (1995). 'Millennium! – Millennium? Das Ostarrichi-Anniversarium und die österreichische Länderausstellung 1996'. In *Österreich in Geschichte und Literatur* 39, pp. 137–55.
Bruckmüller, Ernst (1996). *Nation Österreich. Kulturelles Bewußtsein und gesellschaftlich-politische Prozesse* (2nd edn). Vienna, Cologne and Graz.
Bruckmüller, Ernst and Urbanitsch, Peter (eds) (1996). *Österreichische Länderausstellung, 996–1996. Ostarrichi-Österreich: Menschen – Mythen – Meilensteine*. Horn.
Brünner, Christian (1993). 'Neutralität ohne Eigenschaften – ein Irrtum!' *Profil* 20, pp. 20f.
Brünner, Gisela and Graefen, Gabriele (eds) (1994). *Texte und Diskurse. Methoden und Forschungsergebnisse der Funktionalen Pragmatik*. Opladen.
Bunzl, John (1993). 'Österreich zuerst'. *Das jüdische Echo* 10, pp. 48–50.
Burger, Rudolf (1994a). 'Patriotismus und Nation. Bemerkungen zu einem (nicht nur) öster-reichischen Problem'. *Leviathan* 2, pp. 161–70.
Burger, Rudolf (1994b). 'Vae neutralis! Determination der europäischen Integration in österreichischer Perspektive'. *Levathian* 2, pp. 353–66.
Burger, Rudolf ([1993] 1996). 'Patriotismus und Nation'. In Rudolf Burger, Klein, Hans Dieter, and Schroeder, Wolfgang H. (eds). *Gesellschaft, Staat, Nation*. Vienna, pp. 35–46.
Burke, Peter (1989). 'History as Social Memory'. In Butler, Thomas (ed.). *Memory: History, Culture and the Mind*. Oxford, pp. 97–113.
Campbell, Karlyn Kohrs and Jamieson, Kathleen Hall (1990). *Deeds Done in Words: Presidential Rhetoric and the Genres of Governance*. Chicago and London.
Chilton, Paul and Schaeffner, Christina (1997). 'Discourse and Politics'. In Van Dijk, Teun A. (ed.). *Discourse as Social Interaction*. London, Thousand Oaks and New Delhi, pp. 206–30.
Cicourel, Aaron V. (1969). *Method and Measurement in Sociology*. New York, NY.
Clyne, Michael G. (1995). *The German Language in a Changing Europe*. Cambridge.
Coudenhove-Kalergi, Barbara (1990). 'Die österreichische Doppelseele'. In Rathkolb, Oliver, Schmid, Georg and Heiss, Gernot (eds). *Österreich und Deutschlands Größe: Ein schlampiges Verhältuis*. Salzburg, pp. 56–61.
Csáky, Moritz (1991). 'Historische Reflexionen über das Problem einer österreichischen Identität'. In Wolfram, Herwig and Pohl, Walter (eds). *Probleme der Geschichte Österreichs und ihrer Darstellung*. Vienna, pp. 29–48.
Dachs, Herbert (1994). 'Österreichs Föderalismus zwischen Anpassung und Beharrung'. In

Bundesministerium für Unterricht und Kunst (ed.). *Demokratie in der Krise? Zumpolitischen System Österreichs.* Vienna, pp. 75–86.

de Cillia, Rudolf (1996). 'Linguistic Policy Aspects of Austria's Accession to the European Union'. *New Language Planning Newsletter* 10:3, pp. 1–3.

de Cillia, Rudolf (1998a). *Burenwurscht bleibt Burenwurscht: Sprachenpolitik und gesellschaftliche Mehrsprachigkeit in Österreich.* Klagenfurt/Celovec.

de Cillia, Rudolf (1998b). ' "Dieses zwanzigste Jahrhundert ist für viele Österreicher ein Jahrhundert und eine Geschichte auch des Leidens". Opferthese und österreichische Identität in Politikerreden'. In Kettemann, Bernhard, de Cillia, Rudolf and Landsiedler, Isabel (eds). *Sprache und Politik. Verbal-Werkstattgespräche 1995.* Frankfurt a. M., pp. 119–45.

de Cillia, Rudolf, Menz, Florian, Dressler, Wolfgang and Cech, Petra (1998). 'Linguistic Minorities in Austria'. In Paulston, Christina Bratt and Peckham, Donald (eds). *Linguistic Minorities in Central and Eastern Europe.* Clevedon, pp. 18–36.

de Cillia, Rudolf, Martin Reisigl and Ruth Wodak (1999). 'The Discursive Construction of National Identities'. *Discourse and Society* 10:1, pp. 149–73.

Discourse & Society 4:2 (1993). (Special Issue: *Critical Discourse Analysis.*)

Dokumentation market-Archiv M25 (1993).

Dusek, Peter, Pelinka, Anton and Weinzierl, Erika (1988). *Zeitgeschichte im Aufriß: Österreich seit 1918.* Vienna.

Ecker, Gerold and Neugebauer, Christian (eds) (1993). *Neutralität oder Euromilitarismus: Das Exempel Österreich.* Vienna.

Eemeren, Frans H. van, Grootendorst, Rob and Kruiger, Tjark (1987). *Argumentation: Analysis and Practices.* Dordrecht.

Ehlich, Konrad (1986). 'Funktional-Pragmatische Kommunikationsanalyse – Ziele und Verfahren'. In Hartung, Wolfdietrich (ed.). *Untersuchungen zur Kommunikation – Ergebnisse und Perspektiven* (International Workshop in Bad Stuer, December 1985). Berlin, pp. 15–40.

Ehlich, Konrad (1993). 'Diskursanalyse'. In Glück, Helmut (ed.). *Metzler Lexikon Sprache.* Stuttgart and Weimar, pp. 145–6.

Ehlich, Konrad (1994). 'Einleitung'. In Ehlich, Konrad (ed.). *Diskursanalyse in Europa.* Frankfurt a. M., pp. 9–13.

Elias, Norbert (1992). *Studien über die Deutschen: Machtkämpfe und Habitusentwicklung im 19. und 20. Jahrhundert* (2nd edn). Frankfurt a. M.

Erdmann, Karl Dietrich (1989). *Die Spur Österreichs in der deutschen Geschichte: Drei Staaten, zwei Nationen, ein Volk?* Zurich.

Erdmann, Karl Dietrich (1994). 'Die Spur Österreichs in der deutschen Geschichte'. In Botz, Gerhard and Sprengnagel, Gerald (eds). *Kontroversen um Österreichs Zeitgeschichte.* Frankfurt a. M., pp. 241–65.

Erikson, Erik H. (1959). *Identity and the Life Cycle.* New York.

Euchner, Walter (1995). 'Qu'est-ce qu'une nation? Das Nationsverständnis Ernest Renans im Kontext seines politischen Denkens'. Introduction to Renan, Ernest (1995). *Was ist eine Nation? ... und andere politsche Schriften.* Vienna and Bolzano, pp. 7–39.

Fairclough, Norman (1995). *Critical Discourse Analysis: The Critical Study of Language.* London and New York.

Fairclough, Norman and Wodak, Ruth (1997). 'Critical Discourse Analysis'. In Van Dijk, Teun A. (ed.). *Discourse as Social Interaction.* London, Thousand Oaks and New Delhi, pp. 258–84.

Falkner, Gerda (1995). 'Österreich und die Europäische Einigung'. In Sieder, Reinhard, Steinert, Heinz and Tálos, Emmerich (eds). *Österreich 1945–1995.* Vienna, pp. 331–40.

Der Falter (1995). 'Was war'. 15 June, p. 9.

Faßmann, Heinz and Münz, Rainer (1995). *Einwanderungsland Österreich? Historische Migrationsmuster, aktuelle Trends und politische Maßnahmen.* Vienna.

Fellner, Fritz (1985). 'Das Problem der österreichischen Nation nach 1945'. In Busch, Otto and Sheehan, James (eds). *Die Rolle der Nation in der deutschen Geschichte der Gegenwart.* Berlin, pp. 193–220.

Fellner, Fritz (1994). 'Das Problem der österreichischen Nation nach 1945'. In Botz, Gerhard and Sprengnagel, Gerald (eds). *Kontroversen um Österreichs Zeitgeschichte.* Frankfurt a. M., pp. 216–40.

Fischer, Ernst (1945). *Die Entstehung des österreichischen Volkscharakters.* Vienna.

Francis, Emmerich (1965). *Ethnos und Demos – Soziologische Beiträge zur Volkstheorie.* Berlin.

Freud, Sigmund ([1930] 1982). 'Das Unbehagen in der Kultur (1930)'. In Freud, Sigmund. *Studienausgabe,* Vol. 9: *Fragen der Gesellschaft: Ursprünge der Religion.* Frankfurt a. M., pp. 191–270.

Frey, Hans-Peter and Hausser, Karin (1987). 'Entwicklungslinien sozialwissenschaftlicher Identitätsforschung'. In Frey, Hans-Peter and Hausser, Karin (eds). *Identität: Entwicklungen psychologischer und soziologischer Forschung.* Stuttgart, pp. 3–26.

Friedrichs, Jürgen (1985). *Methoden der empirischen Sozialforschung.* Opladen.

Garscha, Wilfried R. (1994). 'Für eine neue Chronologie der österreichischen Nationsgenese'. In Botz, Gerhard and Sprengnagel, Gerald (eds). *Kontroversen um Österreichs Zeitgeschichte.* Frankfurt a. M., pp. 346–52.

Gärtner, Reinhold (1996). 'Opfer oder Helden? Kriegerdenkmäler aus dem Zweiten Welkrieg in Österreich'. In Manoschek, Walter (ed.). *Die Wehrmacht im Rassenkrieg.* Vienna, pp. 206–20.

Gärtner, Reinhold and Rosenberger, Sieglinde (1991). *Kriegerdenkmäler.* Innsbruck.

Geertz, Clifford (1973a). *The Interpretation of Cultures.* New York.

Geertz, Clifford (1973b). *Dichte Beschreibung.* Frankfurt a. M.

Gehler, Michael and Sickinger, Hubert (1995). 'Politische Skandale in der Zweiten Republik'. In Sieder, Reinhard, Steinert, Heinz and Tálos, Emmerich (eds). pp. 671–83.

Gellner, Ernest (1994). *Nations and Nationalism.* Oxford.

Goffman, Erving (1981). *Forms of Talk.* Oxford.

Goffman, Erving (1990). *Stigma. Notes on the Management of Spoiled Identity.* Harmondsworth.

Goodwin, Ken (1990). 'Anthropomorphizing Nationality. Some Australian and African Examples'. In Zach, Wolfgang (ed.). *Literatures in English. New Perspectives.* Frankfurt a. M., pp. 109–28.

Goschler, Constantin (1992). *Wiedergutmachung.* In Benz, Wolfgang (ed.). *Legenden, Lügen, Vorurteile* (2nd edn). Munich, pp. 222–5.

Greenbaum, Thomas L. (1988). *The Practical Handbook and Guide to Focus Group Research.* Lexington and Toronto.

Groddeck, Wolfram (1995). *Rhetorik über Rhetorik: Zu einer Stilistik des Lesens.* Basel and Frankfurt a. M.

Gruber, Helmut (1991). *Antisemitismus im Mediendiskurs. Die Affäre "Waldheim" in der Tagespresse.* Wiesbaden.

Gruber, Reinhard P. (1988). 'Die Mehrheit ist der Feind des Begriffs'. In Jung, Jochen (ed.). *Reden an Österreich.* Saltzburg and Vienna, pp. 57–67.

Gürses, Hakan (1994). 'Wechselspiel der Identitäten: Bemerkungen zum Minderheitenbegriff'. In *SWS-Rundschau* 4, pp. 353–68.

Gutkas, Karl (1985). *Die Zweite Republik. Österreich 1945–1985.* Vienna.

Haas, Hanns (1994). 'Österreich im "gesamtdeutschen Schicksalszusammenhang?"' In Botz, Gerhard and Sprengnagel, Gerald (eds). *Kontroversen um Österreichs Zeitgeschichte.* Frankfurt a. M., pp. 194–215.

Habermas, Jürgen (1976). *Zur Rekonstruktion des Historischen Materialismus.* Frankfurt a. M.

Habermas, Jürgen (1993). 'Anerkennungskämpfe im demokratischen Rechtsstaat'. In Taylor, Charles and Gutmann, Amy (eds). *Multikulturalismus und die Politik der Anerkennung.*

Frankfurt a. M., pp. 147–96.

Habermas, Jürgen (1996). *Die Einbeziehung des Anderen: Studien zur politischen Theorie.* Frankfurt a. M.

Hagen, Johann Josef (1994). 'Sicherheit und Neutralität im Lichte der europäischen Gesamtentwicklung'. *Journal für Rechtspolitik* 4, pp. 273–82.

Haerpfer, Christian W. (1995). 'Politische Partizipation'. In Sieder, Reinhard, Steinert, Heinz and Tálos, Emmerich (eds). *Österreich 1945–1995.* Vienna, pp. 426–34.

Halbwachs, Maurice (1997). *La mémoire collective.* Paris.

Hall, Stuart (1996a). 'The Question of Cultural Identity'. In Hall, Stuart, Held, David, Hubert, Don and Thompson, Kenneth (eds). *Modernity: An Introduction to Modern Societies.* Cambridge, Mass. and Oxford, pp. 595–634.

Hall, Stuart (1996b). 'Introduction: Who needs "Identity"?' In Hall, Stuart and Du Gay, Paul (eds). *Questions of Cultural Identity.* London, Thousand Oaks and New Delhi, pp. 1–17.

Haller, Max (1996). Elf Thesen zu den Grundlagen und Zukunftsperspektiven der nationalen Identität Österreichs und der Österreicher. In Haller, Max, et al. *Identität und Nationalstolz der Österreicher: Gesellschaftliche Ursachen und Funktionen – Herausbildung und Transformation seit 1945 – Internationaler Vergleich.* Vienna, Cologne and Graz, pp. 501–29.

Haller, Max, Gruber, Stefan, Langer, Josef, Paier, Günter, Reiterer, Albert and Teibenbacher, Peter (1996). *Identität und Nationalstolz der Österreicher: Gesellschaftliche Ursachen und Funktionen – Herausbildung und Transformation seit 1945 – Internationaler Vergleich.* Vienna, Cologne and Graz.

Haller, Max and Gruber, Stefan (1996a). 'Die Österreicher und ihre Nation – Patrioten oder Chauvinisten? Gesellschaftliche Formen, Bedingungen und Funktionen nationaler Identität'. In Haller et al. *Identität und Nationalstolz der Österreicher.* Vienna, Cologne and Graz, pp. 61–147.

Haller, Max and Gruber, Stefan (1996b). 'Die Identität der Österreicher zwischen lokal-regionaler, nationaler und europäischer Zugehörigkeit'. In Haller et al. *Identität und Nationalstolz der Österreicher.* Vienna, Cologne and Graz, pp. 383–430.

Haller, Max and Gruber, Stefan (1996c). 'Der Nationalstolz der Österreicher im internationalen Vergleich'. In Haller et al. *Identität und Nationalstolz der Österreicher.* Vienna, Cologne and Graz, pp. 431–99.

Hanisch, Ernst (1988). 'Ein Versuch, den Nationalsozialismus zu "verstehen"'. In Freytag, Aurelius, Marte, Boris and Stern, Thomas (eds). *Geschichte und Verantwortung.* Vienna, pp. 197–202.

Hanisch, Ernst (1994). *Der lange Schatten des Staates: Österreichische Gesellschaftsgeschichte im 20. Jahrhundert.* Vienna.

Harvey, D. (1996). *Justice, Nature and the Geography of Difference.* London.

Haslinger, Josef (1988). 'Der Umgang der Zweiten Republik mit Krieg und Faschismus'. In Jung, Jochen (ed.). *Reden an Österreich.* Salzburg and Vienna, pp. 68–80.

Heer, Friedrich (1981). *Der Kampf um die österreichische Identität.* Vienna, Graz and Cologne.

Heer, Hannes and Naumann, Klaus (eds) (1995). *Vernichtungskrieg: Verbrechen der Wehrmacht 1941–1944.* Hamburg.

Heinemann, Wolfgang and Viehweger, Dieter (1991). *Textlinguistik: Eine Einführung.* Tübingen.

Heinrich, Hans Georg and Welan, Manfried (1992). 'Der Bundespräsident'. In Dachs, Herbert, Gerlich, Peter, Gottweis, Herbert, Horner, Franz, Kramer, Helmut, Volkmar, Lauber, Müller, Wolfgang C., and Tálos, Emmerich (eds). *Handbuch des politischen Systems Österreichs.* Vienna, pp. 134–9.

Hermanns, Fritz (1982). 'Brisante Wörter: Zur lexikographischen Behandlung parteisprach-licher Wörter und Wendungen in Wörterbüchern der deutschen Gegenwartssprache'. In Wiegand, Herbert Ernst (ed.). *Studien zur neuhochdeutschen Lexikographie 2.* Hildesheim and New York, pp. 87–108.

Höbelt, Lothar (1985). '"Drei Staaten – zwei Nationen – ein Volk?" Kontinuität in der deutschen Geschichte'. *Die Presse,* 7 August, p. 10.

Höbelt, Lothar (1994). 'Österreich = deutsch ≠ bundesrepublikanisch'. In Botz, Gerhard and Sprengnagel, Gerald (eds). *Kontroversen um Österreichs Zeitgeschichte.* Frankfurt a. M., pp. 338–45.

Hobsbawm, Eric J. (1990). *Nations and Nationalism since 1780: Programme, Myth, Reality.* Cambridge.

Hobsbawm, Eric J. and Ranger, Terence (eds) (1983). *The Invention of Tradition.* Cambridge.

Hochschülerschaft der Technischen Universität Wien (1995). *VorSätze-NachSätze. Diskurs über die Republik.* Klagenfurt and Salzburg.

Höll, Otmar (1995). 'Österreichische Außenpolitik'. *SWS-Rundschau* 33:4, pp. 461–7.

Holzinger, Wolfgang (1993a). 'Nationalismus – Versuch einer Annäherung an ein komplexes Thema'. In Guggenberger, Helmut and Holzinger, Wolfgang (eds). *Neues Europa – Alte Nationalismen: Kollektive Identitäten im Spannungsfeld von Integration und Ausschließung.* Klagenfurt/Celovec, pp. 14–38.

Holzinger, Wolfgang (1993b). *Identität als sozialwissenschaftliches Konstrukt. Theoretische Grundlagen und Forschungsfragen.* Unpublished manuscript.

Hölzl, Erik (1994). 'Qualitatives Interview'. In Arbeitskreis qualitative Sozialforschung (ed.). *Verführung zum qualitativen Forschen: Eine Methodenauswahl.* Vienna. pp. 61–8.

Huemer, Friedrun and Manoschek, Walter (1996). 'Wolgograd soll kein Pilgerort werden'. *Informationen der Gesellschaft für politische Aufklärung* 49, pp. 9–10.

Huter, Michael (1994). 'Die Magie der runden Zahlen: Kulturelles Verhalten und Formen der Zeiterfahrung'. In Schmidt-Dengler, Wendelin (ed.). *Der literarische Umgang der Österreicher mit Jahres- und Gedenktagen.* Vienna. pp. 7–16.

Iedema, Roderick A. M. (1997). *Interactional Dynamics and Social Change: Planning as Morphogenesis.* PhD. Dissertation, University of Sydney.

Jäger, Margret (1996). *Fatale Effekte: Die Kritik am Patriarchat im Einwanderungsdiskurs.* Duisburg.

James, Louis (1994). *The Xenophobe's Guide to The Austrians.* London.

Jung, Jochen (ed.) (1988). *Reden an Österreich: Schriftsteller ergreifen das Wort.* Salzburg and Vienna.

Jung, Jochen (ed.) (1995). *Glückliches Österreich: Literarische Besichtigung unseres Vaterlandes.* Vienna.

Kahl, Kurt (1966). 'Das häßliche Deutsch des Österreichers'. *Wort in der Zeit* 5, pp. 27–31.

Kaindl-Widhalm, Barbara (1990). *Demokraten wider Willen? Autoritäre Tendenzen und Antisemitismus in der 2. Republik.* Vienna.

Kaiser, Wolfram, Visuri, Pekka, Malmström, Cecilia, Hjelseth, Arve, Listhaug, Ola and Jenssen, Anders Todal (1994). *Die EU-Volksabstimmungen in Österreich, Finnland, Schweden und Norwegen: Verlauf, Ergebnisse, Motive und Folgen. Forschungsbericht.* Vienna.

Kammerer, Patrick (1995). 'Die veränderten Konstitutionsbedingungen politischer Rhetorik: Zur Rolle der Redenschreiber, der Medien und zum vermeintlichen Ende öffentlicher Rede'. In Dyck, Joachim, Jens, Walter and Ueding, Gerd (eds). *Rhetorik: Ein internationales Jahrbuch* 14, pp. 14–29.

Kargl, Maria (1996). *Der Held von Brüssel: Das Bild Alois Mocks in der EU-Berichterstattung von 'Kronenzeitung' und 'Täglich Alles' als Beispiel für sprachliche Imagekonstituierung.* (M.A. dissertation, University of Vienna.)

Kettemann, Bernhard, Grilz, Wolfgang and Landsiedler, Isabel (1995). *Sprache und Politik: Analyse berühmter Reden.* Retzhof bei Leibnitz.

Khol, Andreas (1990). 'Österreich – Neue Aufgaben in Europa'. *Revue d'Allemagne et des pays de langue allemande* 22:1, pp. 19–34.

Kienpointner, Manfred (1983). *Argumentationsanalyse.* Innsbruck.

Kienpointner, Manfred (1992). *Alltagslogik: Struktur und Funktion von Argumentations-*

mustern. Stuttgart-Bad Cannstatt.

Kienpointner, Manfred (1996). *Vernünftig argumentieren: Regeln und Techniken der Diskussion*. Hamburg.

Kindt, Walter (1992). 'Argumentation und Konfliktaustragung in Äußerungen über den Golfkrieg'. *Zeitschrift für Sprachwissenschaft* 11, pp. 189–215.

Knight, Robert (ed.) (1988). *'Ich bin dafür, die Sache in die Länge zu ziehen': Die Wortprotokolle der österreichischen Bundesregierung von 1945–1952 über die Entschädigung der Juden*. Frankfurt a. M.

Koja, Friedrich (1991). 'Rechtliche und politische Aspekte der österreichischen Neutralität'. *Europäische Rundschau* 19:2, pp. 57–64.

Kolakowski, Leszek (1995). 'Über kollektive Identität.' In Michalski, Krzysztof (ed.). *Identität im Wandel: Castelgandolfo-Gespräche 1995. Institut für die Wissenschaften vom Menschen*. Stuttgart, pp. 47–60.

Koselleck, Reinhart (1989). *Vergangene Zukunft: Zur Semantik geschichtlicher Zeiten*. Frankfurt a. M.

Kramer, Helmut (1991). 'Öffentliche Meinung und die österreichische EG-Entscheidung im Jahre 1989'. *SWS-Rundschau* 31, pp. 191–202.

Kreissler, Felix (1984). *Der Österreicher und seine Nation. Ein Lernprozeß mit Hindernissen*. Vienna, Cologne and Graz.

Kreissler, Felix (1988). 'Nationalbewußtsein und Nationalcharakter: Vom ewigen Anlehnungsbedürfnis der Österreicher'. In Freytag, Aurelius, Marte, Boris and Stern, Thomas (eds). *Geschichte und Verantwortung*. Vienna, pp. 77–90.

Kreissler, Felix (1991). Der Kampf um die österreichische Identität. In Pribersky, Andreas (ed.). *Europa und Mitteleuropa? Eine Umschreibung Österreichs*. Sonderzahl, Vienna, pp. 141–61.

Kreissler, Felix (1993). 'Österreichs Identität und Antiidentität'. *Informationen der Gesellschaft für politische Aufklärung* 37, pp. 3–7.

Kühn, Peter (1992). 'Adressaten und Adressatenkarussell in der öffentlich-politischen Auseinandersetzung'. In Dyck, Joachim, Jens, Walter and Ueding, Gerd (eds). *Rhetorik: Ein internationales Jahrbuch* 11, pp. 51–66.

Kühn, Peter (1995). *Mehrfachadressierung: Untersuchungen zur adressatenspezifischen Polyvalenz sprachlichen Handelns*. Tübingen.

Kuzmics, Helmut (1993). 'Österreichischer und englischer Volkscharakter. Einige Aspekte im Vergleich anhand von belletristischer Literatur'. In Nowotny, Helen and Taschwer, Klaus (eds). *Macht und Ohnmacht im neuen Europa*. Vienna, pp. 123–35.

Laclau, Ernesto (1990). *New Reflections on the Revolution of our Time*. London.

Laireiter, Christian, Schaller, Christian, Sickinger, Hubert, Vretscha, Andreas and Weninger, Thomas (1994). 'Die östereichische EG-Diskussion in den Ländern: Vergleichende Analyse von regionalen Konfliktpotentialen in sechs Bundesländern'. In *Österreichische Zeitschrift für Politikwissenschaft (ÖZP)* 1, pp. 67–88.

Lakoff, George and Johnson, Marc (1980). *Metaphors We Live By*. Chicago.

Lamnek, Siegfried (1989). *Qualitative Sozialforschung Band 2: Methoden und Techniken*. Munich.

Lausberg, Heinrich (1990). *Handbuch der literarischen Rhetorik: Eine Grundlegung der Literaturwissenschaft* (3rd edn). Stuttgart.

Leggewie, Claus (1995). 'Österreich und Europa: Wie westlich ist die Zweite Republik?'. *Österreichische Hochschulzeitung. Magazin für Wissenschaft und Wirtschaft (ÖHZ)* 9, pp. 32–3.

Lévi-Strauss, Claude (1966). 'Natur und Kultur'. In Mühlmann, Wilhelm Emil and Müller, Ernst W. (eds) (1966). *Kulturanthropologie*. Cologne and Berlin, p. 86.

Liebhart, Karin and Reisigl, Martin (1997). 'Die sprachliche Verfertigung des "österreichischen Menschen" bei der diskursiven Konstruktion der nationalen Identität'. In

Bundesministerium für Wissenschaft, Verkehr und Kunst (ed.). *Grenzenloses Österreich*. Vienna, pp. 139–61

List, Elisabeth (1996). '"Wer fürchtet sich vorm schwarzen Mann?" Zur Psychogenese von Fremdenfeindlichkeit, Nationalismus und Sexismus'. In Hödl, Klaus (ed.) (1996). *Der Umgang mit den 'Anderen': Juden, Frauen, Fremde* ... Vienna, Cologne and Weimar, pp. 103–20.

Luif, Paul (1982). 'Österreich zwischen den Blöcken. Bemerkungen zur Außenpolitik des neutralen Österreich'. In *ÖZP* 2, pp. 209–20.

Luif, Paul (1995). 'Die österreichische Europapolitik'. In *SWS-Rundschau* 33:4, pp. 469–73.

Maas, Utz (1984). *'Als der Geist der Gemeinschaft eine Sprache fand'. Sprache im Nationalsozialismus: Versuch einer historischen Argumentationsanalyse*. Opladen.

Manoschek, Walter (1993). *'Serbien ist judenfrei'. Militärische Besatzungspolitik und Judenvernichtung in Serbien 1941/42.* Munich.

Manoschek, Walter (1995). 'Verschmähte Erbschaft: Österreichs Umgang mit dem Nationalsozialismus 1945 bis 1995'. In Sieder, Reinhard, Steinert, Heinz and Tálos, Emmerich (eds). *Österreich 1945–1995*. Vienna, pp. 94–106.

Manoschek, Walter (1996a). 'Die Wehrmacht im Rassenkrieg'. In Manoschek (ed.). *Die Wehrmacht im Rassenkrieg*. Vienna, pp. 9–15.

Manoschek, Walter (ed.) (1996b). *Die Wehrmacht im Rassenkrieg. Der Vernichtungskrieg hinter der Front*. Vienna.

Martin, Denis-Constant (1995). 'The Choices of Identity'. *Social Identities* 1:1, pp. 5–20.

Matouschek, Bernd and Wodak, Ruth (1995). '"Rumänen, Roma ... und andere Fremde": Historisch-kritische Diskursanalyse zur Rede von den "Anderen"'. In Heiss, Gernot and Rathkolb, Oliver (eds). *Asylland wider Willen: Flüchtlinge in Österreich im europäischen Kontext seit 1914*. Vienna, pp. 210–38.

Matouschek, Bernd, Wodak, Ruth and Januschek, Franz (1995). *Notwendige Maßnahmen gegen Fremde? Genese und Formen von rassistischen Diskursen der Differenz*. Vienna.

Matuschek, Stefan (1994). 'Epideiktische Beredsamkeit'. In Ueding, Gerd (ed.). *Historisches Wörterbuch der Rhetorik*, Vol. 2, pp. 1258–67.

Matzner, Egon (1995). 'Plädoyer für die Eigenstaatlichkeit'. *Hochschülerschaft der Technischen Universität Wien*, pp. 37–66.

Mead, George H. (1967). *Mind, Self, and Society from the Standpoint of a Social Behaviorist*. Chicago.

Meissl, Sebastian, Mulley, Klaus-Dieter and Rathkolb, Oliver (eds) (1986). *Verdrängte Schuld – Verfehlte Sühne. Entnazifizierung in Österreich 1945–1955*. Vienna.

Menasse, Robert (1991). *Die sozialpartnerschaftliche Ästhetik*. Vienna.

Menasse, Robert (1995). *Das Land ohne Eigenschaften*. Frankfurt a. M.

Menz, Florian (1994). 'Diskursforschung in Österreich'. In Ehlich, Konrad (ed.). *Diskursanalyse in Europa*. Frankfurt a. M., pp. 139–59.

Miall, Antony (1993). *The Xenophobe's Guide to The English*. London.

Mitten, Richard (1992). *The Politics of Antisemitic Prejudice: The Waldheim Phenomenon in Austria*. Boulder.

Mölzer, Andreas (1988). *Österreich – ein deutscher Sonderfall*. No place given.

Mölzer, Andreas (1991). *Und wo bleibt Österreich? Die Alpenrepublik zwischen deutscher Vereinigung und europäischem Zusammenschluß: Eine Zwischenbilanz*. Berg.

Morgan, David L. (ed.) (1988). *Focus Groups as Qualitative Research*. Sage.

Morgan, David L. (ed.) (1993). *Successful Focus Groups: Advancing the State of the Art*. Newbury Park, London and New Delhi.

Morier, Henri (1989). *Dictionnaire de Poétique et de Rhétorique* (4th edn). Paris.

Muhr, Rudolf (1989). 'Deutsch und Österreich(isch): Gespaltene Sprache – Gespaltenes Bewußtsein – Gespaltene Identität'. *informationen zur deutschdidaktik (ide)* 2, pp. 74–98.

Muhr, Rudolf (ed.) (1993). *Internationale Arbeiten zum österreichischen Deutsch und seinen nachbarsprachlichen Bezügen.* Vienna.

Muhr, Rudolf, Schrodt, Richard and Wiesinger, Peter (eds) (1995). *Österreichisches Deutsch: Linguistische, sozialpsychologische und sprachpolitische Aspekte einer nationalen Variante des Deutschen.* Vienna.

Münkler, Herfried (1994). *Politische Bilder: Politik der Metaphern.* Frankfurt a. M.

Münz, Rainer (1991). 'Wer sind wir? Fragen nach der Identität Österreichs und seiner Bürger'. In Dr. Karl Renner Institut (ed.). *Wir sind wir! Ein Problemaufriß zur politischen Kultur: Studientagung zur politischen Bildung.* Vienna, pp. 6–13.

Neugebauer, Wolfgang (1994). 'Opfer oder Täter'. In Tabor, Jan (ed.). *Kunst und Diktatur.* Baden, pp. 895–8.

Nick, Rainer and Pelinka, Anton (1993). *Österreichs politische Landschaft.* Innsbruck.

Noll, Alfred (1993). 'Neutrales Österreich passé'. In Ecker, Gerold and Neugebauer, Christian (eds). *Neutralität oder Euromilitarismus.* Vienna, pp. 189–201.

Not Without My Daughter (1990). Film, based on the book by Betty Mahmoody and William Hoffer. PATHÉ Entertainment Inc./Metro Goldwyn Mayer. Video produced by Cannon/VMP, 1991.

Nowak, Peter, Wodak, Ruth and de Cillia, Rudolf (1990). 'Die Grenzen der Abgrenzung: Methoden und Ergebnisse einer Studie zum antisemitischen Diskurs im Nachkriegsösterreich.' In Wodak, Ruth and Menz, Florian (eds). *Sprache in der Politik – Politik in der Sprache.* Klagenfurt/Celovec, pp. 128–51.

Nowotny, Helga and Taschwer, Klaus (eds) (1993). *Macht und Ohnmacht im neuen Europa: Zur Aktualität der Soziologie von Norbert Elias.* Vienna.

Österreichisches Statistisches Zentralamt (1993). *Volkszählung 1991: Hauptergebnisse 1.* Vienna.

Österreichische Volkspartei (1996). *Das neue Grundsatz-Programm der Volkspartei* (2nd edn). Vienna.

Ottmers, Clemens (1996). *Rhetorik.* Stuttgart.

The Oxford English Dictionary (1989). *The Oxford English Dictionary. Volume XVI: Soot–Styx* (2nd edn, prepared by J. A. Simpson and E. S. C. Weiner). Oxford, p. 852.

Paier, Günter (1996). 'Menschen im Übergang: Österreichbilder und nationale Identität von Ex- und NeoösterreicherInnen'. In Haller et al., pp. 149–208.

Pelinka, Anton (1985). *Windstille: Klagen über Österreich.* Vienna.

Pelinka, Anton (1988). 'Waldheim in uns'. In Dor, Milo (ed.). *Die Leiche im Keller: Dokumente des Widerstands gegen Dr. Kurt Waldheim.* Vienna, pp. 16–17.

Pelinka, Anton (1990). *Zur österreichischen Identität. Zwischen deutscher Vereinigung und Mitteleuropa.* Vienna.

Pelinka, Anton (1993). 'Ethnische Konflikte in Europa. Die Frage der Identität'. In Nowotny, Helga and Taschwer, Klaus (eds). *Macht und Ohnmacht im neuen Europa.* Vienna, pp. 39–48.

Pelinka, Anton (1994). 'Gefährdet ein EU-Beitritt die Identität Österreichs?' In *Wirtschaftspolitische Blätter* 2, pp. 146–52.

Pelinka, Anton (1995). 'Nationale Identität'. In Projekt-Team 'Identitätswandel Österreichs im veränderten Europa' (ed.). *Nationale und kulturelle Identitäten Österreichs: Theorien, Methoden and Probleme der Forschung zu kollektiver Identität.* Vienna, pp. 28–33.

Pelinka, Anton, Schaller, Christian and Luif, Paul (1994). *Ausweg EG? Innenpolitische Motive einer außenpolitischen Umorientierung.* Vienna.

Pelinka, Anton and Mayr, Sabine (eds) (1998). *Die Entdeckung der Verantwortung: Die Zweite Republik und die vertriebenen Juden. Eine kommentierte Dokumentation aus dem persönlichen Archiv von Albert Sternfeld.* Vienna.

Perelman, Chaim (1980). *Das Reich der Rhetorik.* Munich.

Pernthaler, Peter (1992a). *Das Länderbeteiligungsverfahren an der europäischen Integration.* Vienna.

Pernthaler, Peter (1992b). 'Föderalistische Verfassungsreform: Ihre Voraussetzungen und Wirkungsbedingungen in Österreich'. *ÖZP* 4, pp. 365–88.

Plaschka, Richard G., Stourzh, Gerald and Niederkorn, Jean Paul (eds) (1995). *Was heißt Österreich? Inhalt und Umfang des Österreichbegriffs vom 10. Jahrhundert bis heute.* Vienna.

Plasser, Fritz and Ulram, Peter A. (eds) (1991). *Staatsbürger oder Untertanen? Politische Kultur Deutschlands, Österreichs und der Schweiz im Vergleich.* Frankfurt a. M.

Plasser, Fritz and Ulram, Peter A. (1994). 'Kognitive und affektive Barrieren der Entwicklung eines europäischen Bewußtseins'. In Gerlich, Peter and Neisser, Heinrich (eds). *Europa als Herausforderung: Wandlungsimpulse für das politische System Österreichs.* Vienna, pp. 209–39.

Plett, Heinrich (1989). *Einführung in die rhetorische Textanalyse* (7th edn). Hamburg.

Plitzner, Klaus (ed.) (1995). *Technik – Politik – Identität: Funktionalisierung von Technik für die Ausbildung regionaler, sozialer und nationaler Selbstbilder in Österreich.* Stuttgart.

Pollak, Wolfgang (1992). *Was halten die Österreicher von ihrem Deutsch? Eine sprachanalytische und soziosemiotische Analyse der sprachlichen Identität der Österreicher.* Vienna.

Pollak, Wolfgang (1994a). 'Identität durch Grammelschmalz'. *Der Standard,* 28 April.

Pollak, Wolfgang (1994b). *Österreich und Europa. Sprachkulturelle und nationale Identität.* Vienna.

Prisching, Manfred (1995). 'Geschichten vom Erfolg und vom Versagen'. *Hochschülerschaft der Technischen Universität Wien,* pp. 67–90.

Puntscher-Riekmann, Sonja (1995). 'Die Europäische Union als republikanisches Bündnis – Österreich zwischen Republik und Kerneuropa'. *Hochschülerschaft der Technischen Universität Wien,* pp. 91–115.

Ram, Uri (1994). 'Narration, Erziehung und die Erfindung des jüdischen Nationalismus'. *Österreichische Zeitschrift für Geschichtswissenschaft (ÖZG)* 5:2, pp. 151–77.

Rathkolb, Oliver, Schmid, Georg and Heiss, Gernot (eds) (1990). *Österreich und Deutschlands Größe: Ein schlampiges Verhältnis.* Salzburg.

Räthzel, Nora (1994). 'Cultural Studies und Rassismusforschung in der Bundesrepublik'. IKUS Lectures Nos. 17 and 18.

Reger, Harald (1977). 'Die Metaphorik in der konventionellen Tagespresse'. In *Muttersprache 87,* pp. 259–79.

Reger, Harald (1978). 'Die Metaphorik in der Illustriertenpresse'. In *Muttersprache 88,* pp. 106–31.

Reinprecht, Christoph (1992). *Zurückgekehrt: Identität und Bruch in der Biographie österreichischer Juden.* Vienna.

Reinprecht, Christoph (1995). 'Österreich und der Umbruch in Osteuropa'. In Sieder, Reinhard, Steinert, Heinz and Tálos, Emmerich (eds). *Österreich 1945–1995.* Vienna, pp. 341–53.

Reisigl, Martin (1998). '"50 Jahre Zweite Republik". Zur diskursiven Konstruktion der österreichischen Identität in politischen Gedenkreden'. In Panagl, Oswald (ed.). *Fahnenwörter der Politik. Kontinuitäten und Brüche.* Vienna, Cologne and Graz, pp. 217–51.

Reisigl, Martin (1999). '"1000 Jahre Österreich". Nationale Identitätsstiftung und Mythenbildung im öffentlichen Gedenken der Zweiten Österreichischen Republik'. In Kopperschmidt, Josef and Schanze, Helmut (eds). *Fest und Festrhetorik. Zur Theorie, Geschichte und Praxis der Epideiktik.* Munich, pp. 281–311.

Reiterer, Albert F. (ed.) (1988a). *Nation und Nationalbewußtsein in Österreich: Ergebnisse einer empirischen Untersuchung.* Vienna.

Reiterer, Albert F. (1988b). *Die unvermeidbare Nation: Ethnizität, Nation und nachnationale Gesellschaft.* Vienna.

Reiterer, Albert F. (1993a). 'Österreichische Nation – deutsche Kultur – europäische Identität'. In Nowotny, Helen and Taschwer, Klaus (eds). *Macht und Ohnmacht im neuen Europa: Zur Aktualität der Soziologie von Norbert Elias.* Vienna, pp. 107–22.

Reiterer, Albert F. (1993b). 'Nationen: Erfundene oder ewige Realitäten?' In Guggenberger, Helmut and Holzinger, Wolfgang (eds). *Neues Europa – Alte Nationalismen: Kollektive Identitäten im Spannungsfeld von Integration und Ausschließung*. Vienna, pp. 39–50.

Renan, Ernest ([1882] 1995). 'Was ist eine Nation?' In Renan, Ernest. *Was ist eine Nation? ... und andere politische Schriften*. Vienna and Bolzano, pp. 41–58.

Renan, Ernest (1995). *Was ist eine Nation? ... und andere politische Schriften*. Vienna and Bolzano.

Rex, John (1995). 'Ethnic Identity and the Nation-State: The Political Sociology of Multi-Cultural Societies'. *Social Identities* 1:1, pp. 21–34.

Richmond, Anthony H. (1987). 'Ethnic Nationalism: Social Science Paradigms'. *International Social Science Journal* 11, pp. 3–18.

Richter, Dirk (1994). 'Der Mythos der "guten" Nation: Zum theoriegeschichtlichen Hintergrund eines folgenschweren Mißverständnisses'. *Soziale Welt* 3, pp. 304–21.

Ricœur, Paul (1992). *Oneself as Another*. Chicago and London.

Ringel, Erwin (1984). *Die österreichische Seele: 10 Reden über Medizin, Politik, Kunst und Religion*. Vienna.

Rotter, Manfred (1990). 'Unter Wahrung der Neutralität'. *Die Zukunft* 1, pp. 5–11.

Rotter, Manfred (1995). 'Der Staatsvertrag'. In Sieder, Reinhard, Steinert, Heinz and Tálos, Emmerich (eds). *Österreich 1945–1995*. Vienna, pp. 122–32.

Saner, Hans (1986). 'Von den Gefahren der Identität für das Menschsein'. In Benedetti, Gaetano and Wiesmann, Louis (eds). *Ein Inuk sein: Interdisziplinäre Vorlesungen zum Problem der Identität*. Göttingen, pp. 39–51.

Schaller, Christian (1991). 'Die EG-Debatte in Österreich – Rekonstruktion der Kontroverse in den achtziger Jahren und Thesen zur aktuellen Diskussion'. *SWS-Rundschau* 29:4, pp. 497–508.

Schmid, Georg (1990). '... sagen die Deutschen. Annäherung an eine Geschichte des Sprachimperialismus'. In Rathkolb, Oliver, Schmid, Georg and Heiss, Gernot (eds). *Österreich und Deutschlands Größe*. Salzburg, pp. 23–34.

Schneider, Heinrich (1994). 'Gerader Weg zum klaren Ziel? Die Republik Österreich auf dem Weg in die Europäische Union'. In *ÖZP* 23:1, pp. 5–20.

Schopenhauer, Arthur (1989). *Sämtliche Werke Band 4: Parerga und Paralipomena 1* (2nd edn). Frankfurt a. M.

Schulze, Hagen (1994). *Staat und Nation in der europäischen Geschichte*. Munich.

Schweiger, Günter (1992). *Österreichs Image in der Welt: Ein Vergleich mit Deutschland und der Schweiz*. Vienna.

Seiter, Josef (1995). 'Vergessen – und trotz alledem – erinnern: Vom Umgang mit Monumenten und Denkmälern in der Zweiten Republik'. In Sieder, Reinhard, Steinert, Heinz and Tálos, Emmerich (eds). *Österreich 1945–1995*. Vienna, pp. 684–705.

Sieder, Reinhard, Steinert, Heinz and Tálos, Emmerich (eds) (1995). *Österreich 1945–1995. Gesellschaft – Politik – Kultur*. Vienna.

Silverman, Maxim (1994). *Rassismus und Nation: Einwanderung und die Krise des National-staats in Frankreich*. Hamburg and Berlin.

Smith, Anthony D. (1983). *Theories of Nationalism*. London.

Smith, Anthony D. (1991). *National Identity*. London.

Staudinger, Anton (1994). '"Durch Gedenkfeiern gelegentlich zur Vergessenheit emporgehoben ...": Anmerkungen zur Funktion von Gedenktagen und zur grassierenden Jubiläumshistorie'. In Schmidt-Dengler, Wendelin (ed.). *Der literarische Umgang der Österreicher mit Jahres- und Gedenktagen*. Vienna, pp. 17–24.

Stenographisches Protokoll 40. Sitzung des Nationalrates der Republik Österreich. XIX Gesetzgebungsperiode, Donnerstag 1. und Freitag 2. Juni 1995. Vienna.

Stern, Frank (1991). *Im Anfang war Auschwitz: Antisemitismus und Philosemitismus im deutschen Nachkrieg*. Gerlingen.

Sternfeld, Albert (1990). *Betrifft Österreich*. Vienna.

Stiefel, Dieter (1981). *Entnazifizierung in Österreich*. Vienna, Munich and Zurich.

Stourzh, Gerald (1990). *Vom Reich zur Republik: Studien zum Österreichbewußtsein im 20. Jahrhundert*. Vienna.

Strejcek, Gerhard (1992). 'Ist der Staatsvertrag von Wien obsolet?' *Forum* 465-467, pp. 8–10.

Stuhlpfarrer, Karl (1981). 'Volksabstimmungsfeiern und Geschichtsbild. In *Kärnten – Volksabstimmung 1920. Voraussetzungen – Verlauf – Folgen*. Vienna, Munich and Kleinenzersdorf, pp. 13–27.

SWS-Bildstatistiken (1994). 'Österreich und seine Identität'. *SWS-Rundschau* 32:2, pp. 209–24.

SWS-Bildstatistiken (1995). 'Die "Neue" Europäische Union'. *SWS-Rundschau* 33:4, pp. 453–60.

SWS-Meinungsprofile (1991). 'Der Wert der Neutralität in der Meinung der Österreicher'. *SWS-Rundschau* 31:2, pp. 231–8.

Tabor, Jan (ed.) (1994). *Kunst und Diktatur: Architektur, Bildhauerei und Malerei in Österreich, Deutschland und der Sowjetunion 1922–1956*. Baden.

Tálos, Emmerich (1995). 'Der Sozialstaat – Vom "goldenen Zeitalter" zur Krise'. In Sieder, Reinhard, Steinert, Heinz and Tálos, Emmerich (eds). *Österreich 1945–1995*. Vienna, pp. 537–51.

Tálos, Emmerich and Manoschek, Walter (1994). 'Austrofaschismus, Halbfaschismus, Ständestaat'. In Tabor, Jan (ed.). *Kunst und Diktatur*. Baden, pp. 112–23.

Tàlos, Emmerich and Kittel, Bernhard (1995). 'Sozialpartnerschaft: Zur Konstituierung einer Grundsäule der Zweiten Republik'. In Sieder, Reinhard, Steinert, Heinz and Tálos, Emmerich (eds). *Österreich 1945–1995*, pp. 107–21.

Teuber, Charlotte M. (1993). 'Neutralität war nie ein Neutrum: Der Widerstand der Weisen oder der Anspruch auf Entscheidungsfreiheit'. In Ecker, Gerold and Neugebauer, Christian (eds). *Neutralität oder Euromilitarismus*. Vienna, pp. 14–28.

Thalberg, Hans (1993). 'Auslaufmodell Neutralität'. *Der Standard*, 22 and 23 May, p. 31.

Tibal, André (1936). *L'Autrichien: Essais sur la formation d'une individualité nationale*. Paris.

Toulmin, Stephen Edelston (1964). *The Uses of Argument*. Cambridge.

Traxler, Günter (1995). 'Kollektive Schuld'. *Der Standard*, 3 and 4 June.

Uhl, Heidemarie (1994). 'Erinnern und vergessen'. In Riesenfellner, Stefan and Uhl, Heidemarie (eds). *Todeszeichen: Zeitgeschichtliche Denkmalkultur in Graz und in der Steiermark vom Ende des 19. Jahrhunderts bis zur Gegenwart*. Vienna, pp. 111–96.

Unterberger, Andreas (1992). 'Neutralität: Sinn oder Unsinn?' *Wiener Journal* 2, pp. 11–12.

Van Dijk, Teun A. (in print). 'Critical Discourse Analysis'. In Tannen, Deborah, Schiffrin, Deborah and Hamilton, Heide (eds). *Handbook of Discourse Analysis*. New York et al., page numbers not yet available.

Van Leeuwen, Theo (1996). 'The Representation of Social Actors'. In Caldas-Coulthard, Carmen Rosa and Coulthard, Malcolm (eds). *Texts and Practices: Readings in Critical Discourse Analysis*. London, pp. 32–70.

Van Leeuwen, Theo and Wodak, Ruth (1999). 'Legitimising Immigration Control: A Discourse-Historical Analysis'. In *Discourse Studies* 1:1, pp. 83–118.

Vivelo, Frank Robert (1981). *Handbuch der Kulturanthropologie: Eine grundlegende Einführung*. Stuttgart.

Volmert, Johannes (1989). *Politikerrede als kommunikatives Handlungsspiel: Ein integriertes Modell zur semantisch-pragmatischen Beschreibung öffentlicher Rede*. Munich.

Walter, Ilse (1992). *In diesem Land – Eine Österreich-Anthologie*. Vienna.

Weinzierl, Erika (1993a). '20 Thesen zur österreichischen Identität'. In *Informationen der Gesellschaft für politische Aufklärung* 38, pp. 5–6.

Weinzierl, Erika (1993b). 'Österreichs Identität: Kirche und Politik seit 1918'. *Das jüdische Echo* 10, pp. 58–64.

Weinzinger, Eva (1990). 'Der Landesname AUSTRIA im Mittelalter'. In *Österreich in Geschichte und Literatur (ÖGL)* 34:5–6, pp. 133–44.

Welan, Manfried (1995/1996). 'Der österreichische Bundespräsident'. In Burger, Johann and Morawek, Elisabeth (eds). *Politische Macht und Kontrolle: Informationen zur politischen Bildung.* Vienna, pp. 33–46.

Weninger, Thomas (1991). 'Das österreichische Nationalbewußtsein am Vorabend des EG-Beitritts: Sekundäranalytische Ergebnisse in der 2. Republik'. In *SWS-Rundschau* 31:4, pp. 479–96.

Wiesinger, Peter (ed.) (1988). *Das österreichische Deutsch.* Vienna.

Wodak, Ruth (1995). 'Critical Linguistics and Critical Discourse Analysis'. In Verschueren, Jef, Östman, Jan-Ola and Bloomaert, Jan (eds) (1995). *Handbook of Pragmatics.* Amsterdam and Philadelphia, pp. 204–10.

Wodak, Ruth (1996). *Disorders of Discourse.* New York.

Wodak, Ruth (1997). '"Die Österreicher sind von der Zeitgeschichte nicht gerade mit Samtpfoten behandelt worden". Zur diskursiven Konstruktion österreichischer Identität'. In Römer, Franz (ed.). *1000 Jahre Österreich – Wege zu einer österreichischen Identität: Vorträge anläßlich des Dies Academicus der Geisteswissenschaftlichen Fakultät der Universität Wien am 10. Jänner 1996.* Vienna, pp. 35–67.

Wodak, Ruth, Nowak, Peter, Pelikan, Johanna, Gruber, Helmut, de Cillia, Rudolf and Mitten, Richard (1990). *'Wir sind alle unschuldige Täter'. Diskurshistorische Studien zum Nachkriegsantisemitismus.* Frankfurt a. M.

Wodak, Ruth and Matouschek, Bernd (1993). '"We Are Dealing with People whose Origins One Can Clearly Tell Just by Looking": Critical Discourse Analysis and the Study of Neo-Racism in Contemporary Austria'. *Discourse & Society* 4:2, pp. 225–48.

Wodak, Ruth, Menz, Florian, Mitten, Richard and Stern, Frank (1994). *Sprachen der Vergangenheiten.* Frankfurt a. M.

Wodak, Ruth, de Cillia, Rudolf, Çinar, Dilek and Matouschek, Bernd (1995). *Identitätswandel Österreichs im veränderten Europa: Diskurshistorische Studien über den öffentlichen und privaten Diskurs zur 'neuen' österreichischen Identität (Projektzwischenbericht).* Vienna.

Wodak, Ruth, de Cillia, Rudolf, Reisigl, Martin, Liebhart, Karin, Hofstätter, Klaus and Kargl, Maria (1998). *Zur diskursiven Konstruktion nationaler Identität.* Frankfurt a. M.

Wodak, Ruth and Reisigl, Martin (1999). *Discourse and Discrimination. The Rhetorics of Racism and Antisemitism.* Unpublished manuscript.

Ziegler, Meinrad and Kannonier-Finster, Waltraud (1993). *Österreichisches Gedächtnis. Über Erinnern und Vergessen der NS-Vergangenheit.* Vienna, Cologne and Weimar.

Zimmerman, Eugenia Noik (1989). 'Identity and Difference: the Logic of Synecdochic Reasoning'. *Texte. Revue de Critique et de Théorie Litteraire* 8–9, pp. 25–62.

Zöllner, Erich (1988). *Der Österreichbegriff: Formen und Wandlungen in der Geschichte.* Vienna.

Zoitl, Helge (1991). 'Wir und die anderen: Anmerkungen zur österreichischen Kultur, zum österreichischen Nationalbewußtsein und zum österreichischen Nationalismus'. In Dr. Karl Renner Institut (ed.). *Wir sind wir! Ein Problemaufriß zur politischen Kultur: Studientagung zur politischen Bildung.* Vienna, pp. 14–53.

Index